The Ages of Voluntarism

Cartoon by W. K. Haselden first published in the *Daily Mirror*, 21 May 1925.
Reproduced by permission. Photo © Mirrorpix.

The Ages of Voluntarism

How we got to the Big Society

Edited by

Matthew Hilton and James McKay

Published for THE BRITISH ACADEMY
by OXFORD UNIVERSITY PRESS

Oxford University Press, Great Clarendon Street, Oxford OX2 6DP

Oxford New York

Auckland Cape Town Dar es Salaam Hong Kong Karachi
Kuala Lumpur Madrid Melbourne Mexico City Nairobi
New Delhi Shanghai Taipei Toronto

With offices in

Argentina Austria Brazil Chile Czech Republic France Greece
Guatemala Hungary Italy Japan Poland Portugal Singapore
South Korea Switzerland Thailand Turkey Ukraine Vietnam

Published in the United States by Oxford University Press Inc., New York

First published 2011

British Library Cataloguing in Publication Data
Data available

Library of Congress Cataloging in Publication Data
Data available

Typeset in Palatino by Keystroke, Station Road, Codsall, Wolverhampton
Printed in Great Britain on acid-free paper by
MPG Books Limited, Bodmin, Cornwall

ISBN 978-0-19-726482-9

Contents

Preface and acknowledgements

This book is one outcome of a wider project on the history of non-governmental organisations and voluntary associations in contemporary Britain. We were particularly interested in engaging with non-historians to explore how patterns of voluntarism can inform current understandings of the sector, an interest which has become only more prescient with the launch of the Conservative-Liberal coalition government's 'Big Society' initiative shortly after the British general election of May 2010. It is to be hoped that the nature of historical analyses and historical evidence found in this volume is not forgotten or ignored as politicians seek new relationships with the voluntary sector.

The chapters in the volume arose in the main out of a British Academy workshop, 'The Voluntary Sector in British Society', held in March 2009. The event attracted a large number of historians and social and political scientists, as well as many practitioners from the voluntary sector itself. We would like to thank the audience at this event and to take this opportunity to thank the British Academy for sponsoring and hosting the workshop, and for their ongoing support for this subsequent publication, with particular thanks to Michael Reade, Penny Collins, James Rivington and Brigid Hamilton-Jones. Thanks are also due to the workshop's co-convenor, Pat Thane.

The contributions of attendees and speakers were invaluable in shaping this volume. Particular thanks are owed to John Clarke, Wyn Grant, Bernard Harris and Colin Rochester. We would also like to thank both Lawrence Black and the Academy's anonymous reviewers of the initial drafts of this volume, for their helpful and insightful comments.

Thanks are also due to the Leverhulme Trust, funders of the wider project on which the editors work: Non-Governmental Organisations in Britain, 1945–1997, at the University of Birmingham, Grant number F00094AV, Principal Investigator Matthew Hilton.

Finally, we would like to thank our colleagues on the NGOs in Britain project: Nicholas Crowson, Jean-Francois Mouhot, and particularly Herjeet Marway, whose painstaking work assembling the manuscript was greatly appreciated.

Notes on contributors

Pete Alcock is Professor of Social Policy and Administration at the University of Birmingham and Director of the ESRC Third Sector Research Centre. He has been teaching and researching in social policy for over thirty years and is author or editor of a number of leading books in the field, including *Understanding Poverty* (3rd edition, Palgrave Macmillan, 2006), *Social Policy in Britain* (3rd edition, Palgrave Macmillan, 2008), *The Student's Companion to Social Policy* (3rd edition, Blackwell, 2008) and, with Gary Craig, *International Social Policy* (2nd edition, Palgrave Macmillan, 2009). He has also written widely on social policy, the voluntary sector, social security, poverty and social exclusion, and anti-poverty policy.

Virginia Berridge is Director of the Centre for History in Public Health at the London School of Hygiene and Tropical Medicine, University of London. Her most recent publications include *Marketing Health: Smoking and the Discourse of Public Health in Britain, 1945–2000* (Oxford University Press, 2007) and, as joint editor, *Environment Health and History* (Palgrave Macmillan, forthcoming). Her research interests include health policy, voluntarism, and the history of evidence and policy. She also publishes on the history of illicit drugs, alcohol and HIV/AIDS.

Justin Davis Smith is Chief Executive of Volunteering England and a Visiting Professor at Birkbeck, University of London. His previous jobs include founder and director of the Institute for Volunteering Research, and political assistant to the Rt. Hon. Sir James Callaghan MP (later Lord Callaghan of Cardiff). His publications include *The Attlee and Churchill Administrations and Industrial Unrest* (Frances Pinter, 1990) and, as joint editor, *An Introduction to the Voluntary Sector* (Routledge, 1995).

Nicholas Deakin was Professor of Social Policy and Administration at the University of Birmingham from 1980 to 1998, and has subsequently held appointments as a visiting professor at the University of Warwick and at the Centre for Civil Society, London School of Economics. In 1995–1996, he chaired the Independent Commission on the Future of the Voluntary Sector in England. His most recent books are *In Search of Civil Society* (Palgrave, 2001) and a jointly edited collection, *Welfare and the State* (Routledge, 2003). A collection of essays commemorating the sixtieth anniversary of the publication of William Beveridge's *Voluntary Action*, which he jointly edited and contributed to, was published in 2011.

Eliza Filby has recently completed her doctorate at the University of Warwick. Her thesis explored the interrelationship between religion and politics in 1980s Britain. The book, *God and Mrs Thatcher*, will be published in 2012. Eliza is also the author of the religion and belief chapter in Pat Thane's edited collection, *Unequal Britain* (Continuum, 2010).

Peter Grant is acknowledged as one of the UK's leading practitioners in public and charitable funding. After working in the arts he was director of an inner-city youth charity for eight years. As Director of Operations at the New Opportunities Fund between 1999 and 2005 he developed and delivered over £4.5 billion worth of funding programmes. He then developed the world's first full Masters-level programme in grant-making and philanthropy at Cass Business School, where he is Senior Fellow in Grant-Making, Philanthropy and Social Investment.

Matthew Hilton is Professor of Social History at the University of Birmingham. His previous books include *Smoking in British Popular Culture* (Manchester University Press, 2000), *Consumerism in Twentieth-Century Britain* (Cambridge University Press, 2003), and *Prosperity for All: Consumer Activism in an Era of Globalization* (Cornell University Press, 2009). With James McKay, Nicholas Crowson and Jean-Francois Mouhot he is currently working on *The Politics of Expertise: How NGOs Shaped Modern Britain* (Oxford University Press, 2012).

Helen McCarthy is Lecturer in Modern British History at Queen Mary, University of London. Before taking up her current post, she completed her PhD at the Institute of Historical Research and held a research fellowship at St John's College, Cambridge. Her research interests include the history of popular internationalism, feminism and associational voluntarism. Her first book, *The British People and the League of Nations*, will be published shortly by Manchester University Press.

James McKay is a Postdoctoral Research Fellow at the University of Birmingham. With Nicholas Crowson and Matthew Hilton, he co-edited

NGOs in Contemporary Britain: Non-State Actors in Society and Politics since 1945 (Palgrave Macmillan, 2009). He is currently working on *The Politics of Expertise: How NGOs Shaped Modern Britain* (Oxford University Press, 2012), with Matthew Hilton, Nicholas Crowson and Jean-Francois Mouhot.

Alex Mold is Lecturer in History at the London School of Hygiene and Tropical Medicine. She is the author of *Heroin: The Treatment of Addiction in Twentieth-Century Britain* (Northern Illinois Press, 2008) and, together with Virginia Berridge, *Voluntary Action and Illegal Drugs: Health and Society in Britain since the 1960s* (Palgrave Macmillan, 2010).

Peter Shapely is Senior Lecturer in the School of History, Welsh History and Archaeology at Bangor University. He is the author of *Charity and Power in Nineteenth Century Manchester* (Manchester University Press, 2000) and *The Politics of Housing: Power, Policy and Consumers* (Manchester University Press, 2007). Other relevant publications include 'Tenants Arise! Consumerism, Tenants and the Challenge to Council Authority in Manchester, 1968–92', *Social History*, 31/1, 2006, and 'Planning and Participation in Britain, 1968–1976', written for a special edition of *Planning Perspectives*.

1
The ages of voluntarism

An introduction

MATTHEW HILTON AND JAMES MCKAY

The vitality of voluntarism has long been a cause of concern. Indeed, it is difficult to recall a period when such anxiety was not prevalent. In 1948, after he had helped establish the welfare state, William Beveridge worried about the potential dangers of an all-powerful Leviathan. *Voluntary Action: A Report on the Methods of Social Advance* was the follow up and final part of the trilogy begun with *Social Insurance and Allied Services* (1942) and *Full Employment in a Free Society* (1944). This classic liberal text was written in the shadow of a modern state that Beveridge feared would trample the 'vigour and abundance' of voluntary action; that is, those forms of civic engagement that he held to be 'the distinguishing marks of a free society' and one of 'the outstanding features of British life'.[1] He sought out ways to encourage the continued vitality of voluntary action, it being so central to 'new ways of social advance'. Yet his faith was tinged with pessimism. Not only did 'the coming of the social service state' threaten the traditional role played by many voluntary organisations but social changes had adversely affected the sector too. The redistribution of income since the First World War, the greater enjoyment of leisure by more people (but in smaller parcels for those who had previously enjoyed much more), and the declining influence of the churches all threatened to reduce the impulse and the ability to volunteer.

Beveridge's concerns are common to so many declinist narratives found across the political spectrum and which continue to inform debates about the voluntary sector. The corollary of such a narrative is that some 'golden

---

[1] William Beveridge, *Voluntary Action: A Report on the Methods of Social Advance* (London, 1948), p. 10.

age' must have existed in the past. For Beveridge, that past was the era of Victorian philanthropy, 'a time of private enterprise not only in pursuit of gain, but also in social reform', and to which British citizens were indebted.[2] Furthermore, this debt was owed above all to 'the few', the figures like Shaftesbury, Elizabeth Fry, William Booth and Octavia Hill who, for Beveridge, dominated the scene: 'There is always need for the few – dynamic individuals wholly possessed by this spirit. They call it forth in others; they create the institutions and societies through which it acts; they lead by their example. Voluntary Action depends on its pioneers.'[3] It is a heavily romanticised view, just as much as the views and assumptions of many a political scientist imbued with a Tocquevillian respect for the classic institutions of civil society and democracy, or of social historians keen to mark the Victorian era as the heyday of philanthropy and volunteering.

In contrast, it is the contention of this volume that any such identification of a so-called 'golden age' is neither helpful nor appropriate. Our starting point is that we reject the notion of a voluntarist Garden of Eden from which we have long since been expelled. Instead, the contributions to this collection show how voluntary action has constantly reinvented and redefined itself in response to social and political change. So the fixing of a point when the voluntary sector was somehow 'ideal' is enormously unhelpful; its normativity obscures far more than it reveals, trapping us in an inappropriate declinism that obliterates the sophisticated adaptability of a sector that persists in being marked by diversity and vitality.

In any case, if pressed, most authors will soon move beyond such simplistic interpretations and will point instead to the ongoing work of voluntary organisations amidst a constantly evolving political and social context. Beveridge himself recognised that:

> In face of these changes philanthropy has shown its strength of being able perpetually to take new forms. The Charity Organisation Society has passed over to Family Welfare. Within this century entirely new organisations have arisen, such as the Boy Scouts and Girl Guides, Women's Institutes, the Workers' Educational Association, the National Council of Social Service, Training Colleges for the Disabled, Women's Voluntary Services, and Citizens' Advice Bureaux. The capacity of Voluntary Action inspired by philanthropy to do new things is beyond question.[4]

[2] *Ibid.*, p. 13.
[3] *Ibid.*, p. 152.
[4] *Ibid.*, p. 301.

For the Wolfenden Committee on Voluntary Organisations, reporting thirty years later, change was once again a central theme, driven above all by the developing socio-political environment:

> In summarising the principal developments in social provisions over the last two-hundred years it is possible to identify four main phases. The first, which we will call 'the last phase of paternalism', lasted until 1834. The second, which we will call 'the era of state deterrence and voluntary expansion', covered the years 1834–1905. The third, marked by the emergence of statutory social services, occupied the next forty years. The final phase, which runs from 1945 to the present day, we describe as 'the consolidation of the welfare state'.[5]

The report particularly drew attention to changes in the voluntary sector during the post-war decades. Perceiving a relative lull in the immediate post-war years, it argued that the pace of change then picked up again in the late 1950s, including a reorientation of the sector, to differentiate itself from, and move beyond the limitations of, the welfare state, a 'flowering of mutual-help groups', 'the growth of coordinating bodies at local and national level', the encouragement (particularly through grant support) of the sector by local and national government, and a rise in pressure-group activity.[6]

Eighteen years later, the anticipation of change was an important element of the Deakin report, *Meeting the Challenge of Change* (1996).[7] The adaptive imperative placed upon the voluntary sector came from: changing economic and technological circumstances (particularly globalisation, flexible labour markets, and the knowledge economy); the impact of demographic change and its broader social repercussions; 'political, structural and institutional changes', particularly the future role of the state, and developments in public opinion and, of obvious significance for voluntarism, in the nature of participation.[8]

Simplistic and unhelpful notions of decline, then, should be replaced with an understanding of (even an appreciation for) the role of change. To

---

[5] The Committee on Voluntary Organisations, *The Future of Voluntary Organisations: Report of the Wolfenden Committee* (London, 1978), p. 16.
[6] *Ibid.*, p. 20.
[7] Commission on the Future of the Voluntary Sector, *Meeting the Challenge of Change: Voluntary Action into the 21st Century: The Report of the Commission on the Future of the Voluntary Sector* (London, 1996).
[8] *Ibid.*, pp. 39–43.

borrow Beveridge's phrase, it is voluntarism's 'capacity . . . to do new things' that frames the chapters in this volume. Our collective starting point is that the voluntary sector has continued to thrive, to adapt, to respond to challenges thrown its way, to retreat in certain areas and to grow in others. Our role as historians is to understand the nature of this adaptation, to set out a chronology of evolution, and to point to the most important social, political and economic themes that can explain such change.

The chapters in this collection have therefore been selected because the case studies they examine are emblematic of either the most significant periods in the history of voluntary action since the nineteenth century or the most significant issues that have impacted on the sector. The chapters explore the experience of war, the role of women in public life, the participation of middle- and working-class volunteers, and the rise of new forms of activism, engagement and participation. They show how the voluntary sector has responded to the changes in party politics, during periods of both rising and declining mass membership, and to the institutions of central and local government which have established diverse forms of interaction with the voluntary sector (from direct funding, to partnership and collaboration, and even to hostility and competition). Various chapters examine the role of the voluntary sector within and beyond the welfare state in the 1940s and 1950s, the rise of organisations that more comfortably identify themselves as 'non-governmental' (i.e. NGOs) than as voluntary bodies, and the changing relationship with the state at key moments (for example, during the Attlee governments of 1945–1951, the Thatcher governments of the 1980s, and the engagement with the 'third sector' sought by Tony Blair and Gordon Brown's administrations after 1997).

What emerges is that the concerns that so vexed Beveridge at the end of the Second World War are concerns that still continue to offer challenges and opportunities to the voluntary sector today. The role of the state, rising living standards and changing leisure patterns, social mobility and trust in institutions are subjects as relevant now as they were for Beveridge in 1948, especially as the Conservative-Liberal coalition government embarks upon its 'Big Society' agenda. What is clear, though, is that the strength of the voluntary sector lies in its ability to respond to such challenges, then as now. The stresses these challenges create are ultimately creative as much as they are destructive. The historical explorations of the voluntary sector collected here should warn commentators today that there is much to concern those who work and lead the sector. But, we should not forget, there is also much to be optimistic about in the contribution made by voluntary organisations to democratic life in its broadest sense.

I

The narrative of a voluntary sector in terminal decline can easily be supported by many broader themes of modern British history. If it is assumed that the high-Victorian period represented a golden age of philanthropy then it is easy to suggest that there has been a gradual erosion of its role subsequently. Campaigns on behalf of women and children and for better public health and improved social reform were superseded to an extent by the early welfare reforms of the Edwardian years.[9] The classic public sphere was 'structurally transformed' such that the space for voluntary associations was eclipsed by the tremendous growth of the public and the private, commercial sectors.[10] If female charity workers had constituted their own feminine public sphere, then they too were squeezed by the same processes.[11] By the time of the First World War, the mass mobilisation of the state seemingly brought to an end this apparent heyday of voluntary activity.

Attendant on these changes were not only the social factors listed by Beveridge but also political ones due to the extension of the franchise. The rise of the mass political party politicised public life to an extent that voluntary organisations were seen to be aligned with one of the main political parties. The interwar period saw the emergence of new types of voluntary activity such as the Women's Institutes, the British Legion, Rotary, and the League of Nations Union. These have often been interpreted not so much as independent manifestations of associational life but as extensions of, and supporters of, one of the main political parties.[12] The

[9] G. Finlayson, 'A Moving Frontier: Voluntarism and the State in British Social Welfare', *Twentieth-Century British History*, 1, 1990, pp. 183–206; D. Fraser, *The Evolution of the British Welfare State: A History of Social Policy since the Industrial Revolution* (London, 1973); P. Thane, *The Foundations of the Welfare State*, 2nd edn (London, 1996).

[10] J. Habermas, *The Structural Transformation of the Public Sphere: An Inquiry into a Category of Bourgeois Society*, trans. T. Burger (Oxford, 1992); C. Calhoun (ed.), *Habermas and the Public Sphere* (London, 1992).

[11] Nancy Fraser, *Unruly Practices: Power, Discourse, and Gender in Contemporary Social Theory* (Cambridge, 1989).

[12] R. McKibbin, *Classes and Cultures: England 1918–1951* (Oxford, 2000). For an effective challenge to this interpretation, see H. McCarthy, 'Parties, Voluntary Associations and Democratic Politics in Interwar Britain', *The Historical Journal*, 50, 4, 2007, pp. 891–912.

mass mobilisation of the Second World War, on the home as well as the military front, further brought the state into areas previously occupied by the voluntary sector. The subsequent establishment of the welfare state served to hammer another nail into the coffin of voluntary social services.[13]

The new social movements associated with the 1960s did offer a revival of the voluntary sector's fortunes, though in a rather different form from that of its nineteenth-century predecessors. But the more spectacular moments of activism associated with the peace movement, feminism and environmentalism masked a more persistent decline in the fortunes of the voluntary sector. This is the thesis as put forward by Robert Putnam. In *Bowling Alone* (2000), he provided compelling evidence for the growing unwillingness of ordinary Americans to participate in all forms of associational life, from social movement groups to parent-teacher associations and even leisure and cultural bodies as in the eponymous bowling league.[14] Putnam's emphasis upon decline over time is at its most explicit with his focus on generational change, as the so-called Greatest Generation, which endured the Depression and fought the Second World War, was succeeded in turn by the Baby Boomers and then Generation X, whose own civic-mindedness was a pale shadow of their grandparents'.[15]

Such critiques have been transposed to the British context, with another dimension being added as even those voluntary groups that have enjoyed increasing memberships (such as the environmental movement) have been dismissed as vital components of 'social capital'. Instead, it is claimed, these social movements have developed into highly professionalised NGOs and lobby groups that ask no more of their members than the renewal of direct debit arrangements. Such voluntarism, it is claimed, owes little to healthy social and political engagement and far more to the culture of consumerism: politics becomes a matter of single-issue preference with none of the barriers to exit associated with participation in a traditional voluntary organisation.[16] Indeed, the floodgates of affluence and consumption are rarely kept in check in the debates about voluntary action. Once opened,

[13] N. Deakin, 'The Perils of Partnership: The Voluntary Sector and the State, 1945–1992', in J. Davis Smith, C. Rochester and R. Hedley (eds), *An Introduction to the Voluntary Sector* (London, 1995), p. 40.

[14] R. Putnam, *Bowling Alone: The Collapse and Revival of American Community* (New York, 2000).

[15] *Ibid.*, p. 275.

[16] See, for example, G. Jordan and W. Maloney, *The Protest Business: Mobilizing Campaign Groups* (Manchester, 1997), pp. 17–25.

consumerism sweeps away all other social structures leaving atomised individuals with no option but to shop.

Of course, this narrative is something of an oversimplification. But it does still persist in various forms. One of the most recent revivers of the narrative of decline is Frank Prochaska. In his *Christianity and Social Service in Modern Britain* (2000), Prochaska details with loving care the historical scale of Christian-inspired social service in fields such as education and nursing, only to lament the eclipse of this effort in the twentieth century. The villain here, though, is the Leviathan, rather than Putnam's generational and social change: 'It was not a coincidence that the expansion of government and the contraction of religion happened over the same period, for the modern British state was constructed against religious interests and customs of associational citizenship.'[17]

We remain sceptical of such accounts because of the evidence from today which points to the continued thriving nature of voluntary life. There are around 160,000 charities registered with the Charity Commission of England and Wales.[18] In their 2002 study of *Democracy Under Blair* (2002), David Beetham, Iain Byrne, Pauline Ngan and Stuart Weir found that 156 of the 200 largest charities relied on over 2 million volunteers.[19] A National Survey of Volunteering survey conducted in 1997 found that 22 million people had engaged in some form of voluntary activity (averaging four hours weekly) in the previous year.[20] In 2003, the UK Home Office citizenship survey suggested that more than 20 million people 'were engaged in active community participation', with the trend being one of expansion, rather than decline. Findings for formal volunteering saw a similar upward trend, making a contribution equivalent to around a million full-time workers.[21] These levels of active citizenship were found to have been maintained in a subsequent official study in 2005.[22] Indeed, some scholars have

---

[17] F. Prochaska, *Christianity and Social Service in Modern Britain: The Disinherited Spirit* (Oxford, 2000), p. 150.

[18] http://www.charity-commission.gov.uk/registeredcharities/factfigures.asp (accessed 5 January 2010).

[19] David Beetham, Iain Byrne, Pauline Ngan and Stuart Weir, *Democracy Under Blair: A Democratic Audit of the United Kingdom* (London, 2002), p. 210.

[20] *Ibid.*, p. 211.

[21] T. Munton and A. Zurawan, *Active Communities: Headline Findings from the 2003 Home Office Citizenship Survey* (London, 2004), pp. 1–7.

[22] S. Kitchen *et al.*, *2005 Citizenship Survey: Active Communities Topic Report* (London, 2006), p. 3.

taken such evidence to argue that this is all part of a wider trend of democratic renewal. The forms of participation that many new types of voluntary organisation encourage – demonstrations, signing petitions, consumer boycotts – are noted to be on the rise, suggesting that while political engagement, as measured by voter turnout, is certainly on the decline, civic activism, as directed by the voluntary sector, is not.[23]

We do not wish to go so far as to counter a narrative of decline with one of advance. However, if we pursue a line of constant renewal and adaptation it becomes obvious that many of the specific instances cited as examples of decline can be directly countered. First, it is not so apparent that an expanding state has necessarily encroached upon a terrain formerly held by the voluntary sector. Indeed, as in Jose Harris's analysis of civil society, it is perhaps better not to see the state and the voluntary sector as entirely distinct entities, but as mutually co-constitutive.[24] Often, the state and the voluntary sector have worked hand in hand, giving rise to new opportunities and possibilities, by no means all of which might be identified as co-option. The rediscovery of poverty during the 1960s can be used here as an illustrative example. Triggered above all by social policy experts in the London School of Economics (who themselves were closely allied to the Labour Party), publications such as 'The Meaning of Poverty' (1962) and *The Poor and the Poorest* (1965) used the state's own statistical evidence to highlight the shortcomings of welfare provision, giving rise to pressure groups such as Shelter and the Child Poverty Action Group. These both forced forward statutory welfare provision and were led by individuals whose careers moved between the voluntary and political/statutory spheres. Cases such as these allow one to break down the supposedly clear division between state and society. They also reassert the ongoing agency of actors other than the state, an agency implicitly denied by declinist laments. Constitutive of, and complementary to, the rediscovery of poverty were a flock of voluntary associations – from the Claimants Union and the Disablement Income Group, to Release and the Brook Advisory clinics – which pioneered innovative and much-needed new services. They knew that the man in Whitehall did not necessarily know best, and set about teaching him a thing or two.

[23] Pippa Norris, *Democratic Phoenix: Reinventing Political Activism* (Cambridge, 2002).

[24] Jose Harris, 'Introduction; Civil Society in British History: Paradigm or Peculiarity?', in Jose Harris (ed.), *Civil Society in British History: Ideas, Identities, Institutions* (Oxford, 2003), pp. 1–12.

Secondly, the changing nature of participation in voluntary societies must not be too readily assumed to be in a decline that leads from the philanthropic high-mindedness of the Victorians, to the jam-making social life of the Women's Institute and on to the direct-debit political shopping associated with many NGOs. Indeed, the reporters of *Democracy Under Blair* even go so far as to suggest that while 'cheque book participation' might appear to reduce social capital, it does not necessarily constitute a dis-engagement with politics and thus 'volunteering' in this guise remains as important as ever to democracy. As they put it themselves:

> for reasons of time, much contemporary politics takes place by proxy, but we should not therefore underestimate the role of attentive and critical 'audi-ence', whereby an organisation's members may cheer on its actions from the armchair, or, alternatively, exercise the option of 'exit' if it seems ineffective or in breach of the purpose for which they joined. As long as organisations depend on membership subscriptions for their survival, they cannot afford to get far out of touch with the expectations of their members. And most can rely on being able to mobilise a wider penumbra of potential activists from their armchairs in support of a major issue or event, even if the numbers do not seem large in relation to the total population.[25]

Thirdly, whilst we should not overlook the significance of proxy par-ticipation, we should also not neglect the fact that voluntarism continues to provide varied and extensive opportunities for direct activity. The environmental movement has been a key target for those scathing of 'couch-participation', yet here one sees an enormous range of opportunities for involvement, from the British Trust for Conservation Volunteers' support for more than 2,000 local groups, facilitating the work of more than 100,000 people, to the more politically-oriented lobbying and campaign work undertaken by organisations such as the Campaign to Protect Rural England and Friends of the Earth, with their impressive voluntary local infrastructures.[26] Thinking more broadly, one only has to summon to mind the charity shops that inhabit every British high street to see that the con-cept of proxy participation is only appropriate if carefully, and narrowly, applied.

Fourthly, the link with living standards can be contested as there is no proven link between voluntary giving and the fluctuating fortunes of

---

[25] Beetham *et al.*, *Democracy Under Blair*, p. 216.
[26] Jordan and Maloney, *Protest Business*, p. 170; http://www2.btcv.org.uk/display/facts_and_figures (accessed 5 January 2010).

the economy. Obviously, recessions can have an impact on the voluntary sector, but what analyses there have been of the impact of economic downturns on the sector suggest that this impact will be as diverse as the sector itself. Moreover, measured over the long term, the proportion of income given to charity remains relatively stable, and voluntary organisations continue to be formed during recessions as much as they are through booms.[27]

Fifthly, one should be wary of the implicit (and often explicit) political agenda in much of the declinist analysis. Much of this comes from the New Right, seeking to establish Victorian philanthropy as a period of grace, in order to demonstrate the essential sinfulness of statutory welfare provision. As the director of the Institute of Economic Affairs Health and Welfare Unit argued, 'The story of the voluntary sector in the twentieth century is one of politicisation.' Ceasing to be 'bulwarks of liberty and focal points for collective effort', voluntary organisations had now either been yoked to the state, or 'had come to see their role as pathfinders whose task was to provide a social need in order to legitimise demands for universal provision through the political process'.[28] Hence, Margaret Thatcher's conviction that 'the statutory services can only play their part successfully if we don't expect them to do for us things that we could be doing for ourselves'.[29] The notion that voluntarism and charity ought to be more involved in the provision of social services, amidst the retreat of state provision, is complementary to the argument that the voluntary sector ought not to be engaged politically. Contemporary criticisms of the supposed influence of NGOs in promoting 'burdensome' regulation and constraint upon industry have roots in the 1970s concern that Britain and other industrialised nations had become ungovernable, partly through the political system being clogged up with the demands of pressure groups.[30] This in turn manifested

[27] John Mohan and Karl Wilding, 'Economic Downturns and the Voluntary Sector: What Can We Learn from Historical Evidence?', *History and Policy*, April 2009. Available at: http://www.historyandpolicy.org/papers/policy-paper-85.html (accessed 21 April 2009).
[28] D. Green, 'Foreword', in R. Whelan, *Involuntary Action: How Voluntary is the 'Voluntary' Sector* (London, 1999), p. ix.
[29] Margaret Thatcher, Speech to Women's Royal Voluntary Service National Conference ('Facing the New Challenge'), 19 January 1981, http://www.margaretthatcher.org/speeches/displaydocument.asp?docid=104551 (accessed 6 January 2010).
[30] Anthony Adair, 'A Code of Conduct for NGOs: A Necessary Reform', 1 October 1999, http://www.iea.org.uk/record.jsp?type=book&ID=374 (accessed 6 January 2010); M. Crozier *et al.*, *Crisis of Democracy* (New York, 1975), pp. 12–14.

itself in the Thatcher governments' distaste for 'lobbies', and motivated attacks from the right on international aid and development charities during the 1980s. Of course, the New Right is not alone in bringing ideology to the debate – neo-Tocquevillian social scientists champion a vision of liberal civic life with no less commitment.

Finally, there is a much broader numbers game that has been played over the voluntary sector over the past half-century that makes it inconclusive as to whether there has been a decline even on the most basic measures. Each time evidence is presented of decline, new data emerge that immediately contradict it. Beveridge's worries in 1948, then, soon proved to be ill-founded. In their seminal 1963 work, *The Civic Culture*, Gabriel Almond and Sidney Verba found that membership rates of voluntary organisations were much higher in the United States and the United Kingdom than elsewhere in Europe. While Almond and Verba were keen to point to the qualitative differences in the various forms of participation, their overall conclusions, in terms of the social capital debate, suggest there need be little cause for concern: even relatively passive forms of membership that required little action on the part of supporters improved citizens' feelings of political competence and, thus, helped sustain British democratic life.[31]

In a sense, *The Civic Culture* pointed to a new 'golden age' of participation and voluntary action, one which Robert Putnam has subsequently bemoaned the loss of in US society. Yet, when attempts have been made to apply the findings to Britain, such calls for pessimism seem less certain. Peter Hall, reviewing a number of studies into voluntarism in Britain in 1999, found that while many traditional voluntary groups had indeed seen a decline in membership, others had actually increased their membership, and new groups continued to be founded all the time. A study of over 1,000 organisations conducted in 1992, for instance, found that while one-quarter of them had been founded before 1944, roughly the same amount had been founded in each of the decades of the 1970s and 1980s.[32] Using such raw data alone suggests the narrative is as much open to optimism as it is to pessimism.

[31] Gabriel A. Almond and Sidney Verba, *The Civic Culture: Political Attitudes and Democracy in Five Nations* (Princeton, 1963).
[32] Cited in Peter Hall, 'Social Capital in Britain', *British Journal of Political Science*, 29, 1999, pp. 417–461 (p. 422).

Yet, such squabbling over numbers does not add much to our understanding of the voluntary sector. It is time to move the debate forward. The analysis must shift from the quantitative to the qualitative dimensions. We ought to seek to understand the various relationships individual citizens have had with the different types of voluntary action. Certainly, it will be the case that some forms of participation add more to civic life than others. But, in the first instance, we should not rush to judgement. We should try to understand the different types of engagement on their own terms; to understand the rational decisions taken to engage with voluntary organisations in certain ways. To do so is to understand the context of voluntarism in any one year, decade or period. And to know this context is to know the history of voluntarism.

II

Together, then, what the chapters in this volume do is point to certain themes that are central to the history of voluntary action over the last century. And the history of these themes goes some way to providing a chronological framework for understanding *The Ages of Voluntarism*, a chronology marked by persistent continuities as well as change. If we accept that the voluntary sector cannot be understood as an entity in its own right, then the two broad thematic areas that require further exploration are its relationship with what exists above – the state – and what exists below – society. The history of voluntarism is one of its changing relationships with these two entities. It does not so much occupy a space between the two, but is part of a complex set of relationships and interactions such that its history is inseparable from both.

To engage with this history, it is necessary to reflect upon the definition of voluntary action. For Beveridge, the term encompassed the entirety of 'private action, that is to say action not under the direction of any authority wielding the power of the State', notwithstanding the fact that his report was 'confined to Voluntary Action for a public purpose – for social advance'.[33] Others offer more prescriptive definitions, encompassing, for example, operational and financial independence, the distribution of surpluses in a not-for-profit manner, and the use of volunteers.[34] As we have noted

[33] Beveridge, *Voluntary Action*, p. 8.
[34] B. Knight, *Voluntary Action*, 2nd edn (London, 1993), pp. 73–74.

elsewhere, terminology and definitions tend to carry with them analytical assumptions that do not translate easily across academic disciplines.[35] Indeed, the extensive definitional possibilities on offer explain the popularity of Kendall and Knapp's characterisation of the sector as 'a loose and baggy monster'.[36] Theoretically, we tend towards Beveridge's expansiveness, that voluntary action embraces all associational life, from Sunday football leagues to political party membership and international lobbying organisations. Yet, there are two practical reasons for the more targeted approach taken in this volume. First, the organisational history of many of the more prominent forms of association – political parties and trade unions being cases in point – continues to be well covered by commentators.[37] Second, and perhaps more pertinently, for the purpose of the chapters collected here, is that this volume is not conceptualised as a comprehensive overview of voluntarism. Rather it seeks to tackle specifically the decline narratives outlined above, to champion interpretations of continuity and change, and to highlight specific areas where these have been unduly neglected.

What we are referring to, then, is indeed a 'loose and baggy monster'. In order to uncover the diversity and vitality of the voluntary sector, the chapters in this collection do not adopt a definition that restricts it to, say, philanthropy, legally-constituted charities, or specific types of non-professional activity. To do so would be to establish norms from which any changes must be regarded as abnormal derivations: from such a point, inappropriate narratives of decline soon set in. Yet, the chapters in this collection do not seek to include literally all forms of associational life. Although the voluntary sector seemingly overlaps with, and certainly campaigns on similar issues to, political parties and trade unions, it does not do so with the intention of ultimately obtaining general political power (no matter how minority-based such a political party might be), nor does it, at its core, serve an instrumentalist function for its members (which is the proper role of a trade union).

---

[35] James McKay and Matthew Hilton, 'Introduction', in Nick Crowson, Matthew Hilton and James McKay (eds), *NGOs in Contemporary Britain: Non-State Actors in Society and Politics since 1945* (Basingstoke, 2009), pp. 3–4.

[36] J. Kendall and M. Knapp, 'A Loose and Baggy Monster: Boundaries, Definitions and Typologies', in J. Davis Smith, C. Rochester and R. Hedley (eds), *An Introduction to the Voluntary Sector* (London, 1995).

[37] For recent contributions see: Andrew Thorpe, *Parties at War: Political Organization in Second World War Britain* (Oxford, 2009); J. Lawrence, *Electing Our Masters: The Hustings in British Politics from Hogarth to Blair* (Oxford, 2009).

In definitional terms, the voluntary sector has blurred edges, but it warrants separate study because of its particular role in relationship to society and the state. The changing dynamics of this role are uncovered in the chapters that follow. And the first proposition that must be asserted is that the history of voluntary action is inseparable from the history of the state. Beveridge's concerns that the state might crowd out the voluntary sector as it expands its own social services have proved unfounded. Indeed, as the state has expanded, it has sought new relationships with the voluntary sector, particularly as a form of service provision that either complements the role of the state, or else performs the government's duties to its citizens. This has led to an ongoing debate about the independence of the sector, its co-option through funding and its manipulation into areas that serve the interests of the sitting administration, rather than those of the voluntary organisation itself or the constituency which it seeks to represent. Yet, once viewed over the long term, we should take care not to exaggerate these potential difficulties. Justin Davis Smith has remarked that, by the interwar period, there was already a great deal of 'interdependence' between the state and the voluntary sector.[38]

In part, this was because the developing state continued to rely upon the voluntary sector. Early welfare reforms took account of the role of volunteering and made provisions for the funding of organisations in selected areas. In times of war, such collaboration continued and was extended rather than being pushed to one side. As Peter Grant's chapter demonstrates, an increasingly interventionist state in time of war did not preclude the continued development of a thriving voluntary sector; indeed, it encouraged it, contrary to assumptions in the existing literature. While the scale of volunteering to fight in the First World War has long been appreciated, it is little understood that this was supported by a comparable voluntary effort on the home front, which became more coordinated and regulated (but most certainly not displaced) by the state as the war progressed. Grant outlines three stages in this. First came the establishment of the National Relief Fund (NRF) in 1914, which relied upon the existing voluntary infrastructure to channel support and relief, and operated in the mould of middle-class paternalism. Inconsistencies and delays in the NRF system led to the appointment by the War Office of a Director General of Voluntary Organisations in 1915, charged with ensuring the eradication

---

[38] Justin Davis Smith, 'The Voluntary Tradition: Philanthropy and Self-Help in Britain, 1500–1945', in Davis Smith *et al.*, *Introduction to the Voluntary Sector*, p. 25.

of waste and the maximisation of support for troops. Finally came legislation, in the form of the 1916 War Charities Act, which sought to tackle the small amount of fraudulent activity taking place. Internally, the war encouraged professionalisation and innovation within the charity sector, seeing the development of flag days, direct mail and subscription lists. Externally, it embedded a notion of 'charity working hand-in-hand with state welfare', which would be prominently explored in the 1930s by Elizabeth Macadam's *The New Philanthropy*.[39]

The next stage in the development of the state and the voluntary sector came with Beveridge's own reforms of the 1940s. The establishment of the National Health Service, the welfare state and the era of mass education provided new opportunities for the voluntary sector. Despite widespread predictions of its displacement following the Attlee reforms, Nicholas Deakin has warned elsewhere against seeing the state/voluntarism relationship in the crude terms of a zero-sum game, of growth in one sector necessarily leading to shrinkage in another. Instead, he draws attention to the changes this new situation brought about within the sector: 'new attitudes were developing as new skills were acquired and new tasks addressed, some of them directly generated by the expansion of state functions'.[40]

In his chapter with Justin Davis Smith for this volume, Deakin further elaborates on this theme, arguing against the simplistic and misleading characterisation of the Labour Party in the twentieth century as antagonistic to voluntarism. Speaking in the 1970s, Richard Crossman encapsulated Labour's supposed hostility, arguing that 'We all disliked the do-good volunteer . . . . We despised Boy Scouts and Girl Guides.' This disdain for what was perceived as patronising, middle-class meddling has coalesced with broader developments and attitudes to embed the notion of antagonism. The scientific-rationalist goals of Fabian socialism led away from the vibrant patchwork of grassroots social action, while, with the establishment and development of the welfare state, the mid-twentieth century saw collectivism shouldering many burdens that had hitherto been carried by the sector. Ideologically, it has also suited both New Labour and the New Right to exaggerate the attitude of 'Old Labour', in order to provide

---

[39] See Grant, Chapter 2, this volume, p. 46; Elizabeth Macadam, *The New Philanthropy: A Study of the Relations between the Statutory and Voluntary Social Services: With a War-Time Postscript* (London, 1943 [1934]).

[40] Deakin, 'The Perils of Partnership', pp. 40–42.

15

a rhetorical counter-point for their own political ends. Nevertheless, while opposition to voluntarism has indeed been a theme throughout Labour history, particularly on Labour's hard left, the notion of a broad and consistent antagonism is largely a myth, one based upon a confusion of charity and philanthropy with other forms of cooperation, mutual aid and active citizenship. This latter theme, which Attlee called 'the associative instinct', has been an overlooked, but nevertheless important, constant in Labour's social thought, from Attlee's experiences as a young man at Toynbee Hall, through the promotion of active and local democracy in the 1940s and the revisionist turn away from macro-economics and towards quality of life issues in the 1950s and 1960s, to the 'rainbow coalition' partnerships between local Labour administrations and voluntary groups in the 1980s. In locating coherence amongst different political actors and periods, Deakin and Davis Smith therefore complement the work of Ewen Green on Conservative ideology, where assessments of the coping capacity of civil society, in different areas and at different times, conditioned attitudes towards the appropriate role of the state.[41]

Several commentators have already pointed out that the subsequent history of the post-war state saw the further encouragement of the voluntary sector. The rediscovery of poverty in the 1960s led to greater collaboration with the voluntary sector and this growing sense of co-partnership was formalised through a series of measures in the 1970s. At the civic and regional level, local authorities were permitted to increase their formal funding of voluntary organisations, and at the national level, the Voluntary Services Unit was established in the Home Office. For a variety of ideological and practical reasons the Thatcher governments of the 1980s expanded the number of funding arrangements with the voluntary sector. The centrepiece here was the Community Programme of David Young's Manpower Services Commission, with both financial and moral imperatives overcoming suspicions from the sector (later seemingly confirmed) that the programme was principally designed to massage down politically-difficult unemployment figures.[42] The shock when this funding stream came to an end in the late 1980s marked the culmination of a decades-long crisis the sector had faced over the availability of resources; other challenges centred around new approaches to management within

---

[41] E.H.H. Green, *Ideologies of Conservatism: Conservative Political Ideas in the Twentieth Century* (Oxford, 2002), ch. 9.
[42] Deakin, 'The Perils of Partnership', pp. 56–58.

the public sector, tensions surrounding internal governance, and those centring on policy priorities.[43]

It is within the context of this latter issue, and the oppositional role of the sector in a period of hardship and social unrest, that Eliza Filby explores the impact of Thatcherism, particularly in regard to the Anglican Church. Filby begins by recounting the adaptation of the Church to the expansion of the state in the twentieth century. Two developments – the expansion of state welfare and declining church attendance – have led to a narrative of the displacement of Christian action. In fact, the Church continued to play a leading national and local role, as evidenced by the ongoing relevance of the local parish to fund-raising efforts, the role of Christians in charity work, and of national Christian organisations like Dr Barnardo's and the Children's Society. This is not to say there was no change – as Filby notes, Christian organisations adopted the style and methods of secular voluntarism, and declining denominational identity gave way to rising ecumenical initiative – but overall 'the story is one of reformulation rather than retreat'.[44] The Church was, therefore, a central player in the 1980s when, for ideological as much as practical reasons, the Thatcher governments championed the role of the voluntary sector in retraining and work schemes, in an era of mass unemployment. Church initiative here was led by Church Action with the Unemployed (CAWTU), and framed in a 'non-political', paternalistic way (albeit not always working out that way on the ground). This failure to critique the underlying causes of poverty ran counter to a contemporaneous feeling that 'the task of the Church had changed, its purpose was "not so much to take over the Samaritan role from statutory agents, as to question a system which puts so many people into the ditch"'.[45] The 1985 *Faith in the City* report was key in the articulation of this stance, although the roots of opposition to reactionary social thought can be traced back to nineteenth-century Christian socialism. Again, though, the experience of Church social action in the 1980s defies simple stereotype. *Faith in the City*'s establishment of the Church Urban Fund led to disquiet amongst the Church's middle-class membership, and demonstrated that progressive social thought was not universally shared in the Anglican community.

---

[43] N. Deakin, introductory remarks to 'The Voluntary Sector in 1980s Britain: Witness Seminar', held at the NCVO, London, 11 December 2009.
[44] See Filby, Chapter 7, this volume, p. 137.
[45] See Filby, Chapter 7, this volume, p. 146.

Finally, the Labour governments of 1997 to 2010 brought about further developments in the relationships between the state and the voluntary sector. Increased regulation, competition, corporate backing and the 'contract culture' have led many to worry that the voluntary sector will – or has – become too closely connected to the state. The concern is that such a blurring of boundaries will result in a decline of trust in voluntary bodies, precisely what has helped sustain their popularity with the public.[46] However, in his overview of some of the main changes affecting the sector under New Labour, Pete Alcock demonstrates once again the significance of adaptation and renewal, rather than decline or co-option. The most striking development for the sector during New Labour's period of office was the 2006 creation of the Office of the Third Sector (OTS), 'which brought together policy co-ordination for the voluntary and community sector with previously separate support for social enterprise and co-operatives and mutuals, and was part of a deliberate attempt by government to expand the reach of policy intervention into areas not traditionally associated with voluntary action in the country'.[47] Historically, it inaugurated a new stage in the social welfare role of voluntary action, which has developed since the nineteenth century from leading provision, through complementarity and supplementarity with regard to state welfare programmes in the twentieth century, and into the partnership seen at the start of the twenty-first century. These developments took place within a 'shared discourse' supportive to state-voluntary sector partnership, supported and encouraged through mid-1990s contributions from Nicholas Deakin (from the voluntary sector) and Alun Michael (from the Labour Party), and alongside the complementary notion of the third way, which played such a part in the wider New Labour project.[48] The result was 'a "strategic unity" amongst all the key agents and agencies, who had a collective interest in maintaining and developing the third sector as a space for policy intervention and forward planning'.[49]

---

[46] Fran Tonkiss and Andrew Passey, 'Trust, Confidence and Voluntary Organisations: Between Values and Institutions', *Sociology*, 33, 2, 1999, pp. 257–274.

[47] See Alcock, Chapter 8, this volume, p. 159.

[48] Commission on the Future of the Voluntary Sector, *Meeting the Challenge of Change; Labour Party, Building the Future Together: Labour's Policies for Partnership between Government and the Voluntary Sector* (London, 1997); A. Giddens, *The Third Way: The Renewal of Social Democracy* (Cambridge, 1998).

[49] See Alcock, Chapter 8, this volume, p. 165.

The OTS, therefore, needs to be recognised as a development that both rationalised and built upon the institutional, legal and financial changes of the New Labour years: the establishment of the Active Community Unit, the Civil Renewal Unit, and the Social Enterprise Unit; the development of the national and local Compact agreements, with their institutional complements, the Commission for the Compact, and Compact Voice; legal changes such as the 2006 Charities Act, which reformed the definition of permissible charitable activity, and the establishment of Community Interest Companies; and, perhaps most importantly, significant financial support, through the so-called 'builders programmes', which sought to develop the organisational capacity within the voluntary sector for its new role of partnership. The New Labour years were not a clean break with the past – the principle of partnership came with a long heritage in both theory and practice – but the degree of interest in and support for the sector in the 1997–2010 period marks these years out as a distinct new era of appreciation and engagement.

It is not entirely accurate, therefore, to see the state acting upon the voluntary sector. Rather, their complex interconnections mean they have to be viewed in tandem. Likewise, there exists no straightforward relationship between voluntary action and the wider public. The public supports voluntary bodies for a variety of reasons, matching the variety of organisations found within the sector itself. Therefore, any overview of the history of volunteering and membership of associations must take into account the esteem in which the voluntary sector is held by the public, and the purposes for which it believes the voluntary sector exists.

Much of the relationship between the public and the voluntary sector has been viewed in terms of trust. It is often commented that while trust in politicians has declined over the last few decades, trust in the voluntary sector has remained high. The charitable sector as a whole continues to obtain much support. A survey published by the National Council for Voluntary Organisations (NCVO) in 1998 found that 91 per cent of respondents agreed with the statement, 'I respect what charities are trying to do'.[50] Yet the nature of trust needs to be unpacked. Onora O'Neill has commented that, while we might state that we do not trust journalists, we do trust them to provide, say, accurate football results.[51] Similarly, our high levels of trust in charities might be dependent upon a restricted definition of what

---

[50] 'Blurred Vision – Public Trust in Charities', *NCVO Research Quarterly*, 1, January 1998, p. 1.
[51] Onora O'Neill, *A Question of Trust: The BBC Reith Lectures 2002* (Cambridge, 2002).

charities do. It is interesting to note that in the same survey conducted by the NCVO 89 per cent of respondents agreed that 'charities are about raising money to help the needy'. This is a far more restricted role in comparison to what charities actually do. It is a problem common to the international aid and development sector. Bodies such as Oxfam and Christian Aid enjoy high levels of public trust, but this trust is based on their role in disaster relief. If the public was made fully aware of the tremendous range of activities such voluntary organisations engage in to promote long-term development (including lobbying of domestic and international governments), then the levels of expressed trust would certainly be somewhat lower.[52]

Nevertheless, and notwithstanding these problems of measuring trust, it is quite clear that the wider public looks to the voluntary sector for specific things. These change over time as well as being incredibly varied at any one moment. Indeed, the voluntary sector has adapted over the course of the twentieth century in response to these changing demands of the public, together with the expectations and confidences the public places in it. In an age of mass political parties, therefore, the public has sought in the voluntary sector, alternative, non-sectarian means of addressing social, economic and political issues. The rise of single-issue politics is often associated with the new social movements of the 1960s and 1970s, when the decline in mass party politics set in, but it becomes apparent that the voluntary sector has always been an outlet for political expression beyond the formal party system. Too readily has it been assumed that voluntary organisations that have expressed political opinions have somehow been connected to the wings of the Conservatives, Liberals or Labour. Instead, the voluntary sector has been the means through which society can express other motivations and desires.

In this volume, for instance, Helen McCarthy's examination of the interwar voluntary sector demonstrates that associational life did not come to be dominated by the ideological logic of class-based mass party politics and that it continued to develop an independent voice, oriented towards support for liberal democracy more generally. Her point of departure is A.J.P. Taylor's 'army of busybodies' which, despite historiographical assumptions to the contrary, continued to thrive in the interwar period –

---

[52] See also C. Rochester, A. Ellis Paine, S. Howlett and M. Zimmeck, *Volunteering and Society in the 21st Century* (Basingstoke, 2010), pp. 24–25; Commission on the Future of the Voluntary Sector, *Meeting the Challenge of Change*, p. 35.

not only in terms of political party membership and organised religion, but also through organisations such as the League of Nations Union, the National Council of Women, the Club and Institute Union, and the British Legion. For McCarthy, the 'ideological work' performed by voluntary associations came in two parts. First, it educated and socialised the new mass electorate into the workings of the liberal democratic system, thereby acting as a 'bulwark of democratic values', and contributing to the relative failure of organised communism and fascism to take hold of British society during the period.[53] Second, they assisted in the democratisation of social relations. While class, gender and religious stratification continued to exist, McCarthy argues that it is erroneous to assume, as some commentators have done, that associational life entrenched privilege and anti-progressive values. Instead, limited, but nevertheless significant, ecumenism and gender- and class-mixing meant there was 'a democratising logic at work in the associational cultures of interwar Britain'.[54]

The public supported certain voluntary organisations because they trusted them to better represent their own – or others' – interests. This means that we must move away, yet again, from any idealised imagining of the social structure of the voluntary sector. The emphasis within the new social movement literature on the agency of 'middle-class radicals' with their abstract agendas – in itself a clearly significant development – risks the assumption of the relative insignificance of locality and ongoing working-class action in the post-war decades. On the contrary, working-class groups have consistently sought in voluntary action mechanisms for promoting their concerns. The charge against the welfare state is that it has made its dependants particularly passive recipients of the state's benefi-cence. But as Peter Shapely's chapter on tenants' associations demonstrates, the voluntary sector was also shaped by a working-class culture, even at the height of the welfare state, with the provision of services generating engagement rather than apathy: 'The relationship between the citizen and the state carried greater promises and raised hopes. When these hopes were not fully realised, tenants reacted in frustration.'[55] Tenants' associ-ations provided a vehicle for the assertion of working-class interests in the face of an often unresponsive bureaucracy; in doing so they 'helped to create a new decision-making arena, making a contribution to expanded

---

[53] See McCarthy, Chapter 3, this volume, p. 56.
[54] See McCarthy, Chapter 3, this volume, p. 67.
[55] See Shapely, Chapter 5, this volume, p. 100.

notions of democracy'.[56] That they managed to do so while engaging tenants from across the political spectrum demonstrates 'the essential flexibility and robustness of the voluntary organisation as a form which continued to provide an effective platform for the development of civil society'.[57]

Finally, society continues to place trust in the voluntary sector because it can be seen to deliver. The increasingly complex nature of modern life means that technocratic solutions to problems have been sought over party-political ones. Moreover, as successive governments in the post-Second World War period have 'depoliticised' issues by siphoning them off to expert committees and bureaucratic bodies, the need for expert bodies that can engage in technical disputes over specific subjects has grown. There is thus a certain logic in the rise of the passive direct debit contributor to the modern 'voluntary' organisation. As issues about the environment, public health, international development, and so on, demand expert solutions that go far beyond the competence of ordinary citizens, then so too do these citizens support those organisations they believe they can trust to put the expert case forward.

Undoubtedly, the much commented upon professionalisation of the voluntary sector since the 1940s has had its own internal dynamic. The sheer increase in size and scale of voluntary bodies means that many if not most have had to become far more professional as organisations which seemingly takes them far away from their formerly actively participating members. But the huge increases in membership of new organisations and the funds collected through individual donations show too that professionalism is something the public is willing to support.

This suggests a much more general rise of the modern voluntary agency, one which cannot be solely located in the cultural revolution of the 1960s and the attendant emergence of the 'middle-class radical' attached to post-material 'expressive' politics.[58] In this volume, Virginia Berridge and Alex Mold further explore the heightened professionalism of the voluntary sector as it adapted to the emergence of a new form of activist. But they do so by demonstrating that the 1970s were just as interesting a decade as the 1960s. Different schools of thought have imposed different models

---

[56] See Shapely, Chapter 5, this volume, p. 111.

[57] See Shapely, Chapter 5, this volume, p. 95.

[58] F. Parkin, *Middle Class Radicalism: The Social Bases of the British Campaign for Nuclear Disarmament* (Manchester, 1968).

for understanding voluntary activity during this period. Sociologists like Touraine, Melucci and Habermas have promoted new social movements and the new politics, an extra-parliamentary lifestyle activism, which broke with class-based elitism. Political scientists, on the other hand, have often focused on pressure groups, and, in particular, the differentiation between 'insider' and 'outsider' groups, a classification that relates to both organisational approach and integration in the policy-making process. In their chapter, Berridge and Mold use the case study of voluntary action around smoking and illegal drugs to demonstrate that the distinctions between old and new politics, between insider and outsider groups, simply 'melt away' when closely examined. Instead, they focus attention on the 'in between spaces' of the oppositional models, where organisations merged counter-cultural presentation and thought with more traditional pressure-group and service-provision activity, and combined policy challenge with partnership-working, a balancing act enabled by a surprisingly permissive statutory funding regime.[59] Sophisticated use of the media and of scientific research was relatively novel, and points to the increasing importance of professionalisation and expertise, whereas the importance of sympathy and collaboration amongst policy and political elites has a long heritage. Appealing for subtlety over simplicity, Berridge and Mold conclude that the activity of voluntary groups such as ASH (Action on Smoking and Health) and the Standing Conference on Drug Abuse 'might escape easy categorisation, but it should not escape our attention'.[60]

III

Such developments, as outlined by Berridge and Mold, are clearly ongoing. They give space for an optimistic reading of the state of the voluntary sector today. For all that greater state attention to the voluntary sector has seemingly threatened its independence through the contract culture, it is likely that the public will continue to support and place trust in those voluntary organisations that are better placed to mediate the expectations of the public and the regulations of the state. This may well result in the decline of yet another generation of voluntary agency, just as we have seen

[59] See Berridge and Mold, Chapter 6, this volume, p. 115.
[60] See Berridge and Mold, Chapter 6, this volume, p. 134.

the declining fortunes of philanthropic bodies and mass-member social organisations in earlier decades. Others will be able to adapt and renew themselves according to the changes taking place in state and society. But one thing must remain certain if the history of voluntary action teaches any lessons. If the current plethora of voluntary bodies cannot adapt, new ones will emerge – in different form and with different agendas – to take their place.

This is an important lesson that history brings to policy makers who seek to make the voluntary sector serve agendas other than those it sets itself. At the time of writing, the new Conservative-Liberal coalition government of May 2010 launches upon a 'Big Society' programme that seeks to revitalise the voluntary sector and unleash its potent energy.[61] While much of the detail remains vague, the novelty of these proposals is not so obvious. Indeed, the banning of the use of the term 'the third sector' within Whitehall shortly after May 2010 is an indicator that this is but the latest in a long line of 'new' attempts to forge a relationship between the state and the voluntary sector that did not start with Beveridge, or end with Blair and Brown.

There is the danger that the Big Society proposals are based upon mistaken beliefs about the relationship the voluntary sector has with both state and society. One of the key themes in Prime Minister David Cameron's rhetoric is the problems induced by an over-interfering state. As he put it in July 2010, 'top-down, top-heavy, controlling' government 'has turned able, capable individuals into passive recipients of state help with little hope for a better future. It has turned lively communities into dull, soulless clones of one another.'[62] This has been mixed with a critique of New Labour's approach to the voluntary sector that claims government has had a similar dispiriting and de-incentivising effect.[63] While the former accusation is a common trope of Conservative thought, the latter perhaps holds more empirical validity. As the chapters in this volume attest, the voluntary sector cannot so easily be controlled by external forces: new

[61] For the coalition government's Big Society Programme see 'Building the Big Society', 18 May 2010, available at: http://www.cabinetoffice.gov.uk/media/407789/building-big-society.pdf (accessed 19 July 2010).
[62] Allegra Stratton, 'David Cameron Begins Big Sell of "Big Society"', *Guardian*, 19 July 2010, available at http://www.guardian.co.uk/society/2010/jul/18/four-authorities-experiment-big-society (accessed 19 July 2010).
[63] Phillip Blond, *Red Tory: How Left and Right Have Broken Britain and How We Can Fix It* (London, 2010).

forms of voluntarism emerge, especially if other types, whether through contracting, partnerships or compacts, are seen to be too closely tied to the state's goals. Yet Cameron's proposals represent another form of control, especially since, at base, the Big Society is to be expected to step in where Big Government retreats amidst a drive to reduce public spending. But the state and the voluntary sector are not alternatives. Indeed, they thrive in their relationship to one another. It might be possible, in certain areas of the social services for example, that the voluntary sector can take over from the state, but in other areas, it is just as likely that a revitalised voluntarism will acknowledge its own limits and make claims upon the state for further intervention, increased spending and, in effect, an expansion of Big Government.

Likewise, the chapters in this volume demonstrate the diverse relationships voluntary sector organisations have with the society around them. The sector cannot be reduced to a specific role, or imagined as one particular type of volunteering. However, many of the backers and promoters of the Big Society proposals do just that. In particular, there is a strong strain of socially conservative Anglicanism within those who have become Cameron's advisors. They perceive an opportunity for a Church, supposedly marginalised over the last decade or so during a 'politically correct' programme of support for minority faiths, to re-engage with social issues, its congregations and offshoot associations providing the core of the community initiatives envisaged in the Big Society proposals.[64] Yet this is only one type of voluntary activity, one perhaps suited to the heyday of Anglican worship and membership of the Mothers' Union. Other forms of voluntary organisation, as typified in the case studies presented here, will continue to find alternative forms of expression and alternative solutions that will destabilise any imagined cosy relationship between a retreating state and an amenable voluntary sector.

This lack of control might be the principal lesson for policy makers arising from this volume, but for historians vibrancy, dynamism and diversity must also be noted. Throughout the last century, we have persistently and continuously worried about voluntarism's health and future. Largely this is because we treat the voluntary sector as a prism through

---

[64] Francis Davis, Elizabeth Paulhus and Andrew Bradstock, *Moral, But No Compass: Government, Church and the Future of Welfare* (Chelmsford, 2008); Francis Davis and Brian Strevens, *The Big Society: A View from the South* (Southampton, 2010); Iain Duncan Smith, *Breakthrough Britain: End the Costs of Social Breakdown: Overview* (London, 2007).

which we attempt to observe other phenomena: democracy, civil society, political engagement, and even individual and collective morality. For all that we define and identify the existence of an independent voluntary sector, it is never analysed – and perhaps never should be – as distinct from the society from which it emerges or from the state apparatus within which it is inevitably bound up. It is not something distinct from the world around it. And to understand this context is to see how it has continued to evolve, adapt and transform itself. The voluntary sector has not declined and, as such, its supposed revival is unlikely to prove the panacea that many have perennially hoped it might become. Understanding its changing patterns is key. It is hoped that the chapters in this volume provide a basis for better appreciating the continuities and changes in the voluntary sector.

2

Voluntarism and the impact of the First World War

PETER GRANT

The First World War was a crucial stage in the development of British voluntarism – from the unprecedented scale of activity, and the engagement of women in the war effort, to the pioneering of now-familiar forms of charitable activity – and in re-shaping the relationship between voluntary and state effort. However, the significance of the period has hitherto been obscured by pervasive misunderstandings regarding the history and development of voluntary action. From the wartime perspective, for example, there was no relative 'golden age' of philanthropy in the last decade of the nineteenth century, at least in the sense of a significant increase in charitable giving.[1] Annual income of London charities in 1883–1884 was £4.5 million; by 1912, this total had reached about £8.5 million, and, by 1913, just under £9 million, which meant that voluntary contributions grew approximately in line with national income.[2] What did exist as a backdrop, however, was a highly developed sense of voluntarism. The clearest and most widespread of mutual aid organisations for ordinary people were the trade union and the developing labour movement, and the war years saw a significant increase in union membership. By 1914, trade union membership had doubled from under 2 million at the turn of the century to 4 million, and was to double again, to 8 million, by 1920.

---

[1] See, for example, Frank Prochaska, *The Voluntary Impulse: Philanthropy in Modern Britain* (London, 1988); and Justin Davis Smith, 'Philanthropy and Self-help in Britain 1500–1945', in Justin Davis Smith, Colin Rochester and Rodney Hedley (eds), *An Introduction to the Voluntary Sector* (London, 1995).

[2] The figures exclude 'self-help' or mutual charities such as friendly societies. Source: *Howe's Classified Directory of Metropolitan Charities* (various years).

Friendly societies were also in their heyday during the late nineteenth and early twentieth century and 'by 1900 the membership of affiliated and ordinary friendly societies had risen as high as 5,400,000 (in a United Kingdom population over twenty of about 24 million)'.[3] Whilst sport and the uniformed organisations had a major impact on the male population, there was equal, if not greater, evidence of the potential for voluntary action among the women of pre-1914 Britain. In the 1890s, it has been estimated 'that half a million women volunteers worked full time in charity and another 20,000 were paid officials in philanthropic societies'.[4] There were also many voluntary organisations with a significant membership of working-class women, such as the co-operative movement and the non-conformist churches, but it was women from the 'respectable' working class who were dominant. As Bernard Waites has observed, 'the wives of labourers were relatively untouched by social institutions such as the Cooperative Society and Women's Cooperative Guild which were so significant for artisan families'.[5] Other organisations were more traditional and reflected the deference relationships of late Victorian society. The largest of these were probably the Mothers' Union and allied church-led bodies. Although membership figures are fragmentary, Prochaska has suggested that a million women and children attended these meetings in the Edwardian period.[6]

The foregoing was fertile ground for what became the greatest act of volunteering ever witnessed in this country. Two-and-a-half million men volunteered to fight in a conflict that cost more than 700,000 of them their lives. Hundreds of books have been written about this phenomenon and many more are published every year. But there was another act of volunteering between 1914 and 1918 on at least the same scale, though without the same life-and-death consequences. This was the voluntary effort at home, especially to support the men at the front, in health and sickness, but also to aid numerous other charitable causes. It remains a phenomenon about which little has been written. Even in the relatively few publications

---

[3] Brian Harrison, *Peaceable Kingdom* (Oxford, 1982), p. 178. The statistics come from the *15th Abstract of Labour Statistics*, Parliamentary Papers (PP) Cd 6228, cvii, p. 254.
[4] Prochaska, *Philanthropy*, p. 74. His source is Angela Burdett-Coutts (ed.), *Women's Mission* (London, 1893), pp. 361–366.
[5] Bernard Waites, 'The Effect of the First World War on Class and Status in England, 1910–20', *Journal of Contemporary History*, 11, 1, 1976, pp. 32–33.
[6] Prochaska, *Philanthropy*, p. 381.

that cover the home front, it is not given significant space.[7] Likewise, most histories of British philanthropy and voluntary action either give little space to the First World War or treat it as some kind of 'aberration' or passing phase in the prelude to the establishment of the welfare state.[8] This omission (or something close to it) was recognised by Geoffrey Finlayson when he commented that, 'studies on the influence of war on welfare in the twentieth century . . . have concentrated almost exclusively on the provision of statutory welfare in Britain to the exclusion of an examination of voluntarism'. He went on to note that:

> In any general survey of twentieth-century Britain, there are many references to socialism and collectivism, but few to self-help and charity. The debate on the effects of war on welfare has quite ignored, except by implication, the influence of war on voluntarism and social welfare.[9]

There was a massive increase in charitable voluntary activity during the First World War. Around 11,000 new charities were created, a 30 per cent increase on the number in existence pre-war. Overall, the total fund-raising effort for the war was certainly not less than £100 million and was more likely to have reached £125 to £150 million, and may well have been greater than that.[10] This meant that every man who served in the forces during the war had an average of around £20 to £40 contributed to his support, worth about £1,000 to £2,000 in 2010. During the First World War, the total value of *all* charity investments was £34 million and annual charitable income, of

---

[7] For example two books were published in 2006 on the home front in the Great War. Ian Beckett, in *Home Front 1914–1918* (London, 2006), does give charitable effort some coverage whereas the other, Peter Cooksley, *The Home Front: Civilian Life in World War One* (Stroud, 2006), seems preoccupied with aircraft and airships. Another with nothing to say on voluntary action is E.S. Turner, *Dear Old Blighty* (London, 1980), while Richard Van Emden and Steve Humphries's oral history, *All Quiet on the Home Front: An Oral History of Life in Britain during the First World War* (London, 2003), again contains very little reference to non-uniformed voluntary activity.

[8] By 'voluntary action' I mean activity which is undertaken 'without coercion or compulsion which is deployed through voluntary organisations in the provision of welfare services'. An example of the former is David Owen, *English Philanthropy 1660–1960* (Oxford, 1965). For the 'passing phase' approach see Derek Fraser, *The Evolution of the British Welfare State* (London, 1973), or Pat Thane, *The Foundation of the Welfare State* (London, 1982).

[9] Geoffrey Finlayson, 'A Moving Frontier: Voluntarism and the State in British Social Welfare 1911–1949', *Twentieth Century British History*, 1, 1990, pp. 183, 185.

[10] See Peter Grant, '"An Infinity of Personal Sacrifice": The Scale and Nature of Charitable Work in Britain during the First World War', *War and Society*, 27, 2, 2008.

existing endowed charities, was just £14 million.[11] Therefore, war causes more than doubled pre-war charitable income. With regard to fund-raising for domestic purposes, the increase was even more dramatic, as 40 per cent of pre-war charity income went to overseas missionary activity.[12] The number of people volunteering to help wartime charities on a regular basis ran to at least 1 million, and probably nearer to 2 million, a figure that would compare favourably with the 2.6 million men who volunteered for the armed forces.[13] These numbers are also highly significant in relation to the numbers of women who were employed in other activities during the war. For example, there were only 57,000 in the Women's Auxiliary Army Corps (WAAC), 60,000 in Voluntary Aid Detachments (VADs), and 260,000 in the Women's Land Army. There were also 950,000 'munitionettes', still fewer than the likely numbers who were regularly working for charities. The working classes, especially in the industrial north of England, also contributed a greater degree of support to wartime charities than previously thought. Again contrary to some previous comments, this charitable activity strengthened as the war went on, when the majority of the smaller and exempted charities under working-class control were formed.[14]

Voluntary action and charity were, therefore, of immense significance and, unsurprisingly, there were moves in the direction of state control of charitable activity in support of the war effort. However, this was not a coherently developed policy of government, nor was it by any means a steady, linear process. Rather it was motivated by specific events, or crises, such as concerns as to wasted effort or lack of coordination in the supply of comforts for the troops. In 1915, this, together with public pressure and embarrassments over perceived shortages, led to the establishment by the War Office of the post of Director General of Voluntary Organisations (DGVO), under the highly capable Sir Edward Ward. However, Ward's remit was coordination of supply, not regulation of abuses. Legislation, in

---

[11] *63rd Report of the Charity Commission for England and Wales* (London, 1916).

[12] *Annual Charities Register and Digest 22nd Edition 1913* (London, 1913). It also dwarfs into insignificance the fund-raising efforts of the Boer War, £6 million, which Andrew Thompson describes as 'staggering' ('Publicity, Philanthropy and Commemoration: British Society and the War', in A. Thompson and D. Omissi (eds), *The Impact of the South African War* (Basingstoke, 2002), pp. 99–123.

[13] *Statistics of the Military Effort of the British Empire during the Great War 1914–1920* (London, 1922).

[14] Grant, '"An Infinity of Personal Sacrifice"'.

the form of the 1916 War Charities Act, was almost a last resort entered into when abuses of the charitable system became a significant public issue.[15] Where state intervention did occur, it was often due to a failure to harmoniously integrate the dual charitable impulses of mutual aid and philanthropy with the requirements of a budding state welfare system. Broadly, one can determine three phases of control, which clearly mirrored those in overall state intervention during the war: first, a 'business as usual' phase, attempting to continue the tradition of Victorian paternalistic philanthropy – most notably through the National Relief Fund (NRF), but also with the flourishing of thousands of individual charitable enterprises; second, a crisis point as the scale and duration of the conflict overwhelmed uncoordinated effort, leading in 1915 to the formation of the DGVO and including state control of Belgian charities and takeover of the main charities for prisoners of war; and, finally, state control on a more organised basis with the 1916 War Charities Act.

Paternalistic philanthropy – the NRF

On the outbreak of war, the only organisation concerned with allowances and pensions for servicemen and their dependants was the Commissioners of the Royal Hospital at Chelsea.[16] Their rates of relief remained unchanged from the Boer War, and the massive demands of the new conflict were clearly way beyond their means. The only other source of immediate help came through the local Poor Law Guardians, with the existing mechanisms, rules and rates of relief again unsuited to such emergency needs. There were also two other charitable organisations in existence which provided some assistance to servicemen's families; the Soldiers' and Sailors' Family Association (SSFA), which had been founded in 1885, and the Soldiers' and Sailors' Help Society (SSHS), but on the outbreak of war they were little known and had very few resources.

---

[15] The Act was the first legislation passed in the UK regulating the activities of collecting charities (i.e. those that appealed for funds from the public). Until 1916 only endowed charities were regulated under the supervision of the Charity Commission.

[16] Later on in the war the Royal Patriotic Fund Corporation also became involved but before it was given an extended role in the provision of pensions it confined its activities to 'financial assistance for the families of those who fell in action'. See Graham Wootton, *The Politics of Influence: British Ex-Servicemen, Cabinet Decisions and Cultural Change 1917–57* (London, 1963), ch. 3.

It was clear that if something was to be done quickly then this would have to be through charitable means. Indicating the somewhat haphazard and spontaneous responses to the outbreak of war, there were two royal appeals. The first was on 6 August under the name of the Prince of Wales for a National Relief Fund, whereas the second, on behalf of his grandmother, Queen Alexandra, was specifically for the SSFA. This rather embarrassing situation was quickly remedied when, on 11 August, it was agreed to amalgamate the two schemes under an executive committee, chaired, from October 1914, by Sir George Murray. Though the Fund was established to help alleviate all distress caused by the war, in practice 60 per cent of the proceeds were directed towards naval and military distress.[17] The NRF utilised a network of 300 local relief committees established by the Local Government Board in towns with a population of 20,000 or more, or counties for smaller population centres, to coordinate relief efforts. These committees, though closely involved with the NRF, were also at liberty to raise their own funds and were not centrally controlled. Their significant autonomy could, and did, lead to disagreements with the NRF in London. In some areas, due to the boom in industry later in 1915, their work became less critical as the war continued, even though their early efforts were considerable.

Though some charity leaders – in the existing Charity Organisation Society (COS), Guild of Help and the social welfare movement – were quick to see that the local representation committees had major implications for the relationship between charity and the state, there was no existing national organisation that could identify and recommend potential beneficiaries and administer the NRF on the ground.[18] This role was vital, as the increase in work was so massive with 'the number of wives in receipt of allowances at the outbreak of war [increasing] in a fortnight from 1,500 to 250,000'.[19] The only bodies that fitted the bill were the SSFA, created to help relieve distress in the Boer War, and the even smaller SSHS. They rose from obscurity to become highly significant social welfare networks within a

---

[17] Extracted from the final accounts of the National Relief Fund in *Final Report of the National Relief Fund, March 1921* (London, 1921).

[18] Frederick D'Aeth, 'War Relief Agencies and the Guild of Help Movement', *Progress: Civic, Social, Industrial*, 10, 1915, pp. 140–147; Jane Lewis, 'The Boundary between Voluntary and Statutory Social Service in the Late Nineteenth and Early Twentieth Centuries', *Historical Journal*, 39, 1, 1996, p. 175.

[19] Millicent Garrett Fawcett, 'War Relief and War Service', *Quarterly Review*, 225, 446, 1916, pp. 111–129.

short time from the outbreak of war. Elizabeth Macadam, no great lover of unregulated charitable activity, praised the mobilisation of the SSFA, saying that 'the resurrection of this moribund body at lightning speed is one of the triumphs in the history of voluntary effort'.[20] Just how rapid this increase in activity was is revealed by its work in Liverpool, where the SSFA 'rose from a body of 13 members with no subscription list to a body with 29 district heads, some 700 voluntary workers and an expenditure of £1,000 a week within the first few weeks of war'.[21]

Arthur Marwick has called the whole system of the NRF 'an attempt to integrate private charity and public appeal into Government action'.[22] It was a somewhat uneasy alliance for many reasons, not least the confusion between entitlements and charitable 'gifts'. This led to an unsurprising backlash when Labour leaders criticised the SSFA for treating payments as charity, to be given only if working-class women met their expectations of good behaviour. Labour insisted the money was a right and should be administered by the state.[23] Exacerbating these issues, most of the field work for the SSFA was done by middle-class 'lady visitors' who 'acted as the advocates, disciplinarians, trouble-shooters, and morality police of soldiers' wives'.[24] Despite the continuing uneasy relationship with Labour, the left did see some merit in the method of organisation of the NRF. Very early on, the *Daily Herald* proclaimed that 'local relief committees must be made into "citizen organizations", not mere dispensers of charity'.[25] This was a far-sighted comment. The fact that the committees increasingly had to become more representative and inclusive gave the working class an entrée to, at least, local corridors of power, and the mistake of failing to include trade unionists and other representatives of working people was, generally, not repeated. As the war went on, working-class membership of official committees at both local and national level became the rule rather than the exception. Because the NRF was not state-controlled, the exact remit and powers of the SSFA were also something of a mystery. Individual branches or even individual officials had wide discretion in

---

[20] Elizabeth Macadam, *The New Philanthropy: A Study of the Relations between the Statutory and Voluntary Social Services* (London, 1934), p. 56.

[21] D'Aeth, 'War Relief Agencies'.

[22] Arthur Marwick, *The Deluge: British Society and the First World War* (Boston, 1965), p. 43.

[23] For example in the declaration by the Workers' National Committee at the outbreak of war in 1914: see *The Labour Year Book 1916* (London, 1915), p. 37.

[24] George Robb, *British Culture and the First World War* (Basingstoke, 2002), p. 79.

[25] *Daily Herald*, 10 August 1914.

how they applied the funds, and this led to major inconsistencies. The other main problem – and one still common to emergency appeals to this day – was that of delays in the distribution of the funds. By April 1915, the NRF had realised the remarkable sum of £5 million, but only £2 million had been handed out. The press and the Workers' National Committee had persisted in their criticism and some of the more militant areas outside England were on the verge of open revolt at the dictates of the London-based body.

The National Relief Fund was too much an expression of outdated paternalistic philanthropy, impinging on an area ripe for integration into the embryonic welfare state. More than anything else, it was the moral issue of paternalistic middle- and upper-class 'do-gooders' passing judgement that doomed the entrepreneurial approach, and George Robb is, therefore, perfectly correct in his view that 'the traditional philanthropic ideal of moral reform was out of step with wartime democratic sentiment'.[26] Nevertheless, the NRF raised an enormous sum from all sections of society, though mainly in the early part of the war.[27] It was also a significant precursor for state intervention in the social welfare field and demonstrated that even at a time of enormous expenditure on the war itself, the British economy could sustain such costs. It was 'the unprecedented circumstances of the war [that] had made such massive social spending possible'.[28] The NRF brought the potential of a welfare state a step closer and, by the reaction of the labour movement, which now had to be taken far more seriously to maintain national unity, it put another nail in the coffin of paternalistic philanthropy.

An outbreak of sock-knitting

Following the first flush of response to the war, which especially concerned the hardships of soldiers' dependants and Belgian refugees, there was a

[26] Robb, *British Culture*, p. 79.

[27] The total was just under £7 million of which over 70 per cent was raised in the first nine months, *Final Report of the National Relief Fund*.

[28] Susan Pedersen, 'Gender, Welfare and Citizenship in Britain during the Great War', *American Historical Review*, 95, 1990, pp. 983–1006. The totals paid out year-on-year were (to the nearest million): August 1914–March 1915, £15 million; April 1915–March 1916, £53 million; April 1916–March 1917, £78 million; April 1917–March 1918, £113 million; April 1918–March 1919, £125 million. Source: *Statistics of the Military Effort*, pp. 569–570.

Table 2.1 Main categories of war charities[29]

Comforts for British and Empire troops	28%
Medical support (including hospitals and supplies)	25%
Support for disabled servicemen	13%
Relieving distress at home	11%
Post-war remembrance (including war memorials) and celebration	9%
Aid for refugees and overseas	8%
Assistance to prisoners of war	7%

flourishing of voluntary activity geared in particular towards medical services and troop comforts. Medical services were, to some extent, already systematised and state-controlled, or quickly became so. Voluntary action, especially for women, could be directed to existing medical support agencies. These included VADs, which had been in existence since 1909 (and were administered by the Joint War Committee of the British Red Cross and Order of St John, through the Joint VAD Committee), the Women's Sick and Wounded Convoy Corps, founded by Mrs St Clair Stobart in 1907, and the First Aid Nursing Yeomanry (FANY), founded in the same year by Captain Edward Baker. By 1912, the VADs, of whom two-thirds were women, had a strength of 26,000, and this reached 90,000 by 1918. Even so, with the enormous demands created by the war, there were immediate shortages of medical supplies and comforts for wounded men both abroad and at home.

Existing organisations, like the National Union of Women's Suffrage Societies and the YMCA, were certainly in a much better position to re-focus their activity to war relief, and the improvisation so typical of the early months of the war was, therefore, far easier for bodies with an existing organisation and trained volunteers. But these were supplemented by hundreds of newly created bodies, each dealing with specific aspects of war relief, and thousands of individual, even less coordinated efforts. By the end of the war, charities operating nationally fell under the main categories shown in Table 2.1.

Between them, these organisations used an astonishing range of fund-raising techniques, many of which are still in use today. Flag days, though

---

[29] Source: *War Charities Act 1916: Index of Charities Registered Under the Act to March 1919* (London, 1919). Peter Cahalan, *Belgian Refugee Relief in England During the Great War* (London: Taylor & Francis, 1982), suggests nine main categories: enemy aliens, refugees, war-devastated regions, prisoners of war, convalescent soldiers, the Red Cross, soldiers on leave, comforts for soldiers and civilian distress in England.

not invented during the First World War, sprung to prominence after 1914. Direct mail to potential donors was also used for the first time to any significant extent, with the YMCA and the Church Army employing the technique extensively. Subscription lists for many of the larger funds were published in the national press, most notably for *The Times* appeal, and this was a technique adopted at much more modest levels as well:

> A north-country agricultural village did so well [in raising funds for the NRF] that an inquiry was sent to the chairman of the parish council, if haply he had hit upon a money-raising method that might be recommended to others. It has not been recommended – till now. The village committee had written the names of the subscribers on the blackboard outside the schoolroom every day! How thin is the dividing line between advertisement and publicity![30]

Payroll giving was again not new, but increased significantly. One example of this was in Birmingham, where 'weekly collections have been made in most of the large factories, and about 50,000 workpeople have contributed over £20,000 to the [National Relief] Fund'.[31] The city council in Manchester utilised a similar method:

> The Corporation Officers' Guild proposed a scheme of voluntary weekly contributions . . . and a uniform basis of contribution was decided upon, the officials taxing themselves on the amount of their salaries, the taxes varying from 2¾ to 5 per cent. About one-sixth of the total of the Relief Fund [£30,000 by this date] has been contributed by the officials and employees of the Corporation.[32]

Half-way house – the Director General of Voluntary Organisations

The largest number of organisations were concerned with supplying 'comforts' to British forces, but there were serious questions as to whether comforts were going to the right people. 'Middle-class' regiments, such as the Civil Service Rifles or Honourable Artillery Company, might be well

---

[30] W.E. Dowding, 'The Romance of Voluntary Effort: Part 1 – National Relief Fund', *TP's Journal*, 3, 27, 1915, p. 4.

[31] Alderman W.H. Bowater, Lord Mayor of Birmingham, 'Busy Birmingham: Equipping the Allied Armies', *TP's Journal*, 3, 28, 1915, p. 31.

[32] Alderman Daniel McCabe, Lord Mayor of Manchester, 'Manchester's Motto', *TP's Journal*, 2, 21, 1915, p. 203.

provided for, but what about some of the New Army battalions? Should the supply of such essentials as warm clothing, blankets or field glasses really be left to the vagaries of charitable collections? This last question was uppermost as the harsh winter of 1914–1915 set in, and conditions in the trenches became deplorable. The Home Secretary, Reginald McKenna, was questioned in November 1914 on the subject, and throughout 1915 there was significant correspondence between Major-General Sir John Cowans, Quarter-Master General (QMG) at the War Office, and Lieutenant-General Ronald Maxwell, QMG in France, on the issue, with increasing numbers of letters appearing in the press. Eventually this 'sock scandal' proved the current system of supply of comforts was failing, and the DGVO scheme was announced in November 1915 by Henry Foster, Financial Secretary to the War Office. The Director General himself was to be Lieutentant-Colonel Sir Edward Ward, an unjustly forgotten figure. In 1901, Ward had become Permanent Secretary at the War Office. After significant problems with Hugh Arnold-Foster, the last War Minister of Balfour's adminis-tration, Ward greatly assisted his Liberal replacement, Richard Haldane, with his major army reforms, including re-organising the Army Medical Department, establishment of the Officers Training Corps, and the draw-ing up of mobilisation plans with Douglas Haig, then Haldane's military advisor.

When tasked with War Office re-organisation, Ward drew up a com-pletely new structure and outlined training proposals within a month. He was possibly the first senior figure in Whitehall to realise that the application of business principles to government would bring significant improvements, some nine years before Lloyd-George utilised similar principles in his wartime coalition. He enlisted the services of the Director of the London School of Economics, H.J. MacKinder, who turned the pro-posals into a twenty-one-week curriculum for officials and army officers which began in January 1907. The War Office was, thus, the first govern-ment department to have a coordinated professional training programme. In the debate on the 1908–1909 army estimates, Haldane was able to report to Parliament on the success of the course.[33] It was supervised by a small committee, including Ward, MacKinder, Haig and Sidney Webb, who, despite their radically differing political views, were united in their deter-mination to bring sound business training to both army and civil service.

---

[33] See Ernest M. Teagarden, *Haldane at the War Office: A Study in Organization and Management* (New York, 1976).

With his organisational skills, strong belief in business principles and humanitarianism, Ward was the ideal man for the job of DGVO, a role that, in other hands, could have easily alienated much of the voluntary effort.[34] His office created a register of organisations, with an official certificate both for organisations and workers, and there were 400,000 badge holders by 1918. Communication was maintained with army units in the field to determine their requirements, and a 'comforts pool' was set up in each theatre of war to reduce supply delays.

The two aims of the DGVO were coordination to reduce waste and provision of maximum support for the fighting troops. A press notice was issued on 11 October 1915, and the newspapers commented favourably on both the establishment of the scheme and Ward's appointment in particular. In an editorial under the heading 'The New War Work Scheme, Business Methods Welcomed', *The Times* concluded that:

> Its prime mission is to tell the people of England to make the things which are really wanted and to make them in such quantities as to admit of their being promptly handled by the transport authorities . . . . In other words business methods are to be applied which have hitherto been lacking.[35]

In 1916, the Army Council added to Ward's list of duties the task of providing comforts from Britain for the troops of Allied countries, and this included the US armies that began to reach Europe in 1917. The final totals of items produced under the DGVO scheme and distributed to troops, hospitals and others were prodigious, as detailed in Table 2.2. Ward placed an approximate monetary value on these of £5,134,656.[36] He summarised the work of his department in the following words:

> This great band of voluntary workers will be content to have it recorded that through their efforts the gallant men of our fighting force, whether in health or sickness, have appreciated to the full the efforts of a generous public in providing them an unlimited supply of comforts and gifts of almost every kind, which have helped them to endure the trials and hardships of an active campaign, and which have alleviated their sufferings when lying wounded or sick in hospital. The work of these organisations has done more than any other movement in connection with the war to help and strengthen the

---

[34] In addition to introducing better conditions for 'native' workers with the British army, Ward established recreational and insurance schemes for War Office staff and was a Trustee of the RSPCA, being very active in the prosecution of animal cruelty.

[35] *The Times*, 12 October 1915.

[36] Report on the Director General of Voluntary Organizations.

Table 2.2 Total items supplied by the DGVO

Mufflers	1,742,947
Mittens (pairs)	1,574,156
Helmets (wool)	435,580
Socks (pairs)	3,607,959
Sweaters	123,666
Pyjamas	523,032
Bed jackets and helpless case jackets	325,188
Bed socks	351,764
Operation stockings	154,142
Hospital bags	6,145,673
Bandages of all kinds	12,258,536
Dressings of all kinds	45,503,534
Woodwork articles of all kinds	516,408
Books (via the 'Camps Library')	16,660,000
Cigarettes	232,599,181
Tobacco (lbs)	256,487
Games	62,193
Total	**322,840,446**

morale of our men in the severe trials and difficulties through which they have passed, and has formed a great bond of affection and regard with those left at home.

When the official history of the Great War is written, there will be no more illuminating page than that which records the noble self-sacrifice of the great band of workers at home whose privilege it has been to take their share and play their part in ministering to the needs of our Army, and in having fulfilled their task loyally, faithfully, and in full measure.[37]

The success of Ward as DGVO, achieving economies of scale without stifling local endeavour, meant there was no further adverse press comment regarding troop comforts after 1915. Further, he was certainly one of the first people to bring business methods into the voluntary realm.[38] Significantly, though, it was not only the *stated* aims of the DGVO scheme that were welcomed by the press. *The Times* expected Ward's office to do rather more, hoping that 'the scheme will stimulate the work of *bona fide*

---

[37] Report on the Director General of Voluntary Organizations.

[38] Ward was created the first ever GBE – the highest award of the newly created Order of the British Empire – and his many other activities included being Commissioner of the Metropolitan Police Special Constabulary. He died in 1928 of blood poisoning in the south of France.

associations and will . . . check the operations of certain bodies which are conducted mainly for the benefit of the promoters'.[39] It was clear that some expected rather more of the DGVO than he could deliver. It was, therefore, no surprise when, in March 1916, *Truth* sounded a critical note.[40] Citing the case of the Sailors' and Soldiers' Tobacco Fund, their ire was raised because of the proportion of its overheads.[41] This was an entirely unfair criticism, as control of administrative expenses was certainly *not* one of the intended responsibilities of the DGVO. Ward's remit was insufficient and his powers too limited to expect him to act as a regulator or policeman. It is also important to note that the DGVO was an army-inspired programme run from the War Office. It was intended specifically to deal with issues of concern to that department, namely the efficient supply of comforts and medical requisites to troops, and the deflection of any criticism that the army was either not doing enough, or was failing to coordinate efforts. The roles ascribed by *The Times* and *Truth* were most certainly not those of the War Office but of the Home Department, and Whitehall divisions and rivalries were probably even more significant in 1915 than they are today. In its primary aim of coordinating the collection and distribution of comforts, the DGVO scheme was wholly successful. It continued after the 1916 War Charities Act, despite Ward's concerns that the Act could undermine his own efforts. He, himself, was able to report in June 1917 that 'the response to the Army Council's Scheme for the provision of comforts for general distribution to the Troops in the Field has been highly satisfactory' and the long delays previously reported had ceased.[42]

The DGVO scheme was a half-way house between unregulated and uncoordinated activity, and full legislation. It was designed to solve a specific problem, that of an imbalance in supply of troops' comforts, rather than to control the entire voluntary effort of the country. Based as it was on cooperation rather than legislation, it was inevitable that it worked well when dealing with well-organised, altruistic groups. What it could not do was deal with abuses of philanthropic principles by an unscrupulous minority of individuals who saw an opportunity for personal gain in the upsurge of charitable and voluntary giving initiated by the war.

[39] *The Times*, 12 October 1915.
[40] *Truth* was a Liberal weekly which had made a speciality of exposing financial and charity scandals since the 1880s.
[41] *Truth*, 2046, Vol. LXXIX, 1 March 1916.
[42] DGVO Memorandum 45A, Imperial War Museum, Women, War and Society 1914–1918 Collection, BO1 2/26.

State control – the War Charities Act

The creation of the DGVO dealt with the most urgent aspect of charitable support for Britain's forces. In coordinating supplies of comforts, Sir Edward Ward's department ensured there was less duplication of effort and a more equitable distribution of benefits. As such, the DGVO dealt with abuses at the supply end of charity. However, it had no influence over the collection of charitable funds, which remained open to potential misman-agement or even outright fraud. It was no surprise that some unscrupulous individuals existed who were only too eager to exploit the extraordinary generosity of the public towards war-related causes, and there were very few legal barriers in their way.[43] The Charity Commission, established in 1853, only oversaw those charities with a permanent endowment, and the vast majority of the myriad bodies that sprang up after August 1914 had no intention of establishing an endowment; they existed for immediate financial aid.

One source of pressure for reform was the charities themselves. Recognising that fraudulent operations could have serious implications for public confidence and affect the incomes of legitimate appeals, many charities began to press the authorities for action. A deputation of over twenty organisations, including the COS and War Refugees Committee, headed by the Duke of Norfolk, met with Home Secretary Sir Herbert Samuel, on 3 March 1916. The following month, Samuel appointed an official War Charities Committee, 'to consider representations which have been made in regard to the promotion and management of charitable funds for objects connected with the war, and to advise whether any measures should be taken to secure the better control or supervision of such funds in the public interest'.[44] Giving evidence to the fifth meeting of the com-mittee was the redoubtable Detective Inspector Curry, scourge of wartime charity fraudsters.[45] He carefully listed what he saw as the 'chief evils' that currently existed: the plundering of funds; irresponsible people starting funds; funds conducted either without any committee or with bogus com-mittees; insufficient checks on the expenditure of money; obtaining secret commissions on goods purchased; exaggerated appeals; patrons lending

---

[43] Street collections in London were regulated by the Metropolitan Streets Act, 1903.

[44] PP, Cd. 8287, vi, 1916.

[45] Curry's methods included the first use of (volunteer) women police detectives, the wives of two of his colleagues.

their names to charities without proper inquiry; and, in the case of appeals for the Allies, ignoring the Minister or Ambassador of the country concerned. He handed over a dossier of evidence regarding seven specific war charity scandals. He said that the police 'could without any difficulty have obtained within a few days sufficient information about the promoters [of bogus charities] to shew that they were not suitable persons to have control of such funds'.[46] It is easy to say that these cases were insignificant in relation to the totality of wartime charitable effort, but this is to ignore the impact of fraudulent activity on public opinion, especially in the circumstances pertaining at the time. Given the clear instances of fraud and parasitic activity, it is difficult to argue against the pressure for legislative change, even if some supporters of legislation suggested that fraud was far more widespread than the evidence demonstrates. The Act was passed on the final day of the parliamentary session of 1916. In the final analysis, even if the frauds were unproven or petty, public opinion, and the reputation of *bona fide* charities, demanded some legislative action. In the circumstances, the 1916 War Charities Act was probably as good a piece of legislation as was possible.

The greatest problem with the Act was that it came with very little additional funding, and was open to wide interpretation by each local authority. In London the London County Council (LCC) took a 'hard line'. They scrupulously investigated every application and totally rejected the idea of exemption, partly due to their zealous Chief Clerk, James (later Sir James) Bird, partly because they were better resourced and partly because they were very much in the public eye, especially that of the press. Further away from the capital, local authorities were much more relaxed. In the small West Riding mill town of Todmorden, for example, over 70 per cent of charities were granted exemption from the Act. The LCC was often over-bureaucratic, smaller authorities over-lax. For example, Bird was unhappy that the 17th Lancers Prisoners of War Fund did not have a properly functioning committee that met regularly.[47] Given that their Chairman was Sir Douglas Haig, and most of the others were on active service, the Secretary, Miss S.D. Whitton, rather exasperatedly wrote: 'none of the Regimental Associations for which we are working have had a real Committee Meeting since the War began, the assembling of the members being quite impossible owing to their military duties'. Despite this,

[46] The National Archives (TNA), HO 45/1084/308566/32.
[47] London Metropolitan Archives (LMA), LCC/MIN 8337 (Vol. 3).

Bird still sought their full compliance with the Act. In the end, the Fund arranged for the Regimental Agency (which was registered) to take care of their PoWs.[48]

The actual number of abuses remained quite small (for example the total number of organisations refused registration up to 1919 was just forty-one), and in 1919 the Charity Commissioners reported that 'proceedings were taken against 17 persons appealing to the public on behalf of unregistered War Charities' and that this had resulted in ten convictions. In nine cases the offenders were fined, whilst one was imprisoned.[49] In London, only seventeen organisations were refused registration during the war, and of these six were allowed on appeal.[50] There were just twenty-four cases represented by the Council to the Charity Commission under Section 7 of the Act, i.e. where there was suspicion of fraud. These included the eleven cases cited previously, of which only six proved to be fraudulent. Of the additional thirteen, two, the Red Star Society and Tubs for Tommies, were proven frauds and the police had strong suspicion against at least five others (though none appear to have been prosecuted), but the numbers were still quite small.[51]

Equally, there is also very little evidence of the Act producing significant problems for legitimate charities or over-regulation. In 1917, the Charity Commissioners felt justified in reporting that the Act was working so well it ought to be extended to all charities, saying 'the experience of the working of this Act during the short period it has been in operation has convinced us of the great value of some such control as that afforded by the Act over Charities supported by voluntary contributions'.[52] In this they continued to be supported by many of the major charities. Peter Cahalan too is quite positive in his summary of the Act:

---

[48] Some bureaucratic activity was class-based and led to error and abuse. Bird was indefatigable in investigating the bona fides of Jewish working-class charities and yet allowed the registration of one of the leading fraudsters of the period, Henry Allen Ashton. See LMA LCC/MIN 8338 (Vol. 4), Case No 638 – Koval, Ludmar, Lutsk and District Benevolent Society, and Case No 675 – British-American (Overseas) Field Hospital.
[49] *66th Report of the Charity Commissioners for England and Wales* (London, 1919), p. 9.
[50] LMA, LCC/PC/CHA/1/2.
[51] The five were: the Khaki Prisoners of War Fund; the Stick Crutch Fund; the International Bible Institute War Relief Fund; the British American (Overseas) Field Hospital (LMA, LCC/PC/CHA/1/2); and the Bob Sievier Charity Fund (TNA PRO HO 45/18406/319028/17).
[52] *64th Report of the Charity Commissioners for England and Wales* (London, 1917), p. 8.

> Several old bugbears . . . were stamped out, the Commissioners cracked down on flag days, and poorly-managed charities were compulsorily organised. How successful was the Act? On the whole, it succeeded in eliminating the worst cases of fraud and in forcing some duplicate charities to merge. The WRC and other large organisations were satisfied and the Act silenced the volume of criticism of the eighteen months before its enactment. But small organisations continued to flourish and proliferate.[53]

Many of the same issues came up again in 1939, but under very different circumstances. All parties were far more comfortable with the idea of state control in wartime and welfare provision for dependants was not an issue. With immediate conscription and vastly fewer troops abroad, troop 'comforts' were less prominent. Nevertheless, in January 1940, a new Director General of Voluntary Organisations was appointed. He was Sir Alan Hutchings, who had been Ward's deputy, though he had a far less prominent role than his former boss. A new War Charities Act was also passed in 1940, very similar in general to the 1916 Act (which was repealed), though it included Scotland from the outset, which the 1916 Act did not. The 1940 Act was still in force after the 1960 Charities Act was passed. As late as 1977, there were still 2,250 war charities registered (some of which did not qualify as charities under the 1960 Act) and it was agreed that to repeal the Act might stir up more problems than retaining it, so it was left on the statute book.[54] It was finally superseded by the Charities Act of 1992, which dealt with the control of fund-raising and charitable collections.

Conclusions

The First World War contributed towards an increased professionalisation of the charity sector (many 'modern' fund-raising techniques were invented, for example) and voluntary action was particularly effective due to (in modern parlance) at least three key mission-related criteria being demonstrated: direct feedback mechanisms from beneficiaries; clear performance measures that were shared and understood; and specific aims that were, for the most part, fulfilled through links to state provision.

---

[53] Cahalan, *Belgian Refugee Relief*, pp. 495–496.
[54] TNA HO 279/73, War Charities Act 1940, HO Comments on Goodman Committee Recommendations.

Voluntary action contributed significantly to maintaining morale both on the home front (a visible sign of 'pulling one's weight') and with troops and prisoners of war. Contrary to received opinion, transmitted through war poets and writers such as Siegfried Sassoon and Robert Graves, the vast majority of troops welcomed charitable efforts on their behalf, and were kindly disposed towards benevolence on the home front.

The First World War acted as a catalyst to further, massive, voluntary action. This was especially true for many women, and Jacqueline De Vries has suggested that it was the 'pre-war membership boom in women's social, service and political organizations' that had a significant impact in that it 'provided . . . the "social capital" necessary for winning war'.[55] This involvement of women in war was something entirely new. These 'women volunteers came from a portion of society untapped in earlier wars, the vast network of organised women's groups and associations that had been growing' for several decades before the turn of the twentieth century'.[56] During the war, a host of voluntary organisations were run by these women. Even where the nominal figurehead was a man, and men may have dominated the executive committee, it was often the women who did the day-to-day work. Moreover, it was not only leisured middle- and upper-class women who acted in this capacity, as, again, many writers have asserted.[57] The impact of the pre-1914 explosion of organised sports clubs, boys' organisations, clubs, societies, associations, and women's organisations was profound. Not only did it predispose a large cross-section of society – especially the upper working and middle classes – towards charitable endeavours, but it had many other effects. These ranged from the positive and progressive (unified bodies working across class boundaries), to the less altruistic (including restrictive trade union measures to

---

[55] Quoted in Prochaska, *Philanthropy*, p. 381.

[56] Margaret Vining and Barton C. Hacker, 'From Camp Follower to Lady in Uniform: Women, Social Class and Military Institutions before 1920', *Contemporary European History*, 10, 3, 2001, p. 353.

[57] This is a pervasive myth initiated in many of the contemporary published local histories of war activity and then repeated uncritically ever since. Even the best local histories, such as John Lee's *Todmorden and the Great War 1914–1918: A Local Record* (Todmorden, 1922), concentrate on the middle-class war charities to the exclusion of the significantly greater number of working-class-led charities in the town. Historians who are culpable in this regard include many otherwise outstanding writers such as: Arthur Marwick, *Women at War 1914–1918* (London, 1977), p. 35; Gerard de Groot, *Blighty: British Society in the Era of the Great War* (London, 1996), p. 68; Trevor Wilson, *The Myriad Faces of War: Britain and the Great War 1914–1918* (Cambridge, 1986), p. 159.

prevent the use of unskilled, especially female, labour). Most often, it was the positive that predominated.

The massive voluntary effort of 1914–1918 was the basis of a strength in social capital that gave Britain a distinct edge over Germany. In Britain, voluntary action survived the somewhat half-hearted attempts at state control, both during and after the war. In Germany state control under military direction after 1916 stifled what began as an almost equal flow of voluntary effort. It was the unique and cataclysmic nature of the war that brought about a greater fusion, or integration, of the two elements of voluntary action for social advance, philanthropy and mutual aid, breaking down many of the barriers that had previously existed, most often identified through class differences. This integration was sometimes quite explicit and deliberate, but more often accidental and unstated. Nevertheless, many of the voluntary and charitable movements of the war years combined the two impulses, often in harmonious partnership but occasionally producing class or culture clashes that had repercussions at a national level. It was often where integrative partnership broke down that state intervention was required. After the war, there was a moving apart of the trends, though the two strands were never as distinct again. The developments in voluntary action through the years of war also cemented the transformation of the accepted view of what charity was 'for'. In 1914, the Victorian view of charity as being there to treat the worst excesses of the industrial state probably had equal status with the more modern conception that charity should treat underlying causes. By 1918, the new view, which was much more comfortable with charity working hand-in-hand with state welfare, had decisively gained the upper hand.

3
Associational voluntarism in interwar Britain

HELEN MCCARTHY

Introduction

In his classic history of England during the era of the two world wars, A.J.P. Taylor paid tribute to the innumerable voluntary societies which, in his words, 'protected animals and children; defended ancient monuments and rural amenities; gave advice on birth control; asserted the rights of Englishmen, or encroached upon them. The public life of England', he concluded, 'was sustained by a great army of busybodies, and anyone could enlist in this army who felt inclined to . . . . These were the active people of England and provided the groundswell of her history.'[1] Taylor was not the first and certainly not the last historian to note the richness and resilience of associational voluntarism in Britain. Thanks to a wealth of scholarly literature, much of it produced in the last decade or so, we now know a great deal about the scale and scope of voluntary action in the past, how a broad range of voluntary associations worked and the kinds of people involved, and how such associations related to other historical actors, from the individual, family and the community, to the market and the state.[2] Furthermore, scholars working in a variety of traditions

---

[1] A.J.P. Taylor, *English History, 1914–1945* (Oxford, 1965), p. 175.

[2] This literature is too vast to list here, but for some useful overviews and collections, see, for example, Frank Prochaska, *The Voluntary Impulse: Philanthropy in Modern Britain* (London, 1988); Nick Crowson, Matthew Hilton and James McKay (eds), *NGOs in Contemporary Britain: Non-State Actors in Society and Politics since 1945* (Basingstoke, 2009); Jose Harris (ed.), *Civil Society in British History: Ideas, Identities, Institutions* (Oxford, 2003); M.J.D. Roberts, *Making English Morals: Voluntary Association and Moral Reform in England, 1787–1886* (Cambridge, 2004).

have attempted to address important conceptual questions concerning the functions and effects of associational life, and to weave its shifting dynamics into broader narratives of change and continuity in British society. For some, adopting a classic Tocquevillian perspective, associations have served as the handmaidens of democracy, counterbalancing the power of the state, teaching good citizenship and helping to integrate a complex and diverse society.[3] For others, particularly those located within a Marxist tradition, associations have been actors in class struggle and instruments of social control, reinforcing social hierarchies and, more often than not, inhibiting progressive change.[4]

This chapter aims to offer a fresh perspective on these questions by taking a closer look at Taylor's 'army of busybodies' between the wars, an era of universal suffrage, mass unemployment and nascent consumerism domestically and deepening political crisis on the international stage. Although continuities with the associational cultures of the pre-war period were unmistakable, this chapter argues that social and political changes both at home and abroad reconfigured the world of voluntary action in important ways, altering the 'ideological work' which voluntary associations performed within British society.

This transformation had two key strands. In the first place, associational life became central to the democratisation of the *political* system by playing a major role in socialising, educating and integrating the mass electorate. Voluntary associations became important venues for the practical and symbolic enactment of 'active citizenship', a Victorian discourse which grew in importance following the franchise extensions in Britain and the rise of authoritarian regimes overseas. In the second place, associational voluntarism helped to democratise *social* relations during a period of residual religious divisions, class tensions and shifting gender identities. Whilst certain hierarchies and inequalities were undoubtedly left intact,

---

[3] Brian Harrison, *Peaceable Kingdom: Stability and Change in Modern Britain* (Oxford, 1982); for a more recent example of this tendency, see John Garrard, *Democratisation in Britain: Elites, Civil Society and Reform Since 1800* (Basingstoke, 2002).

[4] This is especially true of historical writing on the nineteenth century. See, for example, Theodore Koditschek, *Class Formation and Urban-Industrial Society: Bradford, 1750–1850* (Cambridge, 1990); Gareth Stedman Jones, *Outcast London: A Study in the Relationship between Classes in Victorian Society* (Oxford, 1971), and 'Working-Class Culture and Working-Class Politics in London, 1870–1900: Notes on the Remaking of a Working Class', in *Languages of Class: Studies in English Working Class History* (Cambridge, 1983); A.P. Donajgrodski (ed.), *Social Control in Nineteenth Century Britain* (London, 1978).

this chapter points to a range of voluntary initiatives which sought – often with success – to prevent such sectional identities from posing a threat to the broader pursuit of social cohesion. The result, it is suggested, was a more equitable distribution of social esteem, if not exactly greater social equality. Naturally, there were some organisations, particularly those pursuing extremist political goals, which do not fit easily into this picture of a liberal, pluralist, associational culture; yet the fact that such organisations were generally unsuccessful in planting deep roots in British civil society is further evidence of the democratic orientation of associational life between the wars, and, indeed, beyond.

Mapping associational life between the wars

Taylor's observations notwithstanding, there existed, until fairly recently, something of a historiographical consensus which held that the interwar period marked an era of associational decline, brought about by the expansion of the central state, the rise of mass consumer culture and the onward march of suburbanisation.[5] As the editors of this volume suggest, this narrative of retreat from a Victorian or Edwardian 'golden age' of voluntarism is neither helpful nor plausible, especially in the light of more recent work carried out by historians of sport, social welfare, youth culture, feminism, education and local government, all of which points towards the conclusion that interwar Britain very much remained the terrain of Taylor's 'army of busybodies'.[6] It is impossible to summarise this vast and fragmented literature here, or indeed to generalise too boldly about such a massive and highly differentiated realm of human activity. A series of brief statistical snapshots, however, can help to convey some sense of the sheer scale of associational activity in this period. In the political sphere, for

[5] Raphael Samuel, 'Middle Class between the Wars', Part I and Part II, *New Socialist*, 9, January/February 1983, pp. 30–36, and 10, March/April 1983, pp. 28–32; Part III, 'Suburbs under Siege', *New Socialist*, 11, May/June 1983, pp. 28–30. For an overview and critique of this 'civic decline' thesis, see Rick Trainor, 'The 'Decline' of British Urban Governance since 1850: A Reassessment', in Rick Trainor and R.J. Morris (eds), *Urban Governance: Britain and Beyond since 1750* (Aldershot, 2000), pp. 28–46.
[6] For further critiques of the civic decline thesis, see David Cannadine, 'The Transformation of Civic Ritual in Modern Britain: The Colchester Oyster Feast', *Past and Present*, 94, 1982, pp. 107–130; Barry Doyle, 'Urban Liberalism and the 'Lost Generation': Politics and Middle-Class Culture in Norwich, 1900–1935', *Historical Journal*, 38, 3, 1995, pp. 617–634.

example, the total number of individual subscribers to the three major parties was probably somewhere approaching 4 million, not counting the many millions of workers who were affiliated to the Labour Party via their trade unions.[7] In addition, some of the largest pressure and interest groups boasted huge memberships. The League of Nations Union (LNU), for example, an advocate of international government, had over 400,000 subscribers at its peak in the early 1930s, whilst the National Council of Women (NCW), an umbrella body for women's organisations, consisted of 17,000 individual members and 1,268 affiliates representing about 2.5 million in total.[8] Amongst male leisure associations, the Club and Institute Union was a giant, with 918,000 registered members in 1929; there were, in addition, 657 Masonic Lodges registered for licensing purposes in 1937, covering 102,000 men, although this was likely to have been only a fraction of the total membership.[9] The British Legion was another notable associational presence, with over 400,000 members around the same time.[10] In the field of youth organisation, the Scout and Guide Associations surpassed all rivals, enrolling perhaps a million or more of the nation's children in 1930.[11] Finally, organised religion remained a major hub of associational activity, despite contemporary fears about declining church attendance. Reliable and comparable figures are hard to find, but in the late 1920s there were around 2.7 million Anglican communicants, 3.3 million members of the various Nonconformist sects, and about 2.6 million members of the Roman Catholic Church, including children.[12]

Aggregate statistics, of course, tell only part of the story; they offer limited insight into the role which associations played in the collective life

---

[7] J. Bates, 'The Conservative Party in the Constituencies, 1918–1939' (unpublished DPhil diss., Oxford University, 1994); Duncan Tanner, 'Labour and its Membership', in Duncan Tanner, Pat Thane and Nick Tiratsoo, *Labour's First Century* (Cambridge, 2000), pp. 248–280.

[8] Helen McCarthy, 'The League of Nations Union and Democratic Politics in Britain, 1919–1939' (unpublished PhD diss., University of London, 2008); Dame Maria Ogilvie Gordon, *An Historical Sketch of the National Council of Women of Great Britain* (London, 1937).

[9] A.M. Carr-Saunders and D. Caradog Jones, *A Survey of the Social Structure of England and Wales, as Illustrated by Statistics*, 2nd edn (Oxford, 1937).

[10] Niall Barr, *The Lion and the Poppy: British Veterans, Politics, and Society, 1921–1939* (London, 2005).

[11] Tammy Proctor, 'On My Honour: Guides and Scouts in Interwar Britain', *Transactions of the American Philosophical Society*, 92, 2, 2002.

[12] Carr-Saunders and Caradog Jones, *Survey*. 'Communicants' referred to those counted in church during Easter Week. If the church electoral role were used, the figure would be 3.6 million for England alone (p. 79).

of local communities. Here contemporary social surveys provide greater assistance. David Caradog Jones, for example, carried out a major study of Merseyside in 1934, where he discovered over 100 political clubs in the district plus a rich array of social, religious and cultural organisations. His survey of about 250 local people revealed that somewhere between 50 and 60 per cent of men of all social classes had attended a club or society during the week in which the survey was taken, whereas nearly all professional women or housewives had, and about half of all female clerks and shop-assistants and 37 per cent of female manual workers and domestic servants.[13] Associations represented an equally central aspect of community life in the villages of Devon, as F.G. Thomas discovered in a study published in 1939. 'A new organisation will find it difficult to find a "free" night in the hall', he observed,

> and equally difficult to discover a possible member in the village who has not already several 'memberships' to finance. The Church, the Chapel, the Women's Institute, the British Legion, the District Nursing Association, the Men's Club, Church Guilds, the Buffaloes, and sports associations will be found in most villages, each intent on securing membership and sub-scriptions.[14]

In his *New Survey of London Life and Leisure* (1930–1935), Hubert Llewellyn Smith noted the growing popularity of cycling clubs, hikers' groups and amateur dramatics societies, together with the enduring appeal of choirs and amateur orchestras and the survival of such collective pastimes as pigeon-fancying, angling, gardening and billiards.[15]

Other accounts, however, revealed a rather more mixed picture, such as Terence Young's well-known study of the working-class Becontree estate, built shortly after the end of the First World War on the edge of east London. Here associational life had to be built up more or less from scratch, with the result, as Young puts it, that 'voluntary institutions, social and religious, have had a great struggle to come into existence in this area'.[16] Although, by 1932, Young counted as many as 590 organisations serving a

---

[13] D Caradog Jones (ed.), *The Social Survey of Merseyside*, Vol. 3 (London, 1934). Caradog Jones's sample, as he himself recognised, was, however, weighted towards those already in contact with a voluntary organisation of some kind.

[14] F.G. Thomas, *The Changing Village: An Essay on Rural Reconstruction* (London, 1939), p. 66.

[15] *The New Survey of London Life and Labour*, Vol. IX, *Life and Leisure* (London, 1935).

[16] Terence Young, *Becontree and Dagenham: A Report Made for the Pilgrim Trust* (London, 1934), p. 26.

population of 103,000, only a relatively small proportion of the community actively participated in their activities. A third of young people attended Sunday schools, but as few as 13 per cent of the adult male population belonged to working-men's clubs, whilst the proportion of women active in women's associations was only marginally higher, at 15 per cent. Furthermore, all the social surveys carried out between the wars noted how participation varied greatly along lines of class, gender, age and, perhaps to a lesser extent, religion. Llewellyn Smith, for example, found that in London rowing and hiking were generally deemed to be middle-class pursuits, whilst the brass band was 'considered to be the working man's orchestra'.[17] Men and women often spent their spare time in separate, homosocial worlds, as evidenced by the huge number of working-men's clubs and Masonic Lodges and the growing popularity of Women's Institutes, Co-operative Guilds and women's sections of the political parties, together with the auxiliary organisations attached to the British Legion, Rotary and Toc H.[18] Sport was notably gendered; in his second survey of York, published in 1935, Seebohm Rowntree discovered that bowls was essentially a male-only pastime.[19] Caradog Jones came to similar conclusions in Liverpool concerning baseball, whilst rounders and hockey were generally viewed as women's games.[20] Young Londoners were amongst the most enthusiastic popularisers of hiking and cycling, as noted by Llewellyn Smith; young men in York, according to Rowntree, were less likely to frequent working-men's clubs; whilst in Liverpool it was older women who made up the core of church congregations across all denominations. In the latter city, Caradog Jones discovered, the legacy of anti-Catholicism fuelled religious antagonisms which infected associational life, not only serving to limit ecumenical cooperation (on which subject, more later) but producing minority political interest groups, such as the Loyal British Patriotic Labour Party and the Liverpool Protestant Party.[21]

These divisions and exclusions draw our analysis away from the task of description and towards a set of more critical questions concerning what might be called the 'ideological work' performed by voluntary associations.

---

[17] *New Survey of London Life*, p. 62.
[18] For homosociality in associational life, see Helen McCarthy, 'Service Clubs, Citizenship and Equality: Gender Relations and Middle-Class Associations in Britain between the Wars', *Historical Research*, 81, 213, 2008, pp. 531–552.
[19] B. Seebohm Rowntree, *Poverty and Progress: A Second Social Survey of York* (London, 1941).
[20] Caradog Jones, *Social Survey of Merseyside*.
[21] *Ibid*.

On the face of it, the stratified nature of participation might appear to undermine 'liberal' interpretations by suggesting that voluntary organisations shored up prevailing power relations, or, to borrow the terminology of political scientist Robert Putnam, served to 'bond' existing interests and identities rather than 'bridge' the divisions between them.[22] Yet differentiation is not in itself proof of an 'anti-democratic' agenda; as the history of the feminist, trade union and civil rights movements demonstrates, organisational separatism could serve as a vehicle for pursuing politically-progressive ends. To evaluate the ideological work of associational voluntarism between the wars, it is necessary to explore its dynamics in much greater depth, and it is to this task that this chapter now turns.

Associational voluntarism and democratisation: political life

By introducing adult suffrage and equalising the voting age for the two sexes, the franchise extensions of 1918 and 1928 effectively completed Britain's transition from *ancien régime* to fully-fledged liberal democracy.[23] The genuinely mass electorate, which sprang into being subsequently, became the object of much fervent speculation amongst politicians, intellectuals, religious leaders, feminists, social reformers and journalists. How would these new voters behave? Were they sufficiently educated to cast their ballots wisely? Would they embrace the values of parliamentary democracy or fall prey to extremist, revolutionary doctrines? Some of the commentary on these questions was deeply pessimistic, drawing upon the insights of the emerging discipline of social psychology and upon pre-war thinkers like Graham Wallas, Gustav le Bon and William James, whose gloomy critiques appeared to suggest that mass democracy would inevitably erode rational, public-spirited citizenship.[24] Yet much of it was cautiously optimistic, viewing the introduction of universal suffrage as an opportunity to renew Britain's political life and to demonstrate the

---

[22] Robert Putnam, *Bowling Alone: The Collapse and Revival of American Community* (New York, 2000).

[23] Some anomalies remained, such as the University and Business franchises. See D.E. Butler, *The Electoral System in Britain since 1918* (Oxford, 1963).

[24] D.L. LeMahieu, *A Culture for Democracy: Mass Communication and the Cultivated Mind in Britain between the Wars* (Oxford, 1988).

democratic capabilities of the British people. The task, as many saw it, was to educate new and existing voters in the responsibilities of citizenship as a means of integrating them into the political system. This theme was evident in many aspects of interwar culture; it was present, for example, in the speeches of party leaders, in the sermons of archbishops and Free Church ministers, in the educational broadcasts of the BBC and in the creative output of a new generation of progressive filmmakers, publishers and artists.[25]

The challenge of creating well-informed, responsible citizens acquired, however, a special significance for voluntary associations. Their vital contribution to nourishing Britain's open, pluralist political culture had long been trumpeted by political theorists, from Edmund Burke to J.S. Mill. This vision of voluntary associations as schools of citizenship became, if anything, even more prominent between the wars. Cambridge intellectual Ernest Barker, for example, who became Chairman of the Community Centres and Associations Committee of the National Council for Social Service in 1930, was a powerful proponent of this view; he argued that the English people's 'habit of doing things together for themselves in voluntary co-operation' was central to their historical development and future cultural well-being.[26] Another prominent voice belonged to Charles Delisle Burns, who used his tenure of the Stevenson Lectureship in Citizenship at the University of Glasgow in 1934 to reflect upon the challenges of prac- tising democratic politics in a modern state. What was required, he argued, was a greater 'sense of the community', by which he meant a more profound appreciation of the ties which bound individuals and groups together.[27] Voluntary associations were well placed to nurture this quality because they attracted 'the "active" type of mind', the men and women who were willing to get involved in public affairs and to hold the state to account; their organisations, Burns remarked, supplied 'a sort of explosive force in the machine, like vaporised petrol in the internal combustion

[25] Philip Williamson, *Stanley Baldwin: Conservative Leadership and National Values* (Cambridge, 1999); John Kent, *William Temple: Church, State and Society in Britain, 1880–1950* (Cambridge, 1992); Abigail Beach, 'The Labour Party and the Idea of Citizenship' (unpublished PhD thesis, University College London, 1996); Richard Weight and Abigail Beach, *The Right to Belong: Citizenship and National Identity in Britain, 1930–1960* (London, 1998).
[26] The quote is from Barker's autobiography, *Age and Youth*, cited in Julia Stapleton, *Englishness and the Study of Politics: The Social and Political Thought of Ernest Barker* (Cambridge, 1994), p. 153.
[27] C. Delisle Burns, *The Challenge to Democracy* (London, 1934), p. 250.

engine, or – as the steam age would have said – like steam in the loco-motive'.[28]

This tendency to insert voluntarism into a Whiggish narrative of Britain's political development and national character was also heavily evident in the public addresses of Conservative leader Stanley Baldwin. It was through the 'triumph of voluntary effort', Baldwin declared in 1923, that 'all the best movements and best things in our country' had sprung, from the Adult Education movement and the Salvation Army to the Boy Scouts.[29] The Conservative Prime Minister even included trade unions, friendly societies and co-operatives in this bracket, remarking in the after-math of the General Strike that such bodies had 'been real pioneers of democratic education in this country, and from them our people have learnt what they could have learnt from no other source whatever'.[30] Baldwin also praised the valuable work carried out by such organisations as the Women's Institutes and Rural Community Councils amongst new female voters, 'preparing them to play the part in the betterment of the whole country which it is essential for everyone to play if democracy is to survive and to prove a blessing and not a curse to the people of this country'.[31]

Commentators frequently contrasted this link between associational activity and the health of Britain's democracy with the weak or non-existent voluntarist traditions evident under totalitarian regimes. For Delisle Burns, democracies and dictatorships required fundamentally different kinds of citizens; for the former, the ideal was the 'easy-going' type, men and women who were 'sociable, clubbable, tending to associate and to work together'.[32] Similar views were expressed at a conference on 'The Challenge to Democracy' convened in 1937 by the Association for Education in Citizenship (AEC), a non-party body promoting formal train-ing in civics as a safeguard against the lure of totalitarian ideologies.[33] The

---

[28] *Ibid.*, pp. 257, 258.

[29] 'Political Education', speech delivered at the Philip Stott College, 27 September 1923, in Stanley Baldwin, *On England: And Other Addresses* (London, 1926), p. 148.

[30] 'The Citizen and the General Strike', extract from a speech delivered at a meeting at Chippenham, 12 June 1926, in Stanley Baldwin, *Our Inheritance* (London, 1928), p. 217.

[31] 'Social Service', address delivered at the Annual Meeting of the Union of Girls' Schools, 27 October 1927, in Baldwin, *Our Inheritance*, p. 204. For Rural Community Councils, see below.

[32] C. Delisle Burns, *Democracy: Its Defects and Advantages* (London, 1929), p. 201.

[33] For the AEC, see *New Statesman and Nation*, 177, 14 July 1934, special supplement on 'Education and Citizenship'.

educationalist Alfred Zimmern addressed this theme by emphasising the importance of participation in public life, which he defined rather pithily as any activity 'where you have to sit round a table and look serious, and have minutes to read, and a secretary, up to the House of Commons and the House of Lords'. He went on to suggest that 'the really successful democracies are the countries with vigorous systems of local government and with very free systems of association and co-operation, countries which offer the widest scope for voluntary organisation and civic spirit'.[34] The economist Arthur Salter echoed the point, ranking 'the enormous development of voluntary associations of all kinds' alongside the formal representative institutions of Parliament and local government as a 'great factor in British democracy'.[35]

Associational voluntarism thus featured within interwar public discourse as a marker of national identity as well as a bulwark of democratic values. This helps to explain why extremist organisations such as the British Union of Fascists (BUF) and the Communist Party of Great Britain (CPGB) – who, after all, must feature in any history of interwar associational life – found it difficult to penetrate more mainstream bodies. Although, in certain regions, the BUF won a few recruits from small shop-keepers', farmers' and rate-payers' associations, on the whole, these and other voluntary organisations remained firmly anchored ideologically in a liberal-democratic framework.[36] An application from the women's section of the BUF to affiliate to the NCW, for example, was turned down in November 1935 on the grounds that, as one member of the Executive put it, the BUF was 'subversive to the existing order in that the individual became the servant of the state rather than the state being the servant of the individual'.[37] Similarly, the strength of pre-existing associational traditions, rooted in the trade union, the working-men's club and pub, was amongst the factors limiting the appeal of Communist politics amongst the

---

[34] Alfred Zimmern, 'Learning and Leadership', in *Constructive Democracy* (London, 1938), p. 165.

[35] Sir Arthur Salter, 'The Challenge to Democracy', in *Constructive Democracy*, p. 204.

[36] Thomas Linehan, *East London for Mosley: The British Union of Fascists in East London and South-West Essex 1933–1940* (London, 1996). For the non-politicisation of farmers' organisations, see John D. Brewer, *Mosley's Men: The British Union of Fascists in the West Midlands* (Gower, 1984), ch. 8.

[37] Minutes of the Executive Committee of the National Council of Women, 22 November 1935, Acc/3613/01/010, London Metropolitan Archives, p. 263.

British working class.[38] This associational diversity held fast amongst many unemployed workers, too, who substituted for their prior workplace ties new forms of associative sociability, typically conducted in reading rooms, labour exchanges, municipal allotments, street corners, cinemas and betting shops. Efforts by both Fascists and Communists to infiltrate these communal settings produced only very limited results.[39]

In short, associational voluntarism was closely identified with the values of democratic citizenship between the wars. Although this was not a new discourse, it gained increased currency after 1918 due to the extensions of the franchise and the growing threat of totalitarian ideologies overseas. As a result, voluntary organisations came to be seen as crucial vehicles for the political education and democratic socialisation of new and existing voters. But how far did these associations nurture these values within their own structures and cultures? Did they democratise social as well as political life?

Associational voluntarism and democratisation: social life

As noted earlier, voluntary associations frequently reproduced the hierarchies and divisions existing in broader society, especially those of class, gender, religion and age. In light of this, some historians, especially those working in the Marxist tradition, have argued against the 'liberal' interpretation of associations as schools of citizenship and vehicles for inclusion.[40] In a set of especially influential readings, Ross McKibbin has suggested that

---

[38] Ross McKibbin, 'Why Was There No Marxism in Britain?' *English Historical Review*, 159, 1984, pp. 297–331; Andrew Thorpe, '"The Only Effective Bulwark Against Reaction and Revolution": Labour and the Frustration of the Extreme Left', in Andrew Thorpe (ed.), *The Failure of Political Extremism in Inter-War Britain* (Exeter, 1988), pp. 11–28.

[39] For failure to radicalise the unemployed see John Stevenson and Chris Cook, *The Slump* (London, 1979), chs 8 and 9. For the associative sociability of the unemployed, see Ross McKibbin, 'The "Social Psychology" of Unemployment in Inter-War Britain', in Ross McKibbin, *Ideologies of Class: Social Relations in Britain 1880–1950* (Oxford, 1991), pp. 228–258. For fascist attempts to penetrate these associational cultures, see Philip M. Coupland, '"Leftwing Fascism" in Theory and Practice: The Case of the British Union of Fascists', *Twentieth Century British History*, 13, 1, 2002, pp. 38–61.

[40] Theodore Koditschek, *Class Formation and Urban-Industrial Society: Bradford, 1750–1850* (Cambridge, 1990).

associational cultures between the wars were deeply class-bound and that their effects were to entrench middle-class anti-socialism and reinforce working-class fatalism.[41] They must be understood, in this respect, as a major part of the explanation for Conservative electoral hegemony and the defeat of organised labour between the wars. Furthermore, these 'civil cultures' were so embedded in British society, McKibbin argues, that they outlived the popular radicalism of the Second World War, explaining in turn why post-war Labour governments struggled to transform Britain into a fully-fledged social democracy. James Hinton came to much the same conclusion in his study of the Women's Voluntary Service (WVS) in the 1940s, an organisation which, he finds, contributed to the continuities of upper- and middle-class power. 'The gulfs in everyday experience that continued to divide housewives on class lines', Hinton writes, 'were simply too great to be bridged effectively in associational life.'[42] Viewed in this light, the social relations of interwar voluntarism exerted a drag on progressive politics, countering the levelling tendencies of the home front and the post-war welfare state and freezing in time the paternalist values of an earlier era.

There can be no denying the fact that Britain was a deeply unequal society between the wars, nor that voluntary associations often served to shore up existing power relations in the manner described by McKibbin and Hinton. Yet a closer look at the dynamics of certain aspects of associational voluntarism reveals a rather more nuanced picture of the ideological work it performed. The character of organised religion, for instance, changed in important ways after the war. One major trend was growing ecumenical cooperation between Anglicanism and Nonconformity, an agenda pushed from above by successive Archbishops of Canterbury committed to restoring church unity, and facilitated from below by the longer-term integration of provincial Nonconformists into a national middle class.[43] Associations played an important role in this process, with a growing number of inter-denominational bodies working to break down the sectarian divisions of old. Toc H, for example, was founded by an

---

[41] Ross McKibbin, *Classes and Cultures: England 1918–1951* (Oxford, 1998), and 'Class and Conventional Wisdom: The Conservative Party and the "Public" in Inter-war Britain', in McKibbin, *Ideologies of Class*, pp. 259–293.

[42] James Hinton, *Women, Social Leadership, and the Second World War: Continuities of Class* (Oxford, 2002), p. 49.

[43] Adrian Hastings, *A History of English Christianity, 1920–2000* (London, 2001); E.R. Norman, *Church and Society in England, 1770–1970: A Historical Study* (Oxford, 1976).

Anglican chaplain, Philip 'Tubby' Clayton, in 1919 as a social club and service organisation which aimed to create 'a Lay Brotherhood, welcoming all Christian men and many who, though seeking Christ, have not yet found Him'.[44] Other inter-denominational initiatives of the period included the Industrial Christian Fellowship, which sent out missioners to tend to the spiritual needs of the manual worker, and the Christian Conference on Politics, Economics and Citizenship (COPEC), a major ecumenical gathering held in 1924 bringing together Anglicans and Nonconformists to discuss how Christianity could best address the problems facing contemporary society.[45]

World peace was just such a problem and one which generated a great deal of cooperation across denominational lines. Many individuals within the churches had forged close links to the Victorian and Edwardian peace movements, but the war injected a new momentum into peace-themed endeavours, triggering, for example, the formation in August 1914 of the World Alliance for Promoting International Friendship through the Churches, under the leadership of the Archbishop of Canterbury.[46] The creation of the League of Nations offered further stimulus to ecumenical initiatives; Anglican and Free Church leaders formed a Standing Committee on the Church and the League of Nations as early as October 1918, whilst the ideal of international cooperation provided a new focus for the work of the World Alliance and for the international 'Life and Work Movement' and its successor, the World Council of Churches.[47] The LNU helped to consolidate this ecumenical trend at grassroots level, with clergymen of all denominations and their congregations forming the organisational backbone of many local branches, whilst inter-denominational services regularly brought Anglicans and Nonconformists together in common cause. The LNU's famous 'Peace Ballot' of 1934–1935, a voluntary referendum on Britain's policy towards the League, offered

---

[44] *The Padre in Toc H* (Toc H Paper No. 2, n.d.), p. 6.
[45] Gerald Studdert-Kennedy, *Dog-Collar Democracy: The Industrial Christian Fellowship 1919–1929* (London, 1982); *The Proceedings of COPEC: Being a Report of the Meetings of the Conference on Christian Politics, Economics and Citizenship, held in Birmingham, April 5–12, 1924* (London, 1924).
[46] Darril Hudson, *The Ecumenical Movement in World Affairs* (London, 1969). See also Daniel Gorman, 'Ecumenical Internationalism: Willoughby Dickinson, the League of Nations and the World Alliance for Promoting International Friendship through the Churches', *Journal of Contemporary History*, 45, 1, 2010, pp. 51–73.
[47] *Ibid.*

further opportunities for cooperation and contact; according to the Dean of Chichester, the Ballot had 'brought the Christian Churches together in positive social action more than anything has done since the war'.[48]

Naturally, there were limits to interwar ecumenism. It remained difficult – although not impossible – to persuade Britain's fast-expanding and tightly-knit Catholic communities to join the movement for church unity.[49] As has been noted, in cities such as Liverpool, with a long history of anti-Catholicism, religious sectarianism continued to structure associational life. Equally, divisions between Anglicans and Nonconformists remained evident at grassroots level; one LNU activist carrying out a caravan tour of English villages in 1931, for example, observed that 'the greatest difficulty in the way of co-operation for a common object was the rivalry between Church and Chapel; if one meeting was conducted under the auspices of the Nonconformists, it was necessary to hold the next on the Rectory lawn'.[50] Nonetheless, it seems clear that religious differences played a far less prominent role in associational life between the wars than in earlier periods. Denominational identities did not disappear, but ecumenical initiatives encouraged greater cooperation between the churches, especially in relation to contemporary social, economic and political problems. This shift was further reinforced by the decidedly non-sectarian nature of many secular organisations, which greatly contributed to the gradual and ongoing integration of Britain's religious communities. Bodies such as the LNU, the NCW, the Women's Institutes, Rotary and the British Legion insisted on keeping religious animosities out of local branch life in order to preserve their broad-based character and facilitate sociability.[51] In 1937, for example, the National Executive reprimanded a local Women's Institute for refusing to let their hall to a pacifist organisation, on the grounds that it was 'unconstitutional for an Institute publicly to denounce views

[48] 'Notes of a delegation received by the Prime Minister at the Foreign Office from Societies Co-operating in the National Declaration on the 23rd July, 1935', PREM 1/178, The National Archives (hereafter TNA), Kew, 9. For the Peace Ballot, see Helen McCarthy, 'Democratizing British Foreign Policy: Rethinking the Peace Ballot, 1934–5', *Journal of British Studies*, 49, 4, 2010, pp. 923–31.

[49] Steven Fielding, *Class and Ethnicity: Irish Catholics in England, 1880–1939* (Buckingham, 1993); James Obelkevich, 'Religion', in F.M.L. Thompson (ed.), *The Cambridge Social History of Britain, 1750–1950*, Vol. III, *Social Agencies and Institutions* (Cambridge, 1990), pp. 311–356.

[50] Marjorie Ascher, 'Spade Work: Carrying the League to the Villages', *Headway*, September 1931, p. 173.

[51] Helen McCarthy, 'Parties, Voluntary Associations and Democratic Politics in Interwar Britain', *Historical Journal*, 50, 4, 2007, pp. 891–912.

which many WI members who belong to the Society of Friends hold'.[52] Rotary held equally fast to its 'no religion' policy, recruiting Anglicans, Nonconformists, Catholics, atheists and even Muslims to its ranks. One of the Wandsworth Club's leading members was Farzand Ali, the imam of Southfields Mosque.[53]

If religious differences became less pronounced in associational terms, what, then, of gender? As noted above, voluntary organisations were often structured along homosocial lines, with men and women inhabiting separate associational worlds. Yet there was a notable increase in opportunities for mixing and sharing responsibility after 1918. This was especially the case for younger men and women, who socialised together through new organisations such as the Youth Hostel Association, the youth sections of the political parties and mixed youth clubs.[54] The Youth Group attached to the Withington branch of the LNU, for example, took advantage of such emergent leisure forms, announcing in 1934 that it planned to hold all its meetings at youth hostels, and later going on to arrange mixed rambles, dances and amateur dramatics.[55] Yet mixing was also evident amongst the older generation; again, LNU branch records reveal a preponderance of married couples serving together on local committees. In Lancaster, for example, Councillor Muriel Dowbiggin ran the local branch with help from her husband, whilst in Ealing, branch chairman Sidney Haynes received stalwart support on the committee from his wife, with the couple regularly hosting meetings in their home.[56] Even if wives often occupied a subordinate or auxiliary role as helpmeet to their husband, this sort of associational mixing was in keeping with the broader trend during this

[52] National Executive Minutes, 8 December 1937, Records of the National Federation of Women's Institutes, The Women's Library, 5/FWI/A/1/1/16, f416-7.

[53] Vivian Carter, *The Romance of Rotary in London* (London, 1948); In her post-war study of Banbury, Margaret Stacey attested to the bridging function of Rotary: 'The club is self-conscious about this position, operating a taboo on politics while carefully balancing power in the club between the Liberal/Free Church and the Conservative/Anglican connexions.' Margaret Stacey, *Tradition and Change: A Study of Banbury* (Oxford, 1960), p. 86. For Farzand Ali, see *Rotary Wheel*, XIX, 204, March 1933, p. 16.

[54] Marcus Collins, *Modern Love: An Intimate History of Men and Women in Twentieth-Century Britain* (London, 2003).

[55] The chairman of the Withington Youth Group was also the honorary secretary of the Manchester branch of the Youth Hostel Association. See McCarthy, 'The League of Nations Union'.

[56] *Lancashire Daily Post*, 12 November 1934. For Haynes, see minutes of the Ealing Branch of the LNU, Ealing Local History Centre, Accession 48.

61

period towards shared leisure amongst middle-class couples.[57] The Rotary movement provided further evidence of this phenomenon; despite it functioning as a male luncheon club, wives were actively involved in its public work to an extent which contrasted sharply with the exclusivity of pre-war gentlemen's clubs and Freemasonry.[58] One Rotarian wife explicitly recognised the significance of her involvement for the balance of power within the home. 'It was felt', she explained in a local newspaper article in 1924, 'that if the women were interested in the work that the men were doing, it would strengthen their hand, and form a united interest in the household.'[59]

On first glance, these illustrative examples might appear to be weighted towards the middle class, the social group which, historically, had provided much of the leadership and funding behind Britain's vibrant voluntary tradition, founding choral societies and hospitals, children's homes and youth clubs, inner-city missions and settlements and countless other charitable and philanthropic initiatives. A great deal of this activity was highly paternalistic in character, designed to instil good habits of thrift and independence amongst the poor and to offer wholesome and sober forms of 'rational recreation' to the working classes as an alternative to the pub or street corner.[60] Working-class people, as we have seen, developed their own associational forms in parallel, often centred on the workplace, neighbourhood or pub or, for the more politically-minded, on the trade union and labour movements. How far did these class cultures break down in the interwar period? It is certainly true, as McKibbin and Hinton suggest, that class identities remained highly salient in structuring associational life, but were they truly unbridgeable? Evidence of cross-class mixing in organisations such as the LNU, the Women's Institutes and the British Legion suggest that this was not always the case. Local branch records

---

[57] Collins, *Modern Love*; McCarthy, 'Service Clubs'. This phenomenon was probably less evident in working-class homes – see Claire Langhamer, *Women's Leisure in England, 1920–1960* (Manchester, 2000).

[58] McCarthy, 'Service Clubs'.

[59] Article from the *Manchester Evening Chronicle* of 12 June 1924, reproduced in *Rotary*, 10, September 1924, p. 294.

[60] For middle-class voluntarism in the nineteenth century, see R.J. Morris, *Class, Sect and Party: The Making of the British Middle Class, Leeds, 1820–1850* (Manchester, 1990); Leonore Davidoff and Catherine Hall, *Family Fortunes: Men and Women of the English Middle Class* (London, 1987); Roberts, *Making English Morals*; Simon Gunn, *The Public Culture of the Victorian Middle Class: Ritual and Authority and the English Industrial City* (Manchester, 2000).

cross-referenced with data from the 1911 Census reveal a number of LNU activists of working-class origins, such as Granville Atack, honorary secretary of the Bury branch and son of a textile worker, or Thomas Seymour, organiser of the Peace Ballot in Darlington, whose occupation was recorded in the Census as 'fitter and turner'.[61] The Women's Institutes recruited ordinary rural housewives alongside the more well-to-do ladies of the shires, whilst the British Legion appealed to ex-servicemen from all walks of life. As the latter's monthly journal put it: 'Within its ranks are the sons of the castle and the sons of the cottage, and with the same spirit that permeated all ranks on the battlefield, all are pulling together with a united effort to further the democratic objects of the Legion.'[62] Church membership was also cross-class in nature between the wars, as were youth organisations such as the Scout and Guide Associations, whilst in many areas amateur dramatics, operatics and historical pageantry facilitated whole-community participation.[63]

The question remains, of course, how far such cross-class associations avoided reproducing class hierarchies within their internal structures. Further, detailed sociological analysis of these and other organisations would provide a fuller picture, but, on the evidence available, it would certainly appear to be the case that middle-class people tended to monopolise positions of leadership. In his study of interwar amateur operatics, for example, John Lowerson finds that even where working-class members formed the majority, as in some Welsh mining communities, their societies were usually led by local professionals or businessmen.[64] Similarly, in a post-war study of 'Squirebridge', an unnamed small English country town, the sociologist Thomas Bottomore calculated that individuals from the top occupational grouping (defined as professional, technical, managerial and executive) held the highest proportion of offices within the 125 voluntary

[61] Information from www.1911.co.uk (accessed 3 July 2009). *Darlington and Stockton Times*, 9 March 1935, p. 3.
[62] *British Legion Journal*, 10, April 1922, p. 219.
[63] Callum Brown challenges the view that working-class church attendance was low during the century, finding that in the 1960s working-class worshippers typically constituted between 50 and 65 per cent of congregations, with higher figures for Roman Catholic churches. See Callum Brown, *Religion and Society in Twentieth-Century Britain* (Harlow, 2006), p. 29; Proctor, 'On My Honour: Guides and Scouts in Interwar Britain'. John Lowerson, *Amateur Operatics: A Social and Cultural History* (Manchester, 2005); for historical pageantry, see Paul Readman, 'The Place of the Past in English Culture, c.1890–1914', *Past & Present*, 186, 2005, pp. 147–199.
[64] Lowerson, *Amateur Operatics*, p. 40.

organisations active in the town. Despite constituting only 16.6 per cent of all memberships, this group accounted for 62.0 per cent of all offices.[65]

Nonetheless, even if, as in earlier periods, it remained the middle classes who possessed the time, resources and self-confidence required for effective social leadership, it would be a mistake to assume that interwar social relations, therefore, continued to fit the paternalistic mould of old. As the occupational structure of the middle class shifted towards managerial and professional employment, a functional emphasis on rational planning and technical expertise replaced, or, perhaps more accurately, reconfigured, older notions of *noblesse oblige*.[66] This was particularly evident within the realm of organised philanthropy, which combined an increasingly professionalised ethos with a greater emphasis on encouraging self-organisation – or what today's voluntary sector leaders might call 'capacity-building' – amongst local communities. This was one of the aims of the National Council of Social Service (NCSS), an umbrella body created in 1919 to encourage greater cooperation amongst voluntary organisations. The Council was closely involved in nurturing a new wave of village-hall building across rural Britain, driven by a desire to extend the range of social, cultural and educational activities available to countryside dwellers. Although there were a few halls already in existence, these were often established through the gift of a local landowner and remained under elite control. The post-war hall, by contrast, was a more democratic affair, funded by a wider range of donors, including the Carnegie Trust and the government's Development Commission, and plugged into a broad network of voluntary organisations, including the Village Clubs Association, the YMCA, the Red Triangle Association, the Women's Institutes, and the Rural Community Councils (RCCs). The RCCs were another NCSS innovation, designed to provide a new infrastructure for community development and self-government, and run by committees drawn from all sections of the local population. Rural historian Jeremy Burchardt finds that, although the old hierarchies proved resistant to change, by the 1930s the traditional elite of landowners and clergymen was often being shouldered aside by '"ordinary" villagers' in the running of the RCCs.[67]

[65] Thomas Bottomore, 'Social Stratification in Voluntary Organisation', in D.V. Glass (ed.), *Social Mobility in Britain* (London, 1954), pp. 349–382.
[66] For changes in the composition of the interwar middle classes, see McKibbin, *Classes and Cultures*.
[67] Jeremy Burchardt, '"A New Rural Civilization": Village Halls, Community and Citizenship

This emphasis on self-organisation provided the central theme for a short documentary film which the NCSS sponsored in 1937 to publicise its work. Directed by Ruby Grierson and Ralph Bond and entitled *Today We Live*, the film depicts two real-life instances of community self-help: the successful conversion of a disused barn into a village hall in rural Gloucestershire, and the creation of an occupational centre by a group of unemployed miners in South Wales. In both cases, the initiative is supplied by local people, who organise whist drives, jumble sales and football matches in order to raise money for their respective endeavours, supplemented by a grant from the NCSS. The NCSS professionals who appear in the film offer advice and guidance, but are minor players, with the focus remaining at all times on the resourcefulness and community spirit of the local residents.

Naturally, *Today We Live* portrayed the NCSS's work in a positive light; the reality elsewhere may have been far more uncomfortable in terms of relations between the classes. Nonetheless, there seems to be little doubt that the interwar middle classes felt less secure in their traditional claims to social leadership following the franchise extensions of 1918. Some voluntary organisations might have boasted 'democratic' constitutions before this date, but it became more important under conditions of universal suffrage to secure broad representation of all sections of the community. This was especially the case for political parties, who could scarcely afford to alienate any class of voters, and for pressure groups like the LNU, whose leaders believed that their ability to influence the government of the day rested on the broad-based nature of their membership.[68] As Lord Robert Cecil, the LNU's long-serving President, put it in 1920: 'No movement on behalf of the League of Nations can be either adequate or effective which is anything short of National – *i.e.*, a movement covering the whole of the British Isles and embracing every class of citizenhood. . . . We shall speak with power and effect only when we can speak on behalf of the Nation as a whole.'[69]

The LNU was not always wholly successful in recruiting across the class spectrum; the salient point, however, is that national leaders and local

in the 1920s', in Paul Brassley, Jeremy Burchardt and Lynne Thompson (eds), *The English Countryside between the Wars: Regeneration or Decline?* (Woodbridge, 2006), p. 34.

[68] Strikingly, Bottomore found that the proportion of offices held by the top occupational group was lowest amongst political organisations, standing at 40.5 per cent, a finding he attributed to the active attempts made by political parties to secure broad representation.

[69] LNU, *The League of Nations Union* (London, 1920), BLPES, LNU/7/1, 228.

activists made strenuous efforts to remedy this failing, conscious of the growing political assertiveness of the working classes and of the dangers of being identified with one narrow social class. Branches organised open-air meetings at factory gates, made announcements during half-time at football matches, arranged for famous sportsmen to address public rallies, and mounted soap-boxes in market squares and on street corners – all in a bid to rouse interest amongst the working classes.[70] Women's Institute leaders were similarly keen to demonstrate the democratic credentials of their movement by encouraging, as one study of 1937 observed, 'the rank and file of the members to take office and to undertake the duties of committee member'.[71] All members – 'from the cottage to the Throne' – paid the same modest subscription of two shillings, regardless of income, and had equal voting rights on matters of policy and governance.[72] As a result the Women's Institute provided, according to another contemporary observer, 'a non-party, all-embracing organisation in which the slow-speaking countrywoman, as much as her readier sisters, could make her voice heard'.[73]

Conclusion

It would be misleading to suggest, on the basis of this limited analysis, that religious divisions, gender differences and class inequalities disappeared from associational life between the wars; they certainly did not. Furthermore, and as noted earlier, it is impossible to generalise too boldly about the associational realm, given its sheer scale and diversity. More detailed analyses of individual organisations or local case studies are required before any conclusive synthesis of the character of interwar associational life – and the ideological work it performed – can be drawn. Nonetheless, on the basis of the evidence presented here, it is possible to point to a number of broad trends which, together, produced an increasingly equal distribution of 'social esteem', if not greater social equality

[70] McCarthy, 'The League of Nations Union'.
[71] Thomas, *The Changing Village*, p. 71.
[72] J.W. Robertson Scott, *The Story of the Women's Institute Movement in England and Wales and Scotland* (Idbury, 1925), p. v.
[73] Janet E. Courtney, *Countrywomen in Council: The English and Scottish Women's Institutes with Chapters on the Movement in the Dominions and on Townswomen's Guilds* (London, 1933), p. 144.

in British society.[74] There was a growing recognition between the wars of the legitimate claim of all social groups – including those previously marginalised or excluded – to democratic citizenship and to an equal share in the development of their local communities. This process was closely linked, in the political sphere, to the franchise extensions of 1918 and the growing threat of totalitarian ideologies overseas, and, in the social and cultural sphere, to broader transformations in the dynamics of organised religion, and in gender and class relations. There was, in short, a democratising logic at work in the associational cultures of interwar Britain. Even if many of the same people were 'in charge' at the end of the period as had been in 1918, their claim to power was arguably less absolute and more open to challenge. A study of the WVS, the Women's Institutes and the British Red Cross from the early 1950s lends support to this picture of a subtly shifting balance of power within associational life. It found that an increasing number of officers were being elected from lowlier occupational groupings, with the wives or female relatives of farmers, market gardeners, minor public officials, small tradesmen, railwaymen and unskilled workers seizing the reins from the titled ladies of the shires.[75] Those ladies, in fact, as the author remarked, could occasionally 'be seen hovering uncertainly at meetings, rather pathetically trying to exercise their old authority'.[76]

That authority, ideologically speaking, was far from finished, even by the 1950s. Yet, as Mike Savage has argued, it lost much of its legitimacy 'in the era of the social democratic welfare state with its insistence on equality and common citizenship rights', and appeared increasingly outdated in an age of growing affluence.[77] One response to this post-war loss of status, Savage argues, was to refashion middle-class identity along less paternalistic and more technocratic lines, giving emphasis to the contribution of professional knowledge and technical expertise to societal advance. Yet, as this chapter has sought to demonstrate, this trend was already apparent within the associational cultures of the interwar decades, and it was accompanied by equally important shifts within religious life and gender

---

[74] The phrase 'social esteem' is used by McKibbin, but exclusively in relation to class, and its redistribution, in so far as such a phenomenon took place, was almost wholly produced by the Second World War. See *Classes and Cultures*, p. 531.

[75] Rosalind Chambers, 'A Study of Three Voluntary Organisations', in Glass, *Social Mobility in Britain*, pp. 383–406.

[76] *Ibid.*, p. 405.

[77] Mike Savage, 'Affluence and Social Change in the Making of Technocratic Middle Class Identities: Britain, 1939–1955', *Contemporary British History*, 22, 4, 2008, p. 470.

relations. If Taylor's 'army of busybodies' provided the groundswell of their nation's history between the wars, then it was a history of democrati-sation – however gradual and uneven in nature – that they helped to forge, and one which continued long beyond 1939.

4
Labour, charity and voluntary action

The myth of hostility

NICHOLAS DEAKIN AND JUSTIN DAVIS SMITH

Introduction

The Labour Party has frequently been represented as having been hostile to voluntary action for most of the twentieth century. In this chapter, we suggest that this view is a misunderstanding, based essentially on the revulsion expressed in the Labour movement against charity, as representing both a class-based and patronising world view, and a repressive and ineffective means for relieving poverty. Rather, we argue that Labour has always been supportive of voluntary action, properly defined, with its roots in mutuality, self-help and active citizenship, and has always seen partnerships between government and voluntary agencies as crucial to the building of a modern welfare state. Such partnerships have taken different forms as the roles, responsibilities and priorities of the partners have changed over time; but the theme is a constant. It follows that New Labour's enthusiastic support for voluntary action when in power after 1997, rather than representing a clear break with the past (as its key architects, Tony Blair and Gordon Brown, have claimed), can better be understood as a continuation of a well-established strand within the Labour movement.

The 'myth' of Labour's hostility

Claims about Labour's hostility to all forms of voluntarism have tended to be cast in general terms.[1] However, there is one conspicuous exception: the much-quoted lecture on the role of the volunteer in the modern social service delivered in 1973 by Richard Crossman, who, as Secretary of State for Social Services in the government of Harold Wilson, had come into close contact with voluntary groups. His starting point was Richard Titmuss's 'remarkable study' of the blood transfusion service and the role in social policy of the 'gift relationship'. Crossman argued that a key cause of social disintegration was 'the frustration of the altruistic motive'. He went on, in what has become the best remembered (and perhaps most influential) part of his text, to denounce Labour for its attitude to charity. 'We all', he said, 'disliked the do-good volunteer and wanted to see him replaced by professionals and trained administrators in the socialist welfare state of which we all dreamed. Philanthropy to us was an odious expression of social oligarchy and churchy bourgeois attitudes. We detested voluntary hospitals maintained by flag days. We despised Boy Scouts and Girl Guides.'[2]

It is this speech, perhaps more than anything else, which has sustained the myth of Labour's hostility to voluntary action. Of course, as we indicate below, there was an element of truth in what Crossman had to say. But Crossman overstated his case. There is also more than a hint of inconsistency – Crossman had discovered the virtues of volunteering as an alternative to state action and was keen to proclaim that from the rooftops. Part of doing so meant over-playing his party's past hostility to charity and misrepresenting opposition to Victorian philanthropy as its current philosophy.

Unfortunately, some future Labour leaders and historians have been inclined to take Crossman's view at face value.[3] And, in a long series of speeches, successive Labour Prime Ministers, Tony Blair and Gordon

---

[1] See, for example, R. Harris and A. Seldon, *Welfare without the State: A Quarter Century of Suppressed Public Choice* (London, 1987); F. Prochaska, *The Voluntary Impulse: Philanthropy in Modern Britain* (London, 1988); F. Prochaska, 'Philanthropy', in F.M.L. Thompson (ed.), *The Cambridge Social History of Britain, 1750–1950*, 3 vols (Cambridge, 1990).

[2] R. Crossman, *The Role of the Volunteer in the Modern Social Service: Sidney Ball Memorial Lecture* (Oxford, 1974).

[3] M. Francis, *Ideas and Policies under Labour, 1945–51* (Manchester, 1997), p. 110.

Brown, have sought to underline the degree of discontinuity between New and Old Labour by deploring what they present as Labour's past hostility to voluntary action.[4] On the surface, the reason is straightforward enough. New Labour's presumed appeal to the electorate was based above all on its claim of *newness*, on its break with the culture, customs and policies of its party's past. Views on voluntarism are convenient candidates for consignment to the category of abandoned fetishes.

But the 'myth' of Labour's hostility to voluntary action is not only found on the left – the right has made its own contribution. From the 1970s onwards, numerous right-wing commentators have sought to portray the period following the end of the Second World War as one characterised by the growth of a monolithic state and the consequent emasculation of voluntary action. For example, Ferdinand Mount has harked back to a 'golden age' of voluntary action in the second half of the nineteenth century. 'All too often', during the twentieth century, he writes, 'we find the State – sometimes wilfully, sometimes out of cackhandedness – smothering the character of the enterprise, turning spontaneous enthusiasm into bureaucratic routine.'[5] A similar claim is made by Robert Whelan in a pamphlet for the Institute for Economic Affairs in 1999. Mourning what he sees as the decline of voluntary agencies after 1945 he places the blame firmly on the Labour government, 'whose members were, in some cases, extremely hostile to voluntary action. There was already, by the 1940s', he writes, 'a long tradition of socialist opposition to voluntarism, which was felt to be a controlling mechanism for keeping the poor in their place and reinforcing the status quo.'[6]

For the right, an attack on what is presented as Labour's centralising statist past has been an essential weapon in its battle to gain acceptance for its alternative vision of a welfare state ordered primarily along pre-1945 lines, with a much reduced role for government and centre stage going to voluntary associations. So, in a much publicised Hugo Young Memorial Lecture in 2009, David Cameron, as Leader of the Conservative Party, attacked the way in which what he represented as a malign Labour tradition of over-dependence on government, in which 'every issue demanded government intervention and every problem could be solved by a state

---

[4] For example, T. Blair, Speech at the ACU Convention, 2 March 2000; G. Brown, Speech at the NCVO Annual Conference, 9 February 2000.

[5] F. Mount, *Clubbing Together: The Revival of the Voluntary Principle* (London, n.d.), pp. 5–6.

[6] R. Whelan, *Involuntary Action* (London, 1999), p. 14.

solution', had snuffed out an alternative tradition on the left of a limited state.[7] As we shall show below, neither version of the myth – neither that created by New Labour as a means of breaking with its past, nor that created by the New Right as part of its vision of a return to a pre-welfare state, 'golden age' of voluntary action – can be substantiated.

The roots of Labour's attitudes

Labour's reformist, rather than revolutionary, character has been one of the basic factors that have helped to shape the nature of the party's relationship with other organisations in civil society. It is true that, at various stages in Labour's history, a significant element within the party have adopted an explicitly Marxist approach and made rhetorical gestures in the direction of a radical break with capitalism – in the late nineteenth century, at the beginning of the 1930s and again in the late 1970s and early 1980s. In so doing, these critics have tended to reject traditional philanthropy as a cover for exploitation, and the language of social service characteristic of late nineteenth- and early twentieth-century voluntary action as hypocritical. The terms in which this rejection has been expressed have varied from time to time; but the messages are the same.[8]

However, after the historic decision at the beginning of the twentieth century to participate in the parliamentary system rather than challenge it from outside, it became necessary for the party to devote attention to ways of addressing the contribution that voluntary action could make towards one of the main objectives of the Labour movement – the improvement of the material circumstances of the working class. There is a long history of involvement of people subsequently influential in progressive politics in voluntary social action – for example, in the settlement movement. Toynbee Hall, in east London, was the classic site for action by middle-class progressives, and this pattern was repeated in all major provincial cities.[9] The father of the welfare state, William Beveridge, and the future Prime Minister, Clement Attlee, are two outstanding examples among many.

---

[7] D. Cameron, Hugo Young Memorial Lecture, 2009.

[8] See, for example, G. Finlayson, *Citizen, State and Social Welfare in Britain 1830–1990* (Oxford, 1994), p. 157; C. Waters, *British Socialists and the Politics of Popular Culture, 1884–1914* (Manchester, 1990); B. Harrison, *Peaceable Kingdom: Stability and Change in Modern Britain* (Oxford, 1983).

[9] A. Briggs and A. Macartney, *Toynbee Hall: The First One Hundred Years* (London, 1984).

But both Beveridge and Attlee, like many other radical progressives, became disillusioned with the settlement approach, for a variety of reasons. One was the question of class, which has provided a second major shaping factor in relations between the Labour movement and voluntary action. There is a strong negative element here: a passionate resistance to the condescension endemic to middle-class charity in all its forms – a criticism not satisfactorily answered by the energetic participation of hearty public school volunteers in boys' clubs or school missions, once a characteristic activity in settlements.

Clement Attlee, who was appointed a lecturer in social work at the London School of Economics in 1912, set out his opposition to charity clearly in the textbook for students that he produced after the First World War:

> Charity is always apt to be accompanied by a certain complacence and condescension on the part of the benefactor, and by an expectation of gratitude from the recipient which cuts at the roots of all true friendliness. The charitable [of the nineteenth century] seem to us today to be smug and self-satisfied. They delighted in sermons to the poor on convenient virtues, and lacked the sharp self-criticism that is the note of society today.[10]

But, he suggests, there is also a positive factor, an alternative model for the provision of welfare: working-class mutual aid and what he calls 'the associative instinct'. This is epitomised in the co-operative movement, and sustained by the institutional structures developed through the friendly societies that evolved in parallel with the trade unions.[11] These developments were fundamental to the growth of the Labour Party and provided an alternative basis for promoting voluntary action.

The third main factor shaping relations was the concern with efficiency, which became a major preoccupation of the reformists within the Labour Party and is associated particularly with the Fabian Society and the Webbs.

---

[10] C.R. Attlee, *The Social Worker* (London, 1920), pp. 9–10. See also F. Beckett, *Clem Attlee, a Biography* (London, 1997).

[11] On Labour's enthusiasm for mutuality and self-help, enshrined in such institutions as the friendly societies, co-ops and Goose and Burial Clubs, see, in particular, E.P. Thompson, *The Making of the English Working Class* (London, 1963). On mutuality as an important (but neglected) strand of voluntary action, see, for example, Finlayson, *Citizen, State and Social Welfare*; J. Davis Smith, 'The Voluntary Tradition: Philanthropy and Self-Help in Britain 1500–1945', in J. Davis Smith, C. Rochester and R. Hedley (eds), *An Introduction to the Voluntary Sector* (London, 1995), pp. 29–35; D. Owen, *English Philanthropy 1660–1960* (Cambridge, MA, 1965); and P. Gosden, *Self Help: Voluntary Associations in Nineteenth Century Britain* (London, 1973).

This concern is reflected in the debate on the future of the Poor Law and the role of voluntary action in the rival reports of the Royal Commission in 1909. The Majority Report, under the persuasive influence of the Charity Organisation Society, favoured the continued dominance of the voluntary response and a reciprocal relationship between charity and the poor laws, as enshrined in the Goschen Minute of 1869. The Minority Report (the work primarily of Beatrice Webb) saw a greater role for the state, although it did not dismiss the importance of charity. It called for the greater use 'of voluntary agencies and of personal service of both men and women of good will', and felt the state should not 'lay its heavy hand on the efforts of the charitable'. But voluntary action should be secondary to the state – analogous to an 'extension ladder', rather than the 'parallel bars' favoured by the Majority Report.[12]

This approach rested in turn on a view of the importance of the state, which required a substantial expansion of its functions and an enhanced role for experts in its governance. These are commonly taken to be the main hallmarks of Fabian socialism, reflected in Sidney and Beatrice Webb's concern with the machinery of government and the potential for achieving reform through application of principles of scientific management, especially in local government.[13] The Webbs' approach was not universally approved within the party. The different, associational tradition with its roots in working-class mutual aid – and hence in voluntary action, properly understood – seemed for a while to offer a genuine alternative, outside the state, which was still distrusted within the Labour movement. But things turned out otherwise, as William Morris observed to Sidney Webb in 1895, shortly before his death: 'the world is going your way at present, Webb, but it is not the right way in the end'.[14]

Partnership in action

From the end of the First World War an increasing number of local authorities came under Labour control as the party rapidly expanded its electoral

[12] Quoted in Finlayson, *Citizen, State and Social Welfare*, pp. 196–197.
[13] Beatrice and Sidney Webb, *A Constitution for the Socialist Commonwealth of Great Britain* (London, 1920).
[14] S. Yeo, 'Notes on Three Socialisms', in C. Levy (ed.), *Socialism and the Intelligentsia* (London, 1987), p. 219.

base. Local government provided the proving ground for a new approach to social policy which necessarily involved forming relationships with voluntary organisations, since a substantial number of key functions in welfare, health and social services were still performed largely by these bodies. Attlee, who began his political career in local government, argued strongly in *The Social Worker* for developing 'partnership in the undertakings of the local authority, supplementing the paid official with the personal service of the volunteer'.[15]

This strengthening of relations between local government and voluntary bodies was described by Elizabeth Macadam as having created a unique partnership – a 'New Philanthropy'.[16] The outstanding example was the London County Council, captured by Labour in 1934 under the leadership of Herbert Morrison, who placed stress on municipal leadership and professionalism in delivery of services, but with a substantial role for voluntary action, especially in child care and schools – the Webbs' 'extension ladder' pushed out still further.[17] Braithwaite estimates that by this time over a third of the total income of registered charities was received from the state as payment for services.[18]

The party made a modest step forward nationally at the General Election of 1935, after which Clement Attlee, who had kept his Limehouse seat in 1931 when the party's big guns had all lost theirs, was elected leader of the party. After his election as leader Attlee found time to produce for the Left Book Club a comprehensive survey of political priorities, *The Labour Party in Perspective*. This is a surprisingly radical document (it was rather ostentatiously 'rediscovered' as such by Tony Benn in the mid-1980s). The stress is mainly on economic policy and planning, with a firm commitment to the central role of the state. But there are several glimpses of a broader approach. Attlee argues strongly for equality as a goal, stating without equivocation that the aim of the socialist state must be to achieve it, and commenting that 'human beings are, of course, unequal, and have diversities of tastes and gifts, but this need not be expressed in wide social inequalities'.[19]

---

[15] Attlee, *The Social Worker*, p. 87.
[16] E. Macadam, *The New Philanthropy* (London, 1934).
[17] B. Harris, 'Voluntary Action and the State in Historical Perspective', *Voluntary Sector Review*, 1, 1, 2010, pp. 25–40.
[18] C. Braithwaite, *The Voluntary Citizen* (London, 1938), p. 171.
[19] C.R. Attlee, *The Labour Party in Perspective* (London, 1937), p. 148.

The other key principle is democracy. Socialists, he says,

> are not concerned solely with material things. They do not think of human beings as a herd to be fed and watered and kept in security. They think of them as individuals cooperating together to make a fine collective life. For this reason, socialism is a more exacting creed than that of its competitors. It does not demand submission and acquiescence, but active and constant participation in common activities. It demands that every individual shall shoulder his or her responsibilities.[20]

And he adds, 'I conceive that in the socialist state there will be, besides the democratic framework of the state and of industry, a great variety of voluntary societies controlled by the members, wherein all the time a training in democracy will be taking place.'[21] This enthusiasm for active citizenship, manifested through voluntary action, was to resurface when Attlee became Prime Minister in 1945.

Whilst the Labour leadership was developing its thinking on the positive role of voluntary action, the same could not be said of broad sections of the trade union movement. The unions had long been hostile to voluntary action, both on class grounds (the image of Lady Bountiful doling out aid to the deserving poor looms large in union mythology) and because of the real (or perceived) threat posed by volunteers to wages and jobs. This hostility came to the fore during the General Strike when volunteers (including enthusiastic bands of students from Oxford and Cambridge) were brought in by the government to break the strike. The memory of 1926 was to cloud relations between the unions and the voluntary movement for more than a generation.[22]

The mass unemployment of the Depression years had created a series of major social problems highlighted in a number of exposés, many of the best known – among them George Orwell's *The Road to Wigan Pier* – published by the Left Book Club.[23] Voluntary action was often seen as a means of addressing some of these problems – slum housing through housing associations, social services by voluntary social work, voluntary activities directly related to the needs of the unemployed. The Voluntary Occupational Centre Movement, which offered a variety of activities to the

[20] *Ibid.*, p. 149.
[21] *Ibid.*, p. 151.
[22] J. Davis Smith, 'An Uneasy Alliance: Volunteers and Trade Unions', in R. Hedley and J. Davis Smith (eds), *Volunteering and Society: Principles and Practice* (London, 1992).
[23] G. Orwell, *The Road to Wigan Pier* (London, 1937).

76

unemployed, including recreation, education and work, was firmly rooted within Labour traditions of self-help and mutual aid. By mid-1935 there were over 1,000 such centres with a total membership of some 150,000.[24] Another form of centre was the Community Centre established on new housing estates, designed to provide a resource for families and promoted by the National Council of Social Service's Community Centres and Associations Committee, intended as 'a new social and cultural nucleus for community life', on 'a self-governing basis'.[25]

The general question of the right place for voluntary action in broader approaches to dealing with social problems was addressed in successive reviews of key areas of social policy, by the newly established progressive think-tank Political and Economic Planning (PEP).[26] These reviews suggested that the integration of voluntary bodies into a coherent strategy would pose difficulties – despite greater professionalisation of their staff, their services were seen as uneven both in quality and in geographical distribution and not susceptible of systematic planning.[27] However, the report on social services comments that, 'Evidently, the salaried staff of the voluntary social services is still growing and its influence is increasing in spite of the expansion of personnel of the statutory services which is also taking place . . . the relations between the two appear to be settling themselves not unsatisfactorily by trial and error.'[28]

Bernard Harris comments on the interwar period that,

> although it may be wrong to argue that the state and the voluntary sector occupied 'separate' spheres at the start of this period it is difficult to deny that they worked much more closely together at the end of it, and this had important consequences for the operation of the voluntary sector on the eve of the Second World War.[29]

This debate on the shape of future relationships was abruptly closed by the outbreak of war. Volunteers were active throughout at every level, not only directly in the war effort but also in coping with the social

[24] R. Hayburn, 'The Voluntary Occupational Centre Movement 1932–39', *Journal of Contemporary History*, 6, 3, 1971, pp. 156–171.
[25] F. and G. Stephenson, *Community Centres* (London, 1942), The Housing Centre, p. 3.
[26] D. Ritschel, *The Politics of Planning* (Oxford, 1997).
[27] For an exploration of these issues see also T.S. Simey, *Principles of Social Administration* (Oxford, 1937); and J. Lewis, *The Voluntary Sector, the State and Social Work in Britain* (Aldershot, 1995).
[28] Political and Economic Planning, *Report on the British Social Services* (London, 1937), p. 174.
[29] Harris, 'Voluntary Action', p. 33.

problems exposed by the experience of war – notably, the consequences of bombing and mass evacuation of children from large cities.[30] The Women's Voluntary Service had been created by the government before the war specifically to address these problems. Citizens Advice Bureaux, also newly hatched, were dealing with 2.5 million enquiries a year by the end of 1942.[31]

But the clear conclusion from experience in wartime was that the state would necessarily have to play a more substantial role and that victory had demonstrated its capacity to mobilise resources in order to do so. The Webbs' one-time protégé, Beveridge, produced in his 1942 report on social insurance a blueprint that well suited the temper of the times: the state as benevolent provider of a common basic standard of welfare; individual action as a voluntary supplement.[32]

Herbert Morrison, as Home Secretary in the wartime coalition, was actively involved in post-war planning issues. He had fought hard for full implementation of Beveridge's proposals (though he had to wind up for the government in the parliamentary debate in which this was resisted, on Churchill's instructions). His wartime speeches and writings set out some lines for post-war policies. For example, in his speech to the Nursery Schools Association in 1943, he picked up themes from the highly influential report *Our Towns*, part sponsored by the NCSS, and used it to identify and praise the pioneering role of voluntary organisations.[33]

PEP had continued its activities in the social planning field throughout the war years. Michael Young, subsequently best known for his work on community and as the archetypal social entrepreneur, acted as Secretary (in effect director) through this period and used the opportunity to produce a number of influential pamphlets on social policy issues in the PEP Planning series. His time as Secretary came to an end when he was head-hunted by Morgan Phillips, secretary of the Labour Party, to join the party's headquarters department. Here he was in large measure responsible for the drafting of the Labour Party manifesto for the 1945 election, *Let Us Face the Future*. His subsequent claim that he inserted as many PEP ideas as he could get past Herbert Morrison should perhaps be taken with a pinch of salt, not least because it still emphasised nationalisation as the means for achieving change.[34]

[30] R. Titmuss, *Problems of Social Policy* (London, 1950).
[31] A.F.C. Bourdillon, *Voluntary Social Services, Their Place in the Modern State* (London, 1945).
[32] W. Beveridge, *Report on Social Insurance and Allied Services* (London, 1942).
[33] J. Welshman, *Churchill's Children* (Oxford, 2010).
[34] A. Briggs, *Michael Young, Social Entrepreneur* (London, 2001), p. 77.

Labour in power

The introduction of the welfare state in Britain after the Second World War marks a watershed in the development of relations between the state and the voluntary sector, though not quite in the way that it has sometimes been believed.[35]

Labour and its leadership were not as statist in their approach to the provision of welfare as is often assumed. It was clear in 1945 that the state would take the lead in the delivery of services, but there was much uncertainty about the way in which the disposition of responsibilities would be organised. Despite the active interest taken by members of the party in the debates about planning there was little evidence of a comprehensive strategy for welfare.[36] As Jose Harris has put it: 'the Welfare State came into being with no clearly defined conception of welfare and no coherent theory of the State'.[37] However, given Labour's past history and concerns, it was inevitable that the new system would take a collectivist form.

Nevertheless, the party and its central figures – in particular, Herbert Morrison as minister responsible for coordinating government social policy – had specific ambitions cast in explicitly socialist terms. Prominent among them was an interest in changing attitudes among the electorate and promoting active democracy. Here, the influence of the Workers' Educational Association (WEA), with which several of the party's intellectuals had been associated (notably R.H. Tawney and Hugh Gaitskell), can be detected.[38]

After the election victory the party's research department carried out an extensive programme of voter and member education, based in part on the model of the wartime Army Bureau of Current Affairs. Material was put out in pamphlet form as a basis for discussion in local parties. Michael Young was responsible for much of this. His biographer Asa Briggs comments: 'close as he was to Morrison, Michael became increasingly uneasy not so much about the machinery of planning – or the continuation of physical controls – as about the Morrisonian pattern of nationalisation. . . . Little had been done, he thought, to close the gap between "them" and "us".'[39]

---

[35] Whelan, *Involuntary Action*.

[36] R. Lowe, *The Welfare State in Britain since 1945* (London, 1999).

[37] J. Harris, 'Political Ideas and the Debate on State Welfare, 1940–45', in H.L. Smith (ed.), *War and Social Change: British Society in the Second World War* (Manchester, 1986), p. 256.

[38] On the WEA see L. Goldman, *Dons and Workers: Oxford and Adult Education since 1850* (Oxford, 1995).

[39] Briggs, *Michael Young*, p. 81.

This emerges very clearly in Young's party discussion pamphlet '*Small Man: Big World*', described as a 'discussion of socialist democracy', which begins the process of revising his thinking. As a preamble, he quotes William Morris: 'individual men cannot shuffle off the business of life on to the shoulders of an abstraction called the state but must deal with each other'.[40] His advocacy of neighbourhood democracy underlines the importance of community, claiming that the role of community associations had increased over the war years and that it should be possible to build on community councils as an instrument of local governance. This activity runs in parallel with Young's continued engagement with PEP and its post-war research theme of active democracy.[41]

Voluntary organisations had their own specific assets to bring to this new post-war situation, apart from the general one of having had a 'good war'. The report of the Nuffield Reconstruction Survey, directed by G.D.H. Cole, on their role helpfully identifies a range of activities that would be particularly relevant to post-war circumstances.[42] Cole and his colleagues saw the voluntary sector acquiring new professional skills and becoming more democratically accountable; they identified several functions as being of particular relevance – child care, youth work, adult education, providing advice and information. Professional casework skills could provide both a guarantee of good quality services and a bridge to the statutory sector, which would serve as a basis for collaboration with the new structures of state welfare.

Public attitudes were perhaps more ambivalent. In spring 1947, Mass Observation included questions on charity and voluntary action in its monthly directives.[43] The responses given, so early into the life of the new Labour government, provide an interesting insight into public attitudes towards charity and the hopes and fears for voluntary action under the Attlee administration.

Opinion was polarised between those who felt that charity was an abomination that had no place in a modern world and those who feared

[40] Quoted in Briggs, *Michael Young*, p. 90.
[41] A. Beach, 'Forging a Nation of Participants: Political and Economic Planning in Labour's Britain', in A. Beach and R. Weight (eds), *The Right to Belong* (London, 1998).
[42] Quoted in Bourdillon, *Voluntary Social Services*.
[43] Mass Observation Archive, April and May 1947, University of Sussex. In citing this material, the authors and editors gratefully acknowledge the help of the Trustees of the Mass Observation Archive, University of Sussex.

for the consequences of an over-bearing state. Perhaps most interestingly for this particular study, some of the respondents revealed their political affiliations, so it is possible to get a taste of how those on the left viewed these developments. As we have already seen in relation to Attlee and other Labour leaders, the hostility to charity on the left ran deep. One musician and author wrote: 'As a thorough-going and (I hope) developing Socialist, I detest it [charity] . . . I am entirely for doing away with all promiscuous "charity"; the state must take care of all the needy.' He went on, in a manner reminiscent of Crossman's later attack, to berate 'the ramshackle condition of "charity" in general; flag days, hospital Saturdays, and the rest of the lazy, thoughtless humbug that takes the place of real socialism'.

However, there were others on the left, keen to draw a distinction between charity and voluntary action, and between the provision of essential public services, which should be the responsibility of the state, and the mass of community action or volunteering, which it was right and proper should remain the preserve of the individual. One respondent, who was secretary of the local Labour Party and active in the trade union NALGO, but who was also active in a vast array of other voluntary roles, including the music circle, community centre, missionary fellowship, charity fêtes, collections and more, summed up this distinction nicely. She did not feel, she wrote, that these volunteer roles should be 'state jobs', but she was adamant that 'hospitals of every kind, magistrates, blind care etc should be all-state concerns'.

The process of setting the structures of the new welfare state in place was completed with the coming into existence of the National Health Service (NHS) in July 1948. The NHS is often taken as the epitome of the Labour welfare reforms. It also represents the one major departure from the general pattern of measures, which had been broadly agreed between the parties before Labour came into office. This was mainly due to the personal approach of the Minister of Health, Aneurin Bevan, who chose to solve the problems of a divided system of hospital management, the weaknesses of which had been clearly exposed during the war, by nationalising all hospitals, both voluntary and local authority controlled. The resulting system could be (and was) represented as a very substantial increase in state power in a crucial area, but it would be wrong to see Bevan's action simply as a reflection of hostility to voluntary action as such.

It is true that Bevan had substantial reservations about charitable funding of hospitals. He told the Commons in 1946 that it was 'repugnant to a civilised community for hospitals to have to rely on private charity

. . . I have always felt a shudder of repulsion when I see nurses and sisters who ought to be at their work . . . going about the streets collecting money for the hospitals'.[44] He also successfully beat off an attempt by Herbert Morrison in Cabinet to keep municipal hospitals under local authority control.[45]

However, Bevan was a passionate proponent of the virtues of comprehensive planning: to guarantee efficiency the system should be run from the centre and subject to accountability through Parliament. As he subsequently put it, the previous situation had been 'a chaos of little or big projects . . . without plan or central direction', so that:

> In place of a rational relationship between all its parts, there arises a patch-quilt of local paternalisms. My experience has taught me that there is no worse enemy to the intelligent planning of a national health service; especially on the hospital side. Warm gushes of self-indulgent emotion are an unreliable source of driving-power in the field of health organisation.[46]

In other circumstances, Bevan was prepared to contemplate a substantial role for voluntary bodies. He told the Commons in 1947 that the government was 'extending the field of voluntary work enormously. What we are doing is to relieve voluntary organisations from the necessity of raising funds.'[47] During the passage of the National Insurance Bill in 1946 he spoke of the government's intention 'to make full use of voluntary organisations', and he accepted certain amendments to safeguard their position.[48] Local authorities were encouraged to provide 'residential accommodation' for the aged through voluntary agencies, 'which they may either subsidise or employ as their agent on agreed terms'.[49]

Moreover, whilst the health reforms undoubtedly reduced the role of voluntary agencies in the direct delivery of services, alternative opportunities for citizen participation were deliberately opened up within the newly created statutory hospitals. Friends groups sprung up throughout the country, providing countless opportunities for people to volunteer within the NHS. One commentator at the time wrote that there were 'many

---

[44] See M. Foot, *Aneurin Bevan: Volume II* (London, 1975), p. 132.
[45] N. Timmins, *The Five Giants: A Biography of the Welfare State* (London, 1995), pp. 116–117. See also K.O. Morgan, *Labour in Power 1945–51* (Oxford, 1984), p. 155.
[46] A. Bevan, *In Place of Fear* (London, 1952), p. 79.
[47] Hansard, *Parliamentary Debates* (House of Commons), 5th ser., vol. 441, col. 1625.
[48] Hansard, *Parliamentary Debates* (House of Commons), 5th ser., vol. 450, col. 2136.
[49] Ministry of Health Circular, 87/46.

ways in which citizens would be made to feel that the public services belong to them – especially when the operative power is vested in a Local Authority. They can participate directly in them as voluntary workers.'[50]

In 1948 William Beveridge (now Lord Beveridge) produced the third in his sequence of reports on different aspects of the future of British society. This third report, *Voluntary Action*, is much less well known than the earlier two on social insurance and full employment. It can be seen as a heroic attempt to redress the balance in favour of activity outside the state, or merely as an afterthought, a reflection of his disillusionment with the role he now occupied – a powerless prophet in the post-war world. The report has substantial recommendations to make about the shape of the future relationship between state and voluntary sector, including the creation of a post of 'Minister-guardian' of the voluntary sector and a state-endowed independent funding body to sponsor future voluntary action.[51]

Beveridge's past eminence earned him a formal response from the Labour government, in the form of a ministerial statement, delivered by Lord Pakenham in the course of a debate in the House of Lords:

> . . . we are convinced that voluntary associations have rendered are rendering and must be encouraged to continue to render, great and indispensable services to the community. I hope that deliberate expression of our basic Governmental attitude will carry far and wide.[52]

According to Pakenham's later account, he had been 'much assisted' in taking this positive line by Herbert Morrison, in his capacity as ministerial coordinator of the government's social policy programme.[53]

In that context, Morrison himself was insistent that Labour wanted to encourage voluntary organisations to take on additional functions. In a speech to the London Council of Voluntary Service in 1948 on 'Social Advance' (a term that echoes the Beveridge report's subtitle), he stressed that the government was anxious to encourage 'the variety and freedom of voluntary action' and to identify ways in which 'statutory and voluntary effort can cooperate efficiently'. In a useful passage he sets out how he thinks the respective roles of state and voluntary sector should be defined:

> It is the responsibility of the statutory side to encourage the variety and freedom of voluntary associations: to consult them in regard to new

[50] T.H. Marshall, 'Voluntary Action', *Political Quarterly*, xx/1–4, 1949, p. 27.

[51] W. Beveridge, *Voluntary Action: A Report on Methods of Social Advance* (London, 1948).

[52] Hansard, *Parliamentary Debates* (House of Lords), 5th ser., vol. 163, cols 119–122.

[53] Lord Longford, *Avowed Intent* (London, 1994), pp. 110–111.

developments . . . . Voluntary associations must not be content to maintain themselves and their own special environment, but interest themselves in getting the wider environment of society right also.[54]

By the end of Labour's period in office, it was clear that the objective of closer collaboration had been met. As the national coordinating body for the voluntary sector in England, the National Council of Social Service concluded that, 'the importance of voluntary organisations was now definitely recognised and the authorities were prepared to regard them as important instruments of community life, not merely as useful agents'.[55] The NCSS annual handbook comments that although there are those with concerns about the extension of the role of the state,

there are many who believe that public and private services are complementary and that there must be a free and open sharing of resources. They believe that the receipt of grants has enabled many organisations to overcome their most serious financial difficulties and to improve the efficiency of their work. They have noted that in practice those organisations that have accepted substantial grants have been left remarkably free of interference or attempts to control their work.[56]

The official record supports these conclusions: the authors of the commentary on the state papers of the period point to the expansion of the voluntary sector's role in the 1948 Children Act and in provision for the elderly, commenting that 'the expansion of voluntary effort took place despite the election of a Labour government committed to the public provision of services'.[57]

Nevertheless, there is some truth in the later assertion of the Wolfenden Committee that, in the period immediately after the war, the voluntary sector had been 'marking time'.[58] But as far as Labour was concerned the essential task of purging the newly created welfare institutions of what Morrison called 'cold charity' had been performed; the stigma of the poor laws had been wiped out. It was perhaps not hyperbole to assert, as T.H. Marshall had done in a thoughtful review in 1949, that in the reformed social services, 'the entire citizen body is organized in a great mutual aid

---

[54] H. Morrison, *The Peaceful Revolution* (London, 1949), pp. 129–130.

[55] C. Basnett, *Voluntary Social Action* (London, 1969).

[56] D.H.W. Hall, *Voluntary Social Services* (London, 1951), pp. 24, 29.

[57] A. Land, R. Lowe and N. Whiteside, *The Development of the Welfare State* (London, 1992).

[58] J. Wolfenden, *The Future of Voluntary Organisations: Report of the Wolfenden Committee* (London, 1978).

society. All contribute, and all are entitled to receive benefits, there is no longer any distinction between the privileged and unprivileged.'[59]

But for mutual aid to function in this way requires the active engagement of citizens in the community – the theme pursued by Young and his colleagues in the Labour research department. The significance of this type of voluntary action – expressed, in terms that were certainly hyperbolic, as 'making socialists' – is essential to a proper understanding of Labour's attitude to voluntarism at this time.[60]

Revisionism and debates about regaining power

Labour went out of office in 1951 and was not to regain power for thirteen years. Its period in opposition provoked much debate on new directions for party policy, the so-called 'revisionism' controversy. Michael Young's close friend Tony Crosland (then still C.A.R.) was one of the main protagonists. His book *The Future of Socialism* is unusual in writing of the period in assuming that some of the major economic questions that had previously agitated the party – in particular, the ownership of industry – were no longer of decisive significance and that the key issues around welfare and equality could be tackled with confidence that the resources would be available to address them. Since Britain was now 'on the threshold of mass abundance', priority could be given to social reform. Here he develops the libertarian case, which set his approach apart at the time, looking to the spheres of 'personal freedom, happiness and cultural endeavour; the cultivation of leisure, beauty, grace, gaiety, excitement and of all the proper pursuits, whether elevated, vulgar or eccentric which contribute to the varied fabric of a full private and family life'.[61]

On social policy, Labour's response to this situation was to seek ways of going 'beyond Beveridge'. This was largely the responsibility of Richard Crossman, who had not held office in the 1945–1951 government, having been distrusted by Attlee; it was an attempt to expand the range of state welfare linked with a new enthusiasm for the concept of planning, drawing on the apparently successful French model of indicative planning and a

---

[59] Marshall, 'Voluntary Action', p. 26.
[60] Francis, *Ideas and Policies under Labour*. See also S. Fielding, P. Thompson and N. Tiratsoo, *England Arise! The Labour Party and Popular Politics in 1940s Britain* (Manchester, 1995).
[61] C.A.R. Crosland, *The Future of Socialism* (London, 1956), p. 355.

developing concern with the efficiency of the machinery of government and the professional skills of those operating it both at local and central level.[62] *Planning for Freedom* is the title that Crossman chose for his essay, which was one of his main contributions to the 'revisionism' debate. However, his discussion is largely confined to economic planning; and, although he refers to the potential significance of consumers as active participants, he concludes that 'there is only one defence for the consumer and that is through his elected representatives, whether in local or national government'.[63]

After Labour's further heavy election defeat in 1959, the influential study *Must Labour Lose?* contained polling evidence analysed by Mark Abrams that appears to dispose of the affluence thesis in its cruder form – increased material prosperity did not appear to (in Abrams's words) seduce the working class from its earlier loyalties and convert them 'into urban peasants determined to resist any party likely to threaten acquisitiveness – and particularly their acquisitiveness'.[64] Rita Hinden, reviewing the results, comments that they show that there is an opening here for a 'real social movement, in which socialists in every locality should be the spearhead . . . the average party member today is starved of meaningful things to do [but] there is always a surprising response when appeals come for help – in money and service'.[65] Here again is the active democracy theme that Michael Young had promoted within and outside the party in the late 1940s, and which led him briefly to promote the idea of a consumers' party with the explicit agenda of empowering citizens against state and market monopolies.[66]

Labour back in office

After what the party chose to term 'Thirteen Wasted Years', Labour returned to power in 1964 and, with the exception of a four-year gap between 1970 and 1974, it was to rule continuously until 1979. In the

---

[62] K. Harris, *Attlee* (London, 1982), p. 411. The story is that Attlee believed that Crossman cheated at tennis; but Harris says that Attlee told him simply that he was 'irresponsible and unstable'.

[63] R.H.S. Crossman, *Planning for Freedom* (London, 1965), p. 73.

[64] M. Abrams and R. Rose, *Must Labour Lose?* (Harmondsworth, 1960), p. 42.

[65] Quoted in Abrams and Rose, *Must Labour Lose?*, p. 115.

[66] Briggs, *Michael Young*, p. 282.

welfare field this period saw the consolidation and expansion of the welfare state apparatus, but also significant changes in attitudes towards voluntary action. This was largely due to the emergence of a new form of voluntary association (including such pressure groups as Shelter and the Child Poverty Action Group) – more radical than its predecessor, more willing to challenge and criticise government action. One left-wing commentator has argued that the voluntary sector 'was revolutionised' in this period by 'the critique of bureaucratic forms of statist welfare'.[67] On Labour attitudes towards these changes, Rodney Lowe comments that on the left of the party, 'these developments were seen as an active concept of citizenship whereby the better off helped those in need with the positive purpose of restoring them to self-sufficiency and thus "full citizenship"'. So 'the increasing number of self-help and pressure groups were seen to be an embodiment of participatory democracy – or even as an effective protest against the "capitalist state"'.[68]

More conventionally, the 1960s saw repeated attempts by government departments to boost the role of voluntary organisations and volunteers. In November 1964 the Ministry of Health issued a circular on *Voluntary Effort in the Health and Welfare Services,* asking all local authorities to 'make full use of their powers to contribute to voluntary organisations whose activities further the development of the health and welfare services'.[69] In 1965 the Home Office appointed a working party to consider the place of voluntary service in the after-care of discharged offenders. Its second report called for a massive expansion of voluntary activity.[70] In April 1968, a Joint Circular from the Department of Education, the Ministry of Health, the Home Office, and the Ministry of Housing was issued on the subject of *Voluntary Community Service by Young People.* It stated that 'the government have been particularly impressed by the widespread enthusiasm of young people to render service to the community. They are concerned that this fund of energy and goodwill should be used to the full, in collaboration with existing statutory and voluntary bodies, so as to support the work already being done and increase the opportunities for voluntary service.'[71]

---

[67] S. Hall, *The Voluntary Sector under Attack* (London, 1989), p. 10.
[68] Lowe, *The Welfare State in Britain,* p. 275.
[69] Ministry of Health, *Voluntary Effort in the Health and Welfare Services,* Circular 18/64, 1964.
[70] Home Office, Home Office Working Party on the Place of Voluntary Service in After-Care, Second Report, 1967.
[71] Ministry of Health, *Voluntary Community Service by Young People,* Joint Circular 15/68, 1968.

In 1969, the Aves report on the role of volunteers in the personal social services was published. It called for greater involvement of volunteers in the public sector and for a national centre to act as a focal point for volunteering.[72] Although not an official report, it was warmly welcomed by the government. Baroness Serota, Minister of State at the Department of Health, said the report had been 'presented at exactly the right time'. Major changes were taking place in statutory/voluntary relations and it was 'essential to re-think the place of voluntary organisations and volunteers in the changing statutory context'.[73]

Unexpectedly turned out of office in 1970, Labour on return to power (equally unanticipated) in 1974 inherited from Heath's Conservative government a formal commitment to closer links between the statutory and voluntary sector in the form of a Voluntary Services Unit located at the Home Office.[74] In 1975, during a debate in the House of Lords on 'Voluntary Service in the Community', Lord Harris, Home Office minister and the government spokesman on voluntary matters, outlined Labour's continuing commitment to voluntary action. 'Even if we had the resources – which we most certainly do not', he said, 'a society in which all human needs were met by the state would be an absurdity.' Although government could do very little about the financial problems voluntary agencies find themselves in, it can, he said, 'play a unique role' in 'encouraging the use of volunteers and the opening of opportunities for them, and in helping the voluntary services to co-ordinate their activities and communicate with all levels of authority'.[75]

This commitment was restated by the Prime Minister himself later that year. Writing in the *Social Services Quarterly*, Harold Wilson argued that 'the role of voluntary organisations is not just a useful adjunct to government services but it is fundamental and irreplaceable. . . . It is a recognition of the distinct, indispensable and socially invaluable role that the voluntary organisations now play in tackling social problems and creating a better society.'[76]

In 1976, the Good Neighbour Campaign was launched, 'to encourage the provision of simple, practical help to old people and others in need and

[72] G. Aves, *The Voluntary Worker in the Social Services* (London, 1969).
[73] National Council of Social Service, 'Report on Conference on the Aves Report, 6 March', unpublished paper, NCSS, 1970.
[74] See Finlayson, *Citizen, State and Social Welfare*, p. 321.
[75] Hansard, *Parliamentary Debates* (House of Lords) 5th ser., vol. 895, cols 1410–1418.
[76] H. Wilson, *Social Services Quarterly*, Winter 1975.

to help build up good neighbourliness'. In 1978, the Labour government responded warmly to the report from the Wolfenden Committee on the future of voluntary organisations, with the Prime Minister, James Callaghan, commenting that 'there will always be competition for government funds. But there is an almost inexhaustible supply of good neighbourliness, of good-hearted people waiting to help. . . .'[77] In 1978, a working party was set up under Stan Orme to look at ways of increasing community action. The group's first report argued that 'the use of volunteers should where possible be extended, especially in areas such as caring for the growing numbers of very elderly people, where the statutory services will have difficulty in meeting demand'.[78] However, the deliberations of the group soon became side-tracked by the public sector strikes of the winter of 1978 which brought into sharp focus once again the uneasy relationship between volunteers and trade unions.[79] A report was circulated to ministers in 1979, but a few weeks later the General Election was called. Labour lost and was to be out of power for eighteen years.

By the end of their period in government, Labour's relationship with voluntary organisations had travelled a long distance from the positions the two parties had occupied in 1945 – the newly created welfare state had bedded down and the scope of its activities and responsibilities had vastly increased. But the voluntary sector had changed too – witness the account by one Labour activist of the growth of mutual aid and campaigning at the expense of charity and philanthropy, and of new opportunities for voluntarism laid out by the Wolfenden Committee.[80] Kendall identifies this as the moment when a new *zeitgeist* increasingly favours voluntary action.[81] And the essential message, of a willingness to look for the means of promoting collaboration between statutory and voluntary sector, remained unchanged.

---

[77] Quoted in M. Brenton, *The Voluntary Sector in the British Social Services* (London, 1985).

[78] P. Stubbings, 'Central Government Policy towards Volunteers' (unpublished MSc thesis, Cranfield Institute of Technology, 1983).

[79] Davis Smith, 'An Uneasy Alliance'.

[80] K. Worpole, 'Volunteers for Socialism', *New Society*, 55, 1981, pp. 199–200.

[81] J. Kendall, 'The UK: Ingredients in a Hyperactive Horizontal Policy Environment', in J. Kendall (ed.), *Handbook on Third Sector Policy in Europe* (Cheltenham, 2009), p. 69.

Towards New Labour

If Labour's thirteen years out of office after 1951 had been traumatic, it was nothing compared to the experience after 1979. Mrs Thatcher's victory at the General Election in that year was followed by three successive further defeats that sent shock waves through the Labour movement.

Labour's attitude to voluntary action reflected this turmoil. The presence of a right-wing government, intent on cutting back the state and contracting out services to the private and voluntary sectors, led to a hardening of hostility towards voluntary action by some on the left. Some local authorities, such as Islington, adopted an aggressively anti-voluntary sector stance; while in Liverpool, where a small Trotskyite sect, Militant Tendency, had taken control, 'open warfare' was declared on voluntary groups and community centres and hostels were closed down. In other areas of the country, a very different pattern emerged. With the national Labour Party impotent in the face of the Thatcherite onslaught, voluntary organisations began to take on the mantle of the main opposition to government policies. A new set of voluntary agencies emerged (mirroring those of the late 1960s) which coalesced around a 'rainbow coalition' of issues, including women's rights and those of black and other ethnic minority groups. Many Labour-controlled local authorities eagerly embraced this new voluntary action and gave it their support. The biggest local authority in the country, the Greater London Council (GLC), courted voluntary agencies at every opportunity, leading one commentator to claim in 1987 that, 'for the last three years of its existence, the GLC was effectively a giant co-ordinating body for the voluntary sector'.[82]

Within the party itself, calls were coming for a more explicitly voluntary sector-minded approach. In 1989, a small grouping within the Labour Party was established by members working in the voluntary sector with the express purpose of forcing the party to adopt a more pro-voluntary sector stance. Labour Community Action's stated aims were: 'to raise awareness in the Labour Party of voluntary sector issues' and 'to influence Labour Party policy with regards to the voluntary sector'.[83] In 1990, the party commissioned a review of voluntary action under the chairmanship of an ex-minister and leading voluntary sector chief executive, Alf Dubs.

---

[82] N. Fielding, 'Feeling Charitable', *New Society*, 10 April 1987, p. 2.
[83] Labour Community Action, *Labour and the Community* (London, 1989).

A consultation document, *Labour and the Voluntary Sector*, was distributed widely to voluntary groups and a series of regional meetings held to gather feedback.[84] In 1992, the fruits of the consultation exercise were distilled in a new publication, *Building Bridges*.[85]

The document represented Labour's fullest expression to date of its commitment to voluntary action: 'We recognise that voluntary action, whether expressed as individual acts of support for friends, neighbours and relatives, through community based collective action or through wider professionally organised bodies, is part of the expression of citizenship.' Old concerns about the threat posed to statutory services were dismissed: 'The inter-dependence of government and the voluntary sector is an established aspect of British society and is warmly welcomed by the Labour Party . . . . We do not believe that voluntary activity is either a threat, or a cheap alternative, to the provision of statutory services.'[86]

One of Tony Blair's own initiatives on succeeding to the leadership of the party on John Smith's death was to commission a review of party policy from Alun Michael, which further extended the party's commitment to working with the voluntary sector in the form of a proposed compact between the two.[87] Thus, when Labour finally returned to power in 1997, it had a ready-made blueprint for governing its relations with the sector, and it speedily embarked upon putting the ideas into practice. In so doing, New Labour went further than any previous administration (either Labour or Conservative) in courting the voluntary sector. But, whether or not this represented a clean break with Labour's past, or simply an extension of previous policies, remains open to question.

Conclusions

On the concept of charity, which represents all that the Labour movement disliked about Victorian attitudes towards poverty and how it should be dealt with, the Labour movement has always had baggage – witness both

[84] Labour Party, *Labour and the Voluntary Sector: A Consultation Document* (London, 1990).
[85] Labour Party, *Building Bridges: Labour and the Voluntary Sector* (London, 1992).
[86] *Ibid.*, p. 1.
[87] Labour Party, *Building the Future Together: Labour's Policies for Partnership between Government and the Voluntary Sector* (London, 1997). For the compact proposal, subsequently implemented, see Home Office, *Compact on Relations between Government and the Voluntary and Community Sector in England* (London, 1998).

Attlee's denunciation quoted above, which was echoed by numerous Labour spokesmen before 1945, and the stress in the 1945 government on the need to purge the taint of the Poor Law. The trade union movement also had long-standing issues with volunteering, seeing it as a threat to the pay and conditions of its members and a source (during periods of major industrial unrest) of enthusiastic strike breakers, although tensions began to thaw during the 1980s and 1990s.[88]

But Labour as a party had a different sort of experience as it moved from political periphery towards taking power, locally as much as nationally. The experience of earlier municipal socialism is important here, and the recognition that volunteers could play an important role in delivering and 'humanising services'.[89]

Volunteering had a political face too. Labour's interest in 'active citizenship' has been a neglected theme. It is cast initially in explicitly political terms ('making socialists') – the kind of comradely community-based political education epitomised by the early twentieth-century Independent Labour Party and developed in the Workers' Educational Association. The 1945 government's commitment to this approach has only recently re-emerged, because the image has been of action through large state bureaucracies created and run by Morrisonian corporations.[90]

Another buried theme is consumer empowerment. This was Michael Young's main contribution, which was picked up by the right wing of the Labour Party (Roy Jenkins as well as Tony Crosland), during and after the revisionism debate, and which linked to another constant Labour theme of participatory democracy and promoting the statutory sector's accountability to the informed citizen.[91]

Meanwhile, the left of the party from the late 1960s on had embraced community action and self-help, partly as a reaction to what was increasingly seen as an over-bearing and unaccountable state. Support for 'rainbow coalitions' of grassroots and single-issue groups was enthusiastically given by Labour-controlled local authorities, and we thus entered an epoch in which 'social service' was abandoned as a theme to describe voluntary engagement. During the same period, there had also been a

[88] Davis Smith, 'An Uneasy Alliance'.
[89] See for example Margaret Cole's description of the positive role of volunteers: M. Cole, *Servant of the County* (London, 1956), pp. 120ff.
[90] See especially Francis, *Ideas and Policies under Labour*.
[91] Michael Young, *The Chipped White Cups of Dover* (London, 1960).

revival of the mutual aid and cooperation theme, another theme with deep roots in the Labour movement but now 'rediscovered'.

The diversity of these different themes means that over the twentieth century there have been a whole range of different responses from different parts of the Labour movement. As well as the positive examples that we have given of constructive engagement, there are other reactions that have been negative. In certain cases they are in conflict – for example, the left's version of municipal socialism produced radically different relationships compared to those promoted in the older version during the interwar period. But, in reaching a judgement on the overall response of the Labour movement, it is important to recognise and understand the varied ways in which these relationships have been formed and developed. This may help us to understand why the crude stereotype of unrelenting statist hostility is simply a myth.

5

Civil society, class and locality

Tenant groups in post-war Britain

PETER SHAPELY

The emergence of the voluntary sector over the last two centuries has been crucial to the development of modern Britain's social fabric. An array of voluntary groups were created across the country, providing an invaluable means of managing communities, developing class identity and smoothing class relations. They offered a range of welfare services and they have supported and promoted numerous social and cultural interests. Historically, the voluntary sector shifted and adapted the same basic formula and framework to social and political changes and technological innovations, highlighting both continuities and changes. This chapter will look at these historical trends and will focus primarily on key aspects of civil society in Britain, an integral part of the voluntary sector which bisects some of the myriad definitions and sub-groups. Civil society became a distinctive and central feature in the historical development of a functioning democratic society from the late eighteenth century. Theoretically, a performing democratic system relies on a healthy civil society. For over 200 years, citizens across the country have joined together over many causes – political, social and economic – campaigning for change, engaging on the political stage and, successfully or otherwise, challenging the power of local and central government. These causes changed over time, from the great moral crusades of Victorian Britain to the new social movements of the post-war period. They also shifted from a predominantly local organisational base to one that had a greater national and international structure. However, many retained several defining characteristics. The durability and adaptability of the voluntary organisation in terms of form and function remained essentially the same. Moreover, every general 'cause' had a plethora of different organisations, each with its own specific *raison d'être*, and they retained a shared discourse based on interpretations of 'rights', 'morality' and 'justice'.

These key characteristics were features in the many tenant groups which emerged from the 1960s. This chapter will focus on the campaigns for justice and rights manifested in the struggle against rent increases and the demand for better houses and living conditions. As will be seen, these groups were diverse in their specific aims and objectives, and in terms of their social and political commitments, underlining both their flexibility as an effective means of protest and their limitations in terms of cohesive social action, but they shared the same sense of moral justification for taking action against local authorities. Moreover, although some became part of national federations, and whilst many were led by educated members of the middle classes, the cause and motivation were usually local, and the call to arms was often only effective if supported by the less advantaged tenants whose grievances the groups were trying to address. Tenant groups came to reflect both the social and economic shifts in society and the essential flexibility and robustness of the voluntary organisation as a form which continued to provide an effective platform for the development of civil society.

The historical context – the voluntary sector and the development of civil society

Study into the origins, structure and character of civil society has attracted a considerable amount of attention over the last few years. Trentmann traces its origins to early modern Europe with its notions of civility, toleration and peace, and to the new society of self-governing clubs and associations operating outside of state interference.[1] Harris has shown how the term 'civil society' began to influence thinking in the 1960s through the work of Habermas and Dahrendorf. A successful civil society is characterised by autonomous social and economic institutions operating independently of the state. It is the embodiment of personal liberty and freedom as well as a new kind of bourgeois society or public sphere, replacing the culture and norms established by royalty and the aristocracy

---

[1] F. Trentmann, 'Introduction', in F. Trentmann (ed.), *Paradoxes of Civil Society: New Perspectives on Modern German and British History* (New York, 2000), p. 3.

with new middle-class values.[2] Britain is generally seen as the nation where civil society first developed, emerging strongly from the eighteenth century (though originating earlier); a 'heartland' where social relations took the form of partnerships, groups and associations largely, or at worst partially, regulated by Parliament.[3]

The rapid expansion of civil society was a consequence of social change brought about through industrialisation and urbanisation. It was a product of a free-market, liberal and pluralistic society. Unlike in other countries, it was not anti-state in its character. Relationships with the state were not an issue.[4] This was an age in which many aspects of the social and political life of the nation were organised by an army emanating from the many voluntary groups. These were supposed to provide a vehicle for liberty and freedom for individuals, no longer bound by the ties of family, patronage or government, though, as Trentmann points out, they were full of paradoxes as many associations were in reality exclusive and influenced by local hierarchies.[5]

In the nineteenth century the state played a minimal role in the everyday organisation and management of local communities. Morris's studies of Edinburgh and Leeds revealed the extent and importance of a wide range of voluntary groups.[6] In cities like Manchester, citizens created a range of voluntary charities covering an array of good causes.[7] These included charities for medical care, social welfare, education, temperance and spiritual reform. The medical care charities included infirmaries, specialist hospitals for women, children, skin, eyes, ear, nose and throat, consumption, cancer, and asylums for the mentally ill. Roberts's work, *Making English Morals*, highlighted the role and impact that moral reform organisations had on Georgian and Victorian England, underlining the impact of their actions on the cultural psyche and the moral fabric of the nation.[8]

---

[2] J. Harris, 'Introduction', in J. Harris (ed.), *Civil Society in British History: Identities and Institutions* (Oxford, 2003), p. 1.

[3] Harris, 'Introduction', p. 3.

[4] J.A. Hall, 'Reflections on the Making of Civility in Society', in Trentmann, *Paradoxes of Civil Society*, p. 50.

[5] Trentmann, 'Introduction', *Paradoxes of Civil Society*, p. 4.

[6] R.J. Morris, 'Structure, Culture and Society in British Towns', in Martin J. Daunton, *Cambridge Urban History of Britain* (Cambridge, 2000); R.J. Morris, *Class, Sect and Party* (Manchester, 1990).

[7] P. Shapely, *Charity and Power in Victorian Manchester* (Manchester, 2000).

[8] M.J.D. Roberts, *Making English Morals: Voluntary Association and Moral Reform in England, 1787–1886* (Cambridge, 2004), p. 298.

In the first part of the twentieth century, charity and associational life still supported the 'public spirit' of the age, providing order and stability in ordinary life. Garside highlights how the Sutton Trust provided clubs and societies for residents, empowering them through the management of facilities such as the bowling greens and meeting halls.[9] By the early twentieth century, however, the structure of civil society was already changing. Throughout the previous century, civil society had been an integral part of urban governance. It was one of the means by which the middle classes became organised and through which they exercised power and authority.[10] However, from the late nineteenth century and throughout the first half of the twentieth century, the middle classes began to retreat from the local and urban landscape, shifting to a culture and identity based on national institutions.[11] Consequently, civil society at the local level no longer had the same relevance. After the Second World War the challenges presented by this change in the structure of urban governance were compounded by the emergence of the welfare state. Colls's study of the post-war period highlights the impact of the decline of civil society in working-class neighbourhoods.[12] British working-class institutions supported and celebrated the common life, taking ideas (political and religious) and welding them to their own experiences.[13] According to Colls, working-class culture and its supportive institutions disintegrated and working-class civil society gradually unravelled.[14] The old community life that he grew up with died and was replaced by a fragmented society. Moreover, civil society was undermined by the rise of quangos, unelected bodies and

---

[9] P. Garside, 'Citizenship, Civil Society and Quality of Life: Sutton Model Dwellings Estates, 1919–39', in R. Colls and R. Rodger (eds), *Cities of Ideas: Civil Society and Urban Governance in Britain, 1800–2000* (Aldershot, 2004), pp. 258–282.

[10] Morris, 'Structure, Culture and Society'. See also Simon Gunn, *The Public Culture of the Victorian Middle Class* (Manchester, 2007), p. 196; R. Trainor, 'The Decline of British Urban Governance since 1850', in R.J. Morris and R.H. Trainor (eds), *Urban Governance: Britain and Beyond since 1750* (London, 2000), pp. 31, 38; B. Doyle, 'The Structure of Elite Power in the Early Twentieth Century City: Norwich 1900–1935', *Urban History*, 24, 2, 1997, pp. 179–199; P. Shapely, 'Governance in the Post-War City: Historical Reflections on Public–Private Regimes', working paper.

[11] Morris, 'Structure, Culture and Society'. See also Gunn, *The Public Culture of the Victorian Middle Class*; Trainor, 'The Decline of British Urban Governance since 1850'.

[12] Colls and Rodger, *Cities of Ideas*, p. 18.

[13] R. Colls, 'When We Lived in Communities: Working-Class Culture and its Critics', in Colls and Rodger, *Cities of Ideas*, p. 306.

[14] *Ibid.*, pp. 306–307.

the gradual erosion of power of local boards, inspectors and commis-sioners, all of which were accountable to local or central government.[15] It might seem that the civil society of the golden age of the nineteenth and early twentieth centuries has been lost.[16]

However, although social, cultural, political and economic develop-ments underpinned significant changes to civil society in post-war Britain, this did not lead to a drift into terminal decline. Political participation gave rise to new social movements.[17] Civil society became more focused on campaigns against the state or to influence government policy. New social movement theorists have argued, for instance, that the peace movement in the 1950s through to the 1980s represented a new order. It is claimed that these peace groups were part of the post-industrial economy and that they were unique and very different from the movements of the old industrial economy. The new movements did not have the same economic concerns as those of the nineteenth century, but were concerned with social issues such as women's rights, gay rights, disability, race and environmental issues.[18] The late 1960s and early 1970s gave rise to a new radical form of civil society which did not necessarily replace but certainly sidelined traditional movements.[19]

The rise of mass media and the expansion of higher education meant more people had a greater awareness of social and political issues. Campaigners for women's rights, gay rights and the fight to protect the environment attempted to challenge and change social and cultural standards and consciousness.[20] People also enjoyed greater mobility, expendable income and spare time. Members of the social movements of the post-war world were overwhelmingly drawn from educated members of the middle classes.[21] Even the historical campaign for equal pay for women, which enjoyed the support of the trade unions, was a cause promoted largely by middle-class women's groups. But, again, this is an

[15] *Ibid.*, p. 306.
[16] J. Garrard, *Democratisation in Britain: Elites, Civil Society, and Reform since 1800* (New York, 2002).
[17] R. Koopmans, 'New Social Movements and Changes in Political Participation in Western Europe', *Western European Politics*, 9, 1, 1996, pp. 28–50.
[18] See A. Lent, *British Social Movements since 1945* (Basingstoke, 2001).
[19] *Ibid.*, pp. 4–5.
[20] A. Touraine, *The Voice and the Eye* (Cambridge, 2001), p. 29.
[21] C. Rootes, 'A New Class? The Higher Educated and the New Politics', in L. Maheu (ed.), *Social Movements and Social Classes: The Future of Collective Action* (London, 1995), pp. 225–226.

overly simplified view of the historical process. Society changed, with far greater fluidity between social groups and much greater levels of higher education amongst traditionally working-class groups. Students did become more radically involved in a series of protests in the late 1960s, though less so in Britain than in other western nations. Britain had a well established network of civil organisations, an institutional framework which evolved over decades. The furore of the 1960s certainly gives an impression of something different and dynamic, a radical Marxist discourse that challenged the economic as well as political order, but, when stripped down, civil society retained many of the key characteristics that had evolved since the nineteenth century. Indeed, many of the issues and debates raised in the late 1960s were an extension of protests, movements and campaigns from the nineteenth century.[22] New Social Movement theory claims that working-class activity was the core of social movements in the industrial age and that the middle classes came to dominate the post-industrial social movements. However, in Britain, civil society was also characterised by large middle-class movements across local urban communities, as well as national groups such as the Anti-Corn Law League. The changes in the character of civil society mirrored the gradual shifts in society and culture, but many of the causes, structures and strategies, formed by like-minded citizens joining together, creating an organising committee, appointing various 'officers' and employing strategies to raise income, actually reflected continuities with the past.

Civil society in action – tenants

Many of these changes and continuities with civil society in the past were highlighted by the tenant groups which emerged in the 1960s. The language and aims of these groups reflected the increasing influence of civil rights, welfare and social consumerism. People became more acutely aware of their 'rights' as citizens. They had a right to health care, welfare benefits and a home. Furthermore, people believed they had a right to articulate their worries and concerns. This growing awareness of rights and demands for increased public participation in political decision-making was recognised, at least in the planning process, in 1968 and 1969, with the Town and

---

[22] H. Nehring, 'The Growth of Social Movements', in P. Addison and H. Jones (eds), *A Companion to Contemporary Britain, 1939–2000* (Oxford, 2007), p. 397.

Country Planning Act and the Skeffington Report, *People and Planning*. Town hall planners were now formally encouraged to engage with people. However, it proved an uncertain process as the notion of 'participation' remained ill-defined.[23] Planning decisions in the early 1970s were still made by local authorities, which so enraged people that many reacted by forming protest groups to campaign against proposals. This was highlighted by the reaction to, and defeat of, the Greater London Development Plan.[24] Opposition to the plan came from across society as an estimated 30,000 people signed a petition objecting to the plan, while the 'Homes before Roads' party won 100,000 votes in London's local election.[25] Associations opposing the plan included middle-class property groups, working-class tenant groups, civic and conservation societies, rate-payers associations, anti-motorway groups and historical societies.[26]

Similarly, the tenant groups that emerged in the late 1960s were a reaction to perceived failings in public policy and, as such, they constituted a defence of their rights against public policy. Their increase in numbers and activities from the 1960s paralleled the rise of the welfare state and the growing awareness of consumer rights. Society had changed and expectations were different. The relationship between the citizen and the state carried greater promises and raised hopes. When these hopes were not fully realised, tenants reacted in frustration. The origins of tenant groups stretched back to the First World War when tenants organised against exploitative landlords in cities like Glasgow and Leeds. Led by the Women's Housing Association, the Glasgow Rent Strike in 1915 was supported by 30,000 tenants and eventually led to a successful rent freeze.[27] Throughout the 1920s, tenant groups were created on a number of new council estates. These groups were not just concerned with defending tenant rights but were also an exercise in social inclusion.[28] In Birmingham,

---

[23] See, for instance, P. Shapely, 'Planning and Participation in Britain, 1968–1976', *Planning Perspectives* (forthcoming, 2011).

[24] J. Davis, '"Simple Solutions to Complex Problems": The Greater London Council and the Greater London Development Plan, 1965–1973', in Harris, *Civil Society in British History*, pp. 249–273.

[25] *Ibid.*, p. 252.

[26] *Ibid.*, p. 256.

[27] John McHugh, 'The Clyde Rent Strike, 1915', *Journal of the Scottish Labour History Society*, 1, 12, 1978, pp. 56–62.

[28] See also P. Garside, 'Citizenship, Civil Society and Quality of Life in Sutton Model Dwelling Estates, 1919–39', in Colls and Rodger, *Cities of Ideas*, pp. 258–282.

for instance, a variety of tenant groups were created that were aimed at encouraging gardening or which arranged lectures and passed on complaints to the council. After the Second World War, tenant associations were created on new overspill estates and in the new towns that sprung up across the country. In the late 1960s and early 1970s, inner-city tenant groups were created, often with a more radical agenda. Urban squatting, for instance, became a feature of housing protests, especially amongst younger groups.[29] Squatting became popular throughout Europe in the 1970s and 1980s.[30]

In Britain, however, squatting was a relatively peripheral feature of tenant action. Although some tenant groups shared certain defining characteristics with the new social movements, they were also sufficiently diverse to make comparisons problematic. Initially, and unsurprisingly, tenant groups were nearly all organised at the local level and were a particular response to a variety of local problems and issues in each neighbourhood. As in the nineteenth century, they were rooted in the communities. Structural changes to urban governance had led to the growth of public–private coalitions which were not connected to communities in the same way as the middle-class elites had been in the nineteenth century. Consequently, small groups emerged to articulate tenant concerns. Up to the early 1970s, rent increases were again the primary motivation for tenant action. In 1958, a demonstration by 5,000 people against the Rent Act resulted in clashes with the police in Trafalgar Square.[31] Most prominent was the St Pancras rent strike of the late 1950s and early 1960s. The strike was in reaction to the Conservative local authority's differential rent scheme. It culminated in a march on the Town Hall, which attracted 4,000 residents, and a petition with 6,000 signatures.[32] By 1960, thirty-five tenant groups in the area had formed the United Tenants Association which led a strike involving 1,400 tenants. The struggle became very bitter throughout the 1960s. Tenants who continued to resist were forcibly evicted. The situation was so bad that the Public Order Act had to be invoked.[33] In the same

[29] See, for example, K.C. Kearns, 'Urban Squatting: Social Activism in the Housing Sector', *Social Policy*, 11, 2, 1980, pp. 21–29.
[30] P. Mitchell, 'Anarchy in the East: The East Berlin Squatting Movement', paper given to the Voluntary Action History Society, University of Birmingham, December 2009.
[31] *Manchester Guardian*, 18 March 1957.
[32] D. Mathieson, *The St. Pancras Rent Strike* (London, 1987), p. 10.
[33] *Ibid.*, p. 24.

year, other London tenant groups went on strike in protest against private landlords.

Economic problems in the late 1960s forced local authorities to increase rents, leading to another series of strikes and civil action. Tenants throughout the country reacted angrily to the rent rises, leading to a number of rent strikes in London, Glasgow, Sheffield and Liverpool.[34] In 1967, the Council Tenants Action Committee, which claimed to represent Newcastle's 36,000 council tenants, threatened to lead a city-wide strike in reaction to rent increases.[35] The council was forced to counter the threat by introducing a comprehensive rebate scheme. The following year in Manchester, the Tenant Action Committee in Miles Platting and Ancoats organised a meeting, attended by 250 residents, at which it was unanimously agreed to strike against rent increases that were being introduced by the city council.[36] They also agreed to encourage over 3,000 tenants to join them in the strike. Opposition to the rent rebate scheme in Sheffield dominated council politics from 1967 to the early 1970s.[37] Thousands of tenants joined the campaign, forcing the council to amend its scheme. It also persuaded many old council members to take early retirement.[38] Tenant groups in Liverpool reacted angrily to the very threat of rent increases. They claimed that if the increases were implemented it would not only lead to a widespread strike but also to a large public demonstration which, they optimistically believed, would attract up to 90,000 tenants.[39] The strike in Skelmersdale lasted eight weeks.[40]

In London, the Conservative-controlled Greater London Council (GLC) proposed to increase rents in 1969 by the maximum allowed under state legislation. Proposals to increase rents in the previous year had already led to rent strikes. They were led by the United Tenants Action Committee which linked numerous local groups. The chair of the GLC's Housing

---

[34] See, for example, L. Hancock, 'Tenant Participation and the Housing Classes Debate' (unpublished PhD thesis, Liverpool, 1994), pp. 146–147. For a detailed account of tenant action by the city's twenty-three different groups in Sheffield see P.A. Baldock, 'Tenants' Voice: A Study of Council Tenants' Organisations, with Particular Reference to Those in the City of Sheffield, 1961–71' (unpublished PhD thesis, Sheffield, 1970–1971), pp. 211–252.

[35] *Guardian*, 19 August 1967.

[36] *Guardian*, 17 September 1968.

[37] C. Binfield, R. Childs, R. Harper, D. Hey, D. Martin and G. Tweedale, *The History of Sheffield 1843–1993* (Sheffield, 1993), p. 145.

[38] *Ibid.*, p. 146.

[39] *Guardian*, 19 February 1968.

[40] *Guardian*, 6 April 1968.

Committee, Horace Cutler, wanted to bring rents into line with private sector rates.[41] Another national demonstration was held in Trafalgar Square, and in Camden 2,000 tenants lobbied a meeting of the local council. The strike took place in November when an estimated 11,000 tenants withheld rent. Another demonstration involving 3,000 tenants was held outside the Housing Minister's home.[42]

In November 1969, the Labour government bowed to pressure and introduced new legislation limiting the level of rent increases. However, the Conservative government's 1972 Housing Finance Act led to further rent increases and resulted in another wave of strike action directed by the National Association of Tenants and Residents. Tenant protests broke out across the country, and, in Clay Cross, Derbyshire, were supported by the Labour council, which refused to implement the rent rise. In London, the new Act resulted in opposition from the Association of London Housing Estates. They claimed the legislation was undemocratic, inflationary and socially divisive.[43] Over eighty rent strikes took place across the country. Similarly, housing cuts by the Labour government of the mid-1970s led to a campaign by the National Co-ordinating Committee Against Housing Cuts.[44]

Besides the frequent campaigns over rents and finances, tenant action was also directed at improving rights and conditions. The middle-class social reform charities, which up to the 1930s had highlighted poor living conditions and campaigned for improvements, had gradually faded.[45] It was small groups of tenants that now became involved in the struggles over slum clearance and to secure money for housing improvements. They emerged as a reaction to government plans to establish General Improvement and Housing Action Areas.[46] The government had decided to move away from expensive rebuilding schemes to the gradual

[41] *Guardian*, 28 November 1969.
[42] Between 1968 and 1971, many campaigns were supported by the Camden-based Poster Workshop which designed and printed a variety of placards, http://www.posterworkshop.co.uk/tenants/index.html
[43] J. Hayes, 'The Association of London Housing Estates and the "Fair Rent" Issue', *London Journal*, 14, 1, 1989, pp. 59–67.
[44] A useful narrative and timeline has been provided by John Grayson, Sheffield Hallam University, http://www.insidehousing.co.uk/story.aspx?storycode=6502482
[45] P. Shapely, *The Politics of Housing: Power, Consumers and Urban Culture* (Manchester, 2007), pp. 110–115.
[46] *Better Homes: The Next Priorities* (London, 1973).

improvement of individual homes or entire districts, believing that, in the majority of cases, it was no longer preferable to attempt to solve housing problems by large new building programmes. Several groups in the early 1970s campaigned for improvement status as opposed to comprehensive slum clearance and redevelopment.[47] Tenant groups challenged local authorities which, initially, adopted a rigid approach to managing housing estates from the top down. Writing for the *Guardian*, Robert Waterhouse claimed that, 'Housing departments are bureaucracies which have fixed and regulated ways of acting . . . . It's all too much for a bureaucracy which likes straight lines and narrow formulas to help it understand let alone process plans.' He wondered, 'will there ever be a fashion for handing ordinary people back the responsibility for creating and looking after their own environment?'[48] Local authorities wanted to retain power over the whole planning, building and managing process. Tenant groups threatened to undermine their position by openly and directly challenging policies. This reticence by local authorities to give a degree of control to tenants was reflected in their attitude towards housing co-operatives. In 1976, Labour's Minister for Housing and Construction, Reg Freeson, claimed that there was very little evidence of town halls taking even the first steps, such as consulting people, or giving them a choice, which might have led to tenants having more control over the management of their houses.[49]

Organised groups wanted a greater voice in the policy decision-making process. These included the likes of Ray Gosling, who was an active campaigner in Nottingham, and the Manchester and Salford Housing Action group (MASHA), which was an umbrella organisation responsible for supporting local initiatives across the region.[50] These groups were often well organised, at the very least partially democratic, and always community-based. Like Victorian voluntary organisations, they made a contribution to participatory democracy and civil engagement. As MASHA continually stressed, they were involved in 'community politics'.[51] However, they were usually relatively modest in size, often had only a

[47] Sheffield, for instance, had at least twenty-three groups campaigning on a number of causes in the 1970s. Baldock, 'Tenants' Voice'. See also Binfield *et al.*, *The History of Sheffield 1843–1993*, p. 146.
[48] R. Waterhouse, 'Marseilles is Different', *Guardian*, 27 October 1977.
[49] *Guardian*, 7 December 1976.
[50] For tenant action in Nottingham, see R. Gosling, *Personal Copy: A Memoir of the Sixties* (London, 1980). For MASHA see Shapely, *Politics of Housing*.
[51] Minutes of Housing Action, 2 April 1973.

limited life span and sometimes were irritated by their partial appeal and impact. While it was possible to motivate tenants in some instances, it could also prove a disappointing and frustrating process because many tenants were doggedly apathetic. Although tenant groups attempted to arrest the arrogance of politicians, or at least make them uncomfortable, their impact varied. Some remained, at best, partially democratic because they failed to recruit sufficient numbers to make any notion of 'democracy' relevant. Gosling, for instance, admitted that his small group had a very limited impact. While they raised awareness of the problems and the issues at stake, support was limited. Gosling had expected an avalanche of mail in response to his campaign against the council, but it never materialised and Gosling admitted that he was 'heartbroken' by the experience.[52] They had delivered 15,000 handbills over one cold weekend in 1967, but had only two responses. People believed either that the plans were not going to affect them, that it was a futile exercise because they could not win against the council, or that they would be victimised if they so much as signed a petition.[53] Despite their best efforts, tenant group campaigns were often unsuccessful. For example, a tenant action committee established in Darlington in 1968 to stop rent increases was disbanded after only four months due to its failure to have any impact on council policy.[54]

Such problems reflected the lack of confidence, stemming from a limited education and knowledge, which prevented many people from getting actively involved. Unlike activists such as Gosling, many tenants did not possess the skills needed to facilitate action. It was a problem echoed across other British cities.[55] Nevertheless, while vocal, organised leaders may often have come from a small group of dedicated and educated individuals, tenants from humble, working-class or poor backgrounds often got involved, especially over rent strikes and specifically targeted campaigns designed to secure resources for housing improvements or rehousing. In the Moss Side district of Manchester, for example, tenant groups held a number of well-attended meetings; organised a petition with 3,000 signatures; organised door-to-door visits to mobilise support against Compulsory Purchase Orders taken out against their properties; carried out a survey of residents' rehousing wishes; produced a newspaper with

[52] Gosling, *Personal Copy*, p. 167.
[53] *Ibid.*, p. 171.
[54] *Guardian*, 10 June 1968.
[55] See Shapely, 'Planning and Participation in Britain, 1968–1976'.

a circulation of 1,400; and provided alternative development designs. They even had a Housing Action Group member elected to the council, polling 767 votes from a 1,000 turnout.[56] Also, in Hattersley, a Manchester overspill estate, residents became mobilised in a campaign which heavily criticised the local authority for the lack of bus services, bus shelters, medical and dental services, shopping facilities, and educational and library services. They also argued for the urgent need to retain the railway link with Manchester.[57]

These struggles were not without success. In 1970, the Acklam Road tenants group in London triumphed in their campaign to be rehoused following the opening of the elevated Westway, which was built only a few feet away from bedrooms.[58] Similarly, a tenant action campaign in Salford, backed by the housing charity Shelter, to force the council to make repairs on houses where demolition had been postponed resulted in a High Court judgment that forced the council to reverse its policy.[59] In Colville Gardens, Notting Hill, groups of tenants started to gather information about rents and cases of harassment by private landlords and, for over a month in the summer, they stopped cars parking down the middle of the road by using home-made signs and volunteer patrols.[60]

Despite the apparent lack of education and confidence, some tenants were clearly prepared to take on council officials in a face-to-face show-down. Tenants in the St Paul's district of Bristol were so angry with the city council's proposals to demolish and redevelop the area against their wishes that a public meeting, attended by over 400 residents, was held. The council brought out its big guns, including the chair of the Housing Committee (Graham Roberts), chair of the Planning Committee (Brian Richards) and the Director of Housing (Cyril Fortune). Residents were not intimidated and vociferously complained that they had not been consulted and that they wanted houses to be improved rather than demolished. Graham Roberts promised to review the plans and hold further public meetings.[61] Similarly, in 1977, Allan Roberts, chair of Manchester's Housing Committee, appeared on *Albert*, a BBC programme, in which he was forced

---

[56] 'Moss Side People's Paper', November 1970, Manchester Central Reference Library.
[57] *North Cheshire Herald*, 4 October 1963.
[58] *Guardian*, 19 January 1971.
[59] *Guardian*, 20 December 1974.
[60] *Guardian*, 25 June 1967.
[61] *Guardian*, 27 July 1974.

to face a group of angry tenants complaining about life in the city's high-rise flats. Roberts had to admit to them and the television audience that, 'all right, these flats were a mistake . . . we know what people want now – they want a house, a front door and a garden. That's what we're giving them.'[62]

Although these challenges to local authorities were focused on specific issues and policies, the underlying motive for some tenant group members was obviously political. Allegiances covered the entire political spectrum. A few were disillusioned with traditional party politics. In 1971, Malcolm Dean wrote a series of articles on the Labour Party and the reasons for the decline in membership. He claimed that many of the younger activists had been more attracted to community action groups, such as the tenant groups, because they enjoyed working directly with people in communities, that they were 'more interested in action than talk'.[63] He believed that community groups had emerged because of reactionary local authorities, both Labour and Conservative, as well as state policies. Many of the young middle-class students were overtly political. A number of left-wing and associated student groups created or came to control tenant groups, and began to use them for broader political purposes. Militant activity was noticeable in some of the big cities, such as Liverpool and Sheffield.[64]

Some tenant groups were conservative in nature and were organised by tenants from working-class and lower middle-class backgrounds. In Manchester, for instance, the decision of the returning Labour council to stop all council house sales in the early 1970s led to a backlash from tenants who had already been promised by the previous Conservative council that they would be able to purchase their homes. At the other end of the political spectrum, in Hulme, the left-wing Manchester Housing Workshop claimed that the major reassessment of the Crescents that took place in 1975 was forced by the Hulme Tenants Association campaign.[65] They believed that it was their media campaign against the council that forced the Housing Committee to give way to demands to rehouse all families with children above the ground floor, in Hulme and four other deck-access estates. Leading Liberals were also involved. Allan Roberts, chairman of the Housing Committee, provided the group with a flat for use as a base and

[62] *Guardian*, 27 October 1977.
[63] *Guardian*, 19 January 1971.
[64] Hancock, 'Tenant Participation', p. 155.
[65] *Hulme Crescents*, Manchester Housing Workshop (Manchester, 1980), p. 18.

advice centre for residents. However, he was to regret his generosity.[66] Roberts became angered at the way the group used the centre for 'political purposes'. He accused Peter Thompson, the centre's coordinator, of turning the 'whole issue of this rights' centre into a political one', and of 'conducting a vendetta against the Labour council'.[67] Thompson, a member of the executive council of the Manchester Liberal Party, was accused of using the centre to undermine the council. Like many of the Victorian voluntary organisations, tenant groups provided a general organisational platform for everyone, irrespective of political or religious beliefs. Just as it had been possible for people from Dissenting or Anglican backgrounds to create their own groups, or for people to establish organisations that rejected sectarian division, so also was it possible for people from the left, centre or right of politics, and for those not interested in political alignment, to create their own tenant societies.

Politics was not the only dimension. Even in Sheffield, which had a reputation for extremist membership, some tenant groups such as the Shiregreen Association were eager to steer clear of left-wing infiltration for fear of the 'Communist smear'.[68] Similarly, in Manchester the MASHA group was acutely aware of the need to avoid being tagged as a left-wing group.[69] However, tenants became united over a common cause and were prepared to conduct aggressive campaigns, irrespective of political persuasion. Although tenant groups were involved in a political struggle, it was not one which belonged exclusively to any traditional political discourse.[70] George Clark, spokesman for the Acklam Road tenants group, claimed that they had been successful in dealing with the GLC because they were politically independent. He stated that, 'if we had had close ties to the Labour Party, dogma would have become involved and we could never have persuaded the Conservative controlled GLC to meet our demands – they would have lost too much face'.[71]

Several groups were distinguished by a gender dimension. Just as they had been in the Victorian period, it was women who were often at the

---

[66] Tenants even occupied the Hulme Project office for seven weeks. See A. Ravetz, *Council Housing and Culture* (London, 2001), p. 230.

[67] *Manchester Evening News*, 6 September 1977.

[68] Hancock, 'Tenant Participation', p. 219.

[69] Shapely, *Politics of Housing*, p. 175.

[70] See, for example, Hancock, 'Tenant Participation', p. 320; Ann Richardson, *Getting Tenants Involved* (London, 1977), p. 242.

[71] *Guardian*, 19 January 1971.

forefront of local campaigns.[72] Mothers in Moss Side created the Moss Side Play Group Association to secure better facilities. They were continually frustrated by the council's failure to provide amenities and to improve living standards. When the Mayor, Alderman Ken Collis, visited the area to hand over a new play bus, he was met by a group of angry and bitter mothers who staged a protest about the failure to provide a substantial play centre and to clear the bug-infested walls in the local maisonettes. Their anger was fuelled by the council's decision to clean up one of the maisonettes, which had been left untouched for months, because of the Mayor's visit.[73] Later, in October 1974, residents of the Moss Side District Centre began a campaign that sought rehousing for people from some of the worst slum flats in the city. Many were involved in a public demonstration, a squat in an empty terraced house and a pram barricade across a busy road during the rush hour. Police were called in to break up the demonstration, arresting one man on an assault charge.[74] Similarly, in 1979, a dozen women from the South Wales Association of Tenants occupied council offices, barricaded themselves into a committee room, chained themselves to a radiator and remained in occupation for three days.[75]

Such solidarity was not always characteristic of tenant activity. Some areas were deeply divided between different groups. In Broadwater Farm, where the population in the mid-1970s was evenly divided between white and black tenants, tensions began to emerge. The established Tenants Association was exclusively white and was regarded with increasing distrust by black residents. Eventually, in 1981, black residents set up their own rival Youth Association, which claimed to offer support and advice to the local black community. In 1983, the council gave the Tenants Association an empty shop to use as an office, which appeared to give them the official authority to deal with local problems, but this increased the antagonism between them and the Youth Association, which, in turn, set up its own youth club, advice centre, estate watchdog and local lobbying group.

Tensions between groups were not necessarily due to racial distrust. In Hulme during the early 1990s, the twelve-tenant group which created

[72] There is a need for more research into female involvement.
[73] *Manchester Evening News*, 15 June 1971.
[74] Shapely, *Politics of Housing*, p. 174.
[75] 'The South Wales Association of Tenants' campaign against damp homes in 1979', www.tenant2u.tripod.com/quotes.html

the Alliance, which was involved in the City Challenge, a scheme for the complete redevelopment of the area, was often affected by strong disagreements and deep divisions.[76] Despite these tensions, the recognition of common ground and shared objectives meant that some local groups, campaigning on local issues, gradually became part of national federations. By the late 1970s, national federations, such as the National Tenants Organisation, were campaigning for tenants' charters and security of tenure, and in the late 1980s a series of campaigns were conducted against the Housing Action Trusts, leading to the creation of new tenant organisations. Protests centred on the sale of council houses and the transfer of the housing stock. Throughout the 1990s, groups continued to emerge as a reaction to government policies, including the National Tenants and Residents Federation, set up in 1992, and the Tenants and Residents Organisation of England. However, despite the rise of national organisations, local tenant groups continued, and continue, to form the backbone of the movement. Tenant groups, such as Sandwell and Kirklees, and tenant management organisations, including, for example, Belle Isle North in Leeds, continue to flourish.

Some of these groups became a formalised and accepted part of the local political process. Tenant groups became more than part of a narrative of the fight for social justice, the struggle against unfair rents and the desire to influence policy or to secure decent facilities. Increasingly, by the mid-1970s, some groups were being used as part of an initiative by local authorities to develop the participation schemes which had been promoted since the late 1960s. The idea was to extend participatory democracy and to bridge the gap between local government and communities by creating forums that would provide a platform for citizen input, a means of opening communication between state and citizen. The idea was to use tenant groups as part of a more systematic approach to consultation and participation. In the early 1970s, some housing departments in London showed an interest in developing tenant participation schemes.[77] In practice, however, some local authorities tried to use the idea of participation to pursue their own agenda, retaining control over the process and remaining dominant in their relationship with the tenant groups.[78] Participation, in practice, was a means of acquiring agreement for local authority policies

---

[76] Shapely, *Politics of Housing*, p. 174.
[77] J.S.G. Rao, 'Power and Participation: Tenants' Involvement in Housing' (unpublished MPhil thesis, Brunel, 1983).

and, thereby, a tool which allowed them to claim legitimacy in the implementation and management of those policies. Yet tenant groups did gradually highlight the need for more effective cooperation between local authorities and people in the communities. From the late 1980s tenant action began to have a partial influence on housing policy in some areas across the country. This was highlighted in the Netherley district of Liverpool, for instance, where tenants carried out a nine-year campaign to demolish homes and rehouse families on the same site. Their pressure eventually led the council to demolish all systems-built units on the estate.

Tenant consultation and participation have become important features of urban politics. These organisations did have a partial impact. Formal groups came and went, but the shift from a rigid and dogmatic approach to housing policy to one which began to recognise tenants' demands had left its mark. Like other social movements in post-war Britain, tenant action had a gradual impact on policy and helped to create a new decision-making arena, making a contribution to expanded notions of democracy.[79] Despite instances of closer levels of cooperation, tenant groups remained independent of the state and local government, generally resisting any attempt to be (mis)used. They remained active in the defence of their communities. Many remained fiercely opposed to and deeply suspicious of all forms of government. Local authorities, in particular, were seen as being responsible for the local housing problems, either because of poor policy decisions or, more often, because of poor management of the housing stock. The Hulme Alliance, for example, expressed a complete and deeply embedded, if not embittered, sense of distrust of the local council. However, many, including those in Hulme, came to work closely and successfully with the council, but they remained part of an independent sector. When they did meet council officials, tenant representatives often felt they were wasting their time. Nevertheless, tenants came to participate in a number of ways, including house design, housing management, schools, shops, open spaces, and planning other facilities. Participation was promoted through groups such as the Tenant Participation Project, and through newsletters, and public meetings and design workshops took place on a regular basis. All

---

[78] See Shapely, 'Planning and Participation in Britain, 1968–1976'; P. Hain, 'The Nationalisation of Public Participation', *Community Development Journal*, 17, 1, 1982.
[79] D. Della Porta and M. Diari, *Social Movements: An Introduction* (Oxford, 1999), p. 25.

Hulme tenants were consulted throughout the design process, in choosing facilities and in managing properties.[80]

Civil society – continuity and change

Despite the problems encountered in trying to build effective participation schemes, tenant participation emerged to become a successful part of the Hulme project. The fact remained that tenant groups were not fixed, institutionalised organisations. They came and went, shifting according to the changing circumstances. This was always one of the underlying features, and strengths, of the voluntary organisation. The organisational format allowed people to create a structured group, which enabled them to coordinate a systematic response to government policies. This flexible structure provided a platform for any group of citizens, sufficiently concerned over an issue, to organise and protest. The voluntary sector continued in the post-war period but in forms that reflected the changing nature and structure of society. Voluntary groups come and go according to the social, economic and political climate. What was relevant in the nineteenth century was not necessarily relevant to post-war Britain. But civil society adapted to these changes. This is precisely why it was still significant. The flexible form of voluntary organisations meant they were still suited to historical flux. In this way, they are a product of both the modern age and the post-modern world. Voluntary organisations were able to react to the wide range of issues that concerned people. In post-war Britain the changes to local economic structures, the continued retreat of the middle classes and the expansion of the welfare state inevitably meant that the structure of civic society would also change. Yet tenant groups, like their nineteenth-century counterparts, helped to create and maintain social capital by bringing like-minded people together over a shared interest or political cause. They partially filled the vacuum created by the restructuring of urban governance and became a vital means of civic engagement, as well as a way of creating communal trust in the face of established networks.[81] As in the nineteenth century, shared interests led to collective action

---

[80] Shapely, *Politics of Housing*, pp. 202–205.
[81] R. Putnam, *Bowling Alone: The Collapse and Revival of American Community* (New York, 2000); J. Coleman, 'Social Capital in the Creation of Human Capital', *American Journal of Sociology*, 94, 1988, pp. 95–120.

through the myriad of voluntary organisations.[82] They transformed individual dissatisfaction into formalised networks, developing trust, providing knowledge and information and drawing on norms of general behaviour and organisational structures and systems that have evolved since the late eighteenth and early nineteenth centuries. They were not necessarily inclusive, but they did, nevertheless, provide a pivotal role in a functioning democracy.

The causes have changed and the methods have been adapted to circumstances, but the discourse of civil society groups – a discourse of perceived rights, morality and justice, no matter how that might be defined – remains essentially the same, as do the basic structures and objectives. Civil society groups have become organised at a global level, though even this is not an entirely new development as many societies had an international profile in the nineteenth century. Equally, many contemporary associations retain a distinctly local focus. Groups have, historically, assembled over a common cause, formed an organising committee, appointed various 'officers', defined their own rules and parameters, produced their own literature and conducted their own campaigns. They exist for as long as the cause, or support for the cause, continues. Welfarism, consumerism and a growing awareness of individual 'rights', the decline of bi-polar politics and rise of single-issue politics, the rise of the mass media and especially television, a growing interest and connection to the 'national' and 'international', and the structural changes to urban governance meant that civil society had to adapt to new circumstances. In doing so, civil society also reflected these social and political changes. In some respects, it is still adjusting to social and economic upheaval – but in other respects, by its very nature, it always will be.

---

[82] M. Alessandrini, 'Is Civil Society an Adequate Theory?', *Third Sector Review*, 8, 2, 2002, pp. 105–119.

6

Professionalisation, new social movements and voluntary action in the 1960s and 1970s

VIRGINIA BERRIDGE AND ALEX MOLD

Introduction

> After thirty-two months, ASH has established itself as an authoritative body, and is now in a position to mount a challenge to the tobacco industry and interests. If we continue to 'react', rather than 'create' news, it is likely that any reduction in smoking will be sporadic and temporary; if, however, we establish our targets and concentrate our resources, we could achieve far reaching results – and en route add to our resources. . . . We can offer potential donors or supporters no object of sympathy. We are neither a campaign on behalf of a deprived sector of the population, nor are we raising money for an objective which can be dealt with by raising funds alone. We have no specific constituency, and we have a variety of opponents who will use every trick in the book – and many not even in the appendices – to stop us. Because we are a cause to which the public at large is either opposed or apathetic we can only raise funds and support by creating an atmosphere in which 'anti-smoking' becomes not only acceptable but even fashionable.[1]

Mike Daube, Director of ASH (Action on Smoking and Health), reporting to the organisation's AGM in 1973, articulated a clear vision for this new style of pressure group. In doing so, he also raised questions about the type of social movements which characterised that decade. This chapter takes a fresh look at the changes which took place in the 1960s and 1970s. These decades are typically characterised as being marked by the rise of a new

---

[1] Contemporary Medical Archives Centre (hereafter CMAC), Wellcome Library, ASH archive SA/ASH/B.1/3 report to ASH AGM 14 June 1973.

style of politics and activism, described as 'new social movements' (NSM). Numerous commentators have pointed to the existence of a 'new' kind of politics from the late 1960s onwards. Theorists such as Alain Touraine, Alberto Melucci and Jurgen Habermas posited that new social movements (the civil rights movement, the women's movement, the gay rights movement, the peace movement, the environmental movement, and so on) were representative of a 'new' politics: a politics that operated outside Parliament and traditional political institutions, a politics that dealt with new struggles based on identity, culture and lifestyle.[2] The category of the political was extended by movements which had no explicit political affiliation, but which made matters of identity (gender, sexuality) and lifestyle the subject of protest and activism. The 'new' politics was no longer about class but was concerned with quality of life, equality, individual self-realisation, participation and human rights.[3]

As exciting and dynamic as the new social movements were, they are only part of the story of voluntary action during the 1960s and 1970s. In this chapter we argue that new social movements and their relationship to voluntarism need historicising in a way which recognises greater complexity. Christopher Moores, in a recent study of the National Council for Civil Liberties during the 1960s, has drawn attention to what he calls the 'progressive professionals', occupying an 'in between space' between the politics of the new social movements and the politics of the pressure group.[4] We build on this analysis and take it further in two ways. First, we suggest that there were 'in between spaces' within organisations that appeared to conform to the NSM image but which, in reality, occupied an indeterminate zone between the activities of a pressure group and a 'new left' associated with extra-parliamentary movements and the counter-culture. This type of space was particularly notable in the field of public health activism. We examine the activities of Action on Smoking and Health (ASH); this and related health organisations were both pressure group and social movement, with a powerful image of voluntary activity and concern. Centrally driven and organised with a limited membership base, they drew strength from an image, rather than a reality, of mass

---

[2] A. Touraine, *The Voice and the Eye* (Cambridge, 1981); A. Melucci, *Nomads of the Present* (London, 1988); J. Habermas, 'New Social Movements', *Telos*, 49, 1981, pp. 33–37.

[3] Habermas, 'New Social Movements', p. 33.

[4] C. Moores, 'The Progressive Professionals: The National Council for Civil Liberties and the Politics of Activism in the 1960s', *Twentieth Century British History*, 20, 4, 2009, pp. 538–560.

activism. We argue that the NSM image was a useful 'badge'; that organisations like ASH adopted a distinctive media-focused style, supported by reference to science; and that they were both close to and at a distance from government. Second, new voluntary organisations were established during the 1960s and 1970s which did not fit the NSM mould, even though many had counter-cultural connections, as they were primarily focused on offering new kinds of services to those in need. Considering the example of voluntary organisations which provided services for illicit drug users points to the existence of another kind of 'in between space'. Many of these groups, such as the Community Drug Project (CDP), presented a new community-based counter-cultural image, but they also drew on long-standing notions of social and voluntary concern and on professional expertise.

The amalgamation of old and new politics can also be seen in the nature of the relationship between certain voluntary organisations and the state during the 1960s and 1970s. What NSM-style groups like ASH and the service-providing organisations like the CDP shared was their positioning between the state and 'pure', 'unambiguous' voluntarism; they worked in close collaboration with the state, but were not part of it.[5] This close, yet at the same time distant, relationship to the state can be seen in patterns of funding. Although many drug voluntary groups operated with an autonomous image, and this was part of their attraction, they came to be largely funded by the state. Such support, however, did not lead to the incorporation of voluntary groups within the state: in the 1970s, government funding for voluntary organisations was hands-off, leaving considerable leeway for independent action. We suggest that the close, and yet distant, relationship between voluntary groups and the state was not so much a case of 'governing at a distance' but rather a pragmatic reaction to the potency of the challenge offered by new kinds of voluntary action, as government sought to draw on the expertise offered by such groups to deal with difficult problems in innovative ways.

[5] D. Billis, *Organising Public and Voluntary Agencies* (London, 1993), pp. 163–166.

Public health activism and new social movements: Action on Smoking and Health (ASH)

Smoking was emblematic of a new lifestyle-focused public health in the post-war years. The decline of infections and the rise of chronic disease brought with it a public health based on the science of risk factor epidemiology and focused on the prevention of conditions with a lengthy, behaviourally related gestation, smoking-related heart disease among them. The rise of smoking as a health issue typified and pioneered the new approach. Reports produced by medical professionals – the Royal College of Physicians (RCP) reports on smoking published in 1962 and 1971 – placed smoking centrally on the public policy agenda and were important in the initiation of the new public health.[6] Of particular significance for this new agenda was an anti-tobacco organisation, Action on Smoking and Health (ASH), founded in 1971 in the wake of the publication of the second Royal College report.

Throughout its early history, ASH exemplified a mix of old and new politics. A new activist organisation, it was also rooted in professional and governmental public health politics. The initiative for its founding came from two leading public health doctors, Charles Fletcher and Keith Ball, both members of the RCP committees, Fletcher as secretary. But civil servants, notably the Chief Medical Officer, George Godber, were also involved. Godber saw the formation of ASH as part of his strategy to goad government into action on smoking by pressure from without.

> If the RCP will start it and the HEC [Health Education Council] also take part we would have something very different from the interdepartmental committee. A voluntary group may be a thorn in our flesh – but only if we are inert and deserve it. This is one of our biggest health problems . . . . We really must show we are in earnest.[7]

From the start, ASH was positioned as an outsider organisation but in reality with a close connection to interests within government.

It was in 1973 that its emergent NSM image began to become more visible and a positive asset. The part-time secretary of ASH, Dr John

[6] V. Berridge, *Marketing Health: Smoking and the Discourse of Public Health In Britain, 1945–2000* (Oxford, 2007).
[7] The National Archives (hereafter TNA), MH 154/169 Minute from George Godber, 18 June 1969.

Dunwoody, a former junior minister in the Department of Health and an ex-MP, left the organisation. He was replaced by Mike Daube, a non-medical radical activist who had worked with the campaigner Des Wilson at Shelter. Daube brought with him Wilson's campaigning style and media consciousness. He reflected later:

> It seemed to me when I came into ASH that here was a pressure group campaign that was ripe. It hadn't been properly used. You had your villain. You had your St George and the dragon scenario, you had your growing ecology bandwagon, growing interest in consumerism. It seemed there were a lot of prospects of making something out of it.[8]

This was the tone of ASH's activities throughout the 1970s. The organisation was intensely media-conscious at a time when media structures were changing to accommodate this type of approach. The rise of independent television and the establishment of the specialist health and science correspondents in the media underpinned these developments.[9] The new tone was intensely hostile to 'the industry', another NSM-style radical characteristic. Daube would buy a single share in a tobacco company and would then turn up to ask well-reported questions at the company AGM. ASH collaborated with the journalist Peter Taylor and Thames TV's *This Week* programmes. Daube operated according to the American activist text *Rules for Radicals* – 'rule one is to personalise the problem – the people running the major companies are responsible for those deaths'.[10] A major aim was to keep tobacco on the front pages: the story did not matter but the media coverage did. ASH created news in a way which has become more familiar since. Daube set up a media storm over the issue of a low-tar cigarette called Westminster Abbey. He contacted a journalist and suggested:

> 'I wonder what Westminster Abbey think of that, why don't you ask them.' She phoned up W.A. and they said, no, we don't know about it. Ten minutes later I phoned up as Mike Daube from ASH and they said, 'Funny, we have just had a journalist on to us asking about this.' I said, 'really, well it shows how wide the interest is.'[11]

---

[8] CMAC, SA/ASH William Norman collection R.12 Box 77, interview with Mike Daube, no date but c.1975–1976.

[9] For these developments see K. Loughlin, 'Networks of Mass Communication: Reporting Science, Health and Medicine in the 1950s and 60s', in V. Berridge (ed.), *Making Health Policy: Networks in Research and Policy after 1945* (Amsterdam, 2005), pp. 295–322.

[10] Interview with Mike Daube by Virginia Berridge, 11 March 1999.

[11] ASH archive, Norman interview with Daube.

Then a piece appeared in the journal *Adweek* and Westminster Abbey sent Daube a copy. He wrote to the Dean of the Abbey complaining, the Dean consulted lawyers, and he and the journalists were phoning up and keeping in touch. It was what Daube called the 'rapier and stiletto' approach – now better known as 'spin'.

But alongside this radical campaigning image was a different set of relationships within government. ASH was an insider as well as an outsider organisation. ASH was not primarily a membership organisation and increasingly its funding came direct from government sources. By 1978, 90 per cent of its income came from the DHSS. This was not tied to a service provision role in the way government funding of the voluntary sector developed in the 1980s and 1990s, or indeed as funding was directed earlier to the drugs voluntary sector. Rather the health department funded ASH to represent a force to be reckoned with outside government. In the network of relationships which characterised smoking policy in the 1970s, it was useful for health interests and politicians to be able to point to a pressure group apparently representing growing public opinion which prevented them from taking certain policy lines or which supported particular courses of action. Later in the 1980s it was said that government funding of voluntarism reduced the activist role in favour of service provision. But in the 1970s government was also funding activism as a way of putting pressure on itself. Governments operated a policy balancing act in which they were prepared to fund the alternative voices.

This role was clearest under the Labour government of 1974–1979 and during David Owen's tenure as Minister of Health from 1974 to 1976. Owen, a keen non-smoker, had plans to bring tobacco substitutes, which were then under development as a harm-reduction replacement for tobacco, under the regulatory provisions of the 1968 Medicines Act. They would be controlled like medicines; the implication was that tobacco would also eventually be regulated in this way. Matters came to a head in 1976 when the MP Robert Kilroy Silk was putting through a private member's bill on the subject. Kilroy Silk was a friend of Owen's, but, Owen, as minister, could not offer direct help. ASH fulfilled a vital role as go between. A senior civil servant was allowed to brief Daube on the implications of the proposed bill, and this was the conduit of information to Kilroy Silk. The intervention gave Owen the leverage he needed to press ahead against competing interests. ASH at the same time maintained its overt activist oppositional role, selectively leaking information to urge the minister on to greater action. Owen referred to this dance of interests later – he used the Commons, ASH attacked him, and there was also contact with sympathetic sections of the industry.[12]

ASH was also in discussion with the Treasury, helping to secure the higher taxation policies for cigarettes put through by the Chancellor, Denis Healey.[13] Similar relationships operated in the answering of parliamentary questions (PQs), where Daube would be rung up from within government for help in answering them; or would encourage the planting of questions. But there was always a limit to the opposition. 'With several PQs I have discussed with them what the terms of the PQ should be. Because I want to embarrass them, obviously, in some ways, but I don't want to ask the kind of really embarrassing question. It is not my job just to make life difficult.' So the activist NSM image was useful to government in an 'insider' way, a set of relationships which clearly depended on the personalities and the politics involved as well as the changing public relations of health activism at this time.

In this mix science was an activist tool and strategic support. This was something new. There had been anti-tobacco organisations before ASH, just as there had been anti-opium and anti-alcohol ones in the nineteenth and early twentieth centuries. These however relied more on a mass membership, or pretensions to it, and they rarely used science. Earlier anti-tobacco organisations had used a moral argument, that of the selfishness of the smoker in polluting the atmosphere.[14] In the 1970s this form of argument was replaced, or rather reformulated, in two ways. Initially, the new science of risk factor epidemiology became a key activist tool. And where scientific evidence of this type was lacking, recourse to human rights replaced or rather reformulated the moral arguments of the nineteenth and early twentieth centuries. By the end of the 1970s, ASH had moved its policy agenda towards a focus on the rights of the non-smoker, in contradistinction to the industry's stress on the rights of the smoker. A conference in which ASH was involved, on 'The Rights of the Non-Smoker', was held at the King's Fund in London in the late 1970s. This human rights

[12] This is referred to in the William Norman interview with Daube and also in an interview with Owen. Wellcome Library, ASH archive, SA/ASH, William Norman collection, R.24, Box 79, interview with David Owen, 20 January 1976.

[13] M. Daube, 'The Politics of Smoking: Thoughts on the Labour Record', *Community Medicine*, 1, 1979, pp. 306–314.

[14] M. Hilton and S. Nightingale, '"A Microbe of the Devil's Own Make": Religion and Science in the British Anti Tobacco Movement, 1853–1908', in S. Lock, L. Reynolds and E.M. Tansey (eds), *Ashes to Ashes: The History of Smoking and Health* (Amsterdam, 1998), pp. 41–77.

focus predated the science of passive smoking, which became a key part of the activist case when the relevant scientific papers were published in the early 1980s. In this sense passive smoking, which gave scientific justification for a focus on the non-smoker, was a 'science waiting to happen', with human rights and the moral case as its precursor.

The 'ASH model' became a dominant mode within public health in the 1970s. Organisations sprang up to campaign on other public health lifestyle issues. The Coronary Prevention Group (CPG), for example, was established by a similar group of health activists at the end of the 1970s. Its Canterbury conference in 1983 and a report on heart disease published in 1984 displayed many of the tactics which ASH had pioneered, and some of the same people were involved.[15] ASH itself did not remain the dominant organisation in the smoking field. In the 1980s, under a Conservative government, it was less influential at the policy level. The model of public health activism changed, with networks and partnerships between organisations replacing the influence of one dominant organisation. In the UK, the British Medical Association (BMA) became part of these networks. Its older image as the doctors' trade union was being replaced by a focus on human rights which also marked its response to HIV/AIDS.[16]

ASH was an example of a new type of public health activism in the 1970s which gained its legitimacy through an 'outsider' image while nonetheless operating on the inside track of policy making. Yet this was not the only model for voluntary action in the health field: a rather different set of 'outsider' and 'insider' relationships developed around the response to illegal drug use. New drugs organisations established at this time were not so involved in policy making, nor did they act as pressure groups. But their image was also an 'outside' one, part of the counter-culture. This image was superimposed on a practice which drew on longer-standing practices of social and voluntary concern. Moreover, drug voluntary organisations were gradually drawn 'inside' as the government came to recognise their value in dealing with some of the problems posed by illicit drug use.

---

[15] See LSHTM archive papers of the Coronary Prevention Group, currently uncatalogued.
[16] V. Berridge, *AIDS in the UK: The Making of Policy, 1981–1994* (Oxford, 1996).

New services for illicit drug users: community-based street agencies and national-level organisations

Illicit drugs were not in the public health mainstream in the 1960s and 1970s but rather operated within the field of mental health and psychiatry, with a focus also on criminal justice approaches. Here we concentrate on two types of new organisation: local community-based groups, providing services outside the medico-psychiatric mainstream; and national drug voluntary organisations. There were undoubted tensions between the statutory services, the Drug Dependence Units (DDUs) run by consultant psychiatrists, and the community-based street agencies, but almost all of these voluntary groups received some funding from statutory sources. Various branches of both local and national government supported these community-based groups but there was also funding for national organisations like the Standing Conference on Drug Abuse (SCODA). This suggests that the state recognised the value of these groups, perhaps not in spite of, but because of, their different approach to drug use. Such an approach was part of a wider growth of statutory interest in the work of voluntary organisations in the 1960s and 1970s. Reports assessing the role of the voluntary sector published in this period, including the Aves Report of 1969 and the Wolfenden Report of 1978, pointed to the importance of voluntary organisations and their ability to complement, supplement, extend and influence statutory provision.[17] Financial support for voluntary organisations from statutory sources increased in the drugs field and more widely. Yet, stronger financial ties to the state also raised the possibility of diminishing independence, something many voluntary groups resisted. SCODA, for example, wanted its relationship with the state to be based on 'partnership not patronage'.[18] To a great extent, this desire appears to have been realised.

---

[17] G.M. Aves, *The Voluntary Worker in the Social Services: Report of a Committee Jointly Set up by the National Council of Social Service and the National Institute for Social Work Training* (London, 1969). The idea that voluntary organisations should 'complement, supplement, extend and influence' statutory provision was put forward by the Wolfenden Report. See Joseph Rowntree Trust, *The Future of Voluntary Organisations* (London, 1978), p. 26.

[18] DrugScope Library, hereafter DL 14039, The First SCODA Report, 1974.

Community-based street agencies

In the late 1960s a number of local organisations were created to meet the needs of a growing population of drug users. Particularly important were local community-based groups, known collectively as 'street agencies'. Such agencies formed to provide services for drug users including counselling, advice and sometimes simply a 'place to be'. These groups grew out of a variety of different inspirations and approaches, including pastoral Christian theology and radical social work, something which highlighted the existence of a diverse and vibrant network of voluntary organisations around illegal drugs in this period.[19] The presence of such a range of groups also points to a degree of uncertainty around drug use. Illegal drug use on any scale was a comparatively new problem and the absence of clear expertise around drugs meant that the field was relatively open to new ideas and organisations. Psychiatric expertise was beginning to develop around the treatment of addiction at the DDUs, but there was a feeling amongst many groups that statutory services for drug users were inadequate. The professional input into community-based drug services was notable, but the roots of these organisations derived from various traditions in the drug field, including the role of medical professionals. This was a slightly different pattern from that found within the parallel field of mental health where, as Nick Crossley has shown, health activism in this period was initially led by psychiatrists, translating later on into a powerful user movement.[20] In the case of illicit drugs, professionals worked alongside those with less conventional backgrounds from the outset. Again, as with public health activism, an image of the 'new' masked close connections with pre-existing interests in the area.

Such an interaction of new and old influences can be found in the work of the Community Drug Project. The actual driving force behind the establishment of the CDP was that of the psychiatrist Dr Griffith Edwards and his newly created Addiction Research Unit (ARU) at the Institute of Psychiatry. Edwards already had considerable experience of working with voluntary organisations in the alcohol field, and he also played a key role in the establishment of the Phoenix House therapeutic community for

---

[19] For more detail on these groups and the role they played, see Alex Mold and Virginia Berridge, *Voluntary Action and Illegal Drugs: Health and Society in Britain since the 1960s* (Basingstoke, 2010).

[20] N. Crossley, *Contesting Psychiatry: Social Movements in Mental Health* (London, 2005).

drug users.[21] The CDP, which was based in Camberwell, was designed to provide practical services for drug users, but its main aim was to encourage users to enter treatment. The CDP was intended to 'establish an atmosphere where the addict can begin to see constructive alternatives to his drug use'.[22] The whole project was aimed at 'treating the problem of drug addiction at the community level'.[23]

'Community' was an essential concept to the work of the CDP, but this term seems to have had a variety of different meanings, each with slightly different implications. Edwards's notion of 'community' appears to have been at least partly derived from ideas about community care and more specifically community psychiatry. Although the term 'community care' is itself imprecise and has changed over time, it has generally been used to describe a shift away from hospital-based treatment to care in the community which took place as a result of the steady reduction in the number of psychiatric inpatients following the Hospital Plan in 1962.[24] Edwards stated in a letter to Captain John Brown, Secretary to the Trustees of the Attlee Memorial Foundation, and later Chair of the CDP's management committee, that, 'We [the ARU] feel too that this is very much an experiment in community [his underline] psychiatry.'[25]

It was clear that the CDP regarded drug use as a community problem requiring a community-based solution, but there was a difficult relationship between those managing the CDP and the clients attending the centre. Involving users in the running of the project raised very real issues about who 'owned' the CDP, about its outlook and general purpose. Staff at the CDP became frustrated with 'an increasing number of attenders using CDP as a drug orientated centre as opposed to a social work support centre'. They felt the more 'positive' clients were being pushed out by those who wanted to use the centre as a place to 'crash', 'fix', 'deal' and 'score'.[26] Staff

---

[21] See B. Thom, *Dealing with Drink: Alcohol and Social Policy – from Treatment to Management* (London, 1999), pp. 91–94; and T. Cook, 'It Was the Bad Apple: The Alcohol Recovery Project', in H. Curtis and M. Sanderson (eds), *The Unsung Sixties: Memoirs of Social Innovation* (London, 2004), pp. 97–115.

[22] Private Papers of Professor Griffith Edwards, hereafter PP/GE, File 19, CDP Annual Report, 1968–1969.

[23] PP/GE File 19, Proposal for a community centre for drug addicts by the Addiction Research Unit, Institute of Psychiatry, no date [1968].

[24] V. Berridge, *Health and Society in Britain since 1939* (Cambridge, 1999), pp. 34–37; C. Webster, *The National Health Service: A Political History* (Oxford, 2002) pp. 54–55.

[25] PP/GE File 4A, Letter from Griffith Edwards to John Brown, 18 July 1968.

[26] PP/GE File 18, Annual Report: Community Drug Project 1977–78.

124

felt that they were in danger of 'colluding' with the 'drug lifestyle' and that the project was becoming a 'community dustbin'.[27] A particular source of tension was over the injecting or 'fixing' room. In 1975 restrictions were placed on the use of the fixing room, with users only being allowed to inject on the premises at agreed times, but by 1976 injecting was banned altogether. Staff felt that it was 'impossible for the addicts to sustain any commitment to positive change in an atmosphere still dominated by the fixing room'.[28] In fact, the CDP was one of the last agencies to close its fixing room: both the Hungerford Project and the Blenheim Project had done so a few years previously.[29]

Alongside this level of user participation, the CDP also wanted to encourage the local community to become involved in the project. This stemmed from their view of drug use as a community problem requiring a community solution. Edwards wanted the local community to be 'truly involved in a helping and caring role', with volunteers working with professionals at the CDP.[30] However, reaction from the local community to the project was not always so positive. A number of residents formed a protest group which complained that the CDP had 'thrust' the project upon a local community already experiencing a number of social problems.[31] Yet, it was this emphasis on community, no matter how contested, that marked out what the CDP were doing from the statutory services for drug users. The work that the CDP and the other street agencies were doing was, however, much more than 'filling gaps' in state provision: it was offering a different approach to dealing with the problem of drug use.

The significance that the government came to attach to such an approach can be seen in changes in the way these organisations were funded, as financial backing shifted from philanthropic sources to the state. The CDP had initially been supported by the Attlee Foundation, a charitable trust, specifically because 'the Trustees believe that it is their duty to use the funds which are available to them . . . to work in fields which are

---

[27] *Ibid.*; PP/GE File 18, Annual Report: Community Drug Project 1974–75.

[28] PP/GE File 18, Circular regarding fixing room: copies to trustees, management committee and the DDUs, 9 December 1976.

[29] N. Dorn and N. South, *Helping Drug Users: Social Work, Advice Giving, Referral and Training Services of Three London Street Agencies* (Aldershot, 1985), pp. 13, 23–25.

[30] PP/GE File 19, Letter from Edwards to Mr Shifrin, 7 July 1969; PP/GE File 4A, List of anticipated questions and proposed answers from a press release on the CDP, no date [July 1968].

[31] PP/GE File 19, Letter from Captain Brown to Mr Shifrin, 4 July 1969.

125

complementary to government and national policy, but for which no government funds are available'.[32] But, by the early 1970s, the CDP's costs could not be met by charitable sources of income alone, and there was a feeling amongst the project's staff and trustees that as the CDP had proven its worth, it 'should now be financed by public funds'.[33] The CDP thus approached a series of statutory bodies. Although the Home Office were 'in no doubt about the value of the project' and the Department of Health and Social Security (DHSS) 'had high regard for the work of the CDP and was most anxious that it should continue operating', support from central government was initially unforthcoming, as the CDP was considered to be a local organisation, requiring local funding.[34] The project therefore turned to the London Boroughs Agency (LBA), which gave the CDP £12,000 in 1972, as well as finding money to support another street agency (the Hungerford Project) and a number of residential facilities, including Phoenix House.[35] The LBA continued to support the CDP, but even these funds became insufficient, and in 1982 the DHSS agreed to give money to the CDP and two other street agencies to prevent them from closing.[36]

This central support for a local project despite a stated intention not to fund such groups attests to the value which the government placed on the work of the CDP and organisations like it. Indeed, such funding for specific voluntary organisations was not that uncommon: the drug legal charity Release received a grant from the Home Office to support its activities during this period, through the Voluntary Services Unit.[37] This support was in line with a general increase in central funding for voluntary organisations in all areas, and the drugs field was clearly no exception. It was estimated that in 1975, £700,000 had been awarded to voluntary groups

---

[32] PP/GE File 4A, List of anticipated questions and proposed answers from a press release on the CDP, no date [July 1968].

[33] PP/GE File 18, Community Drug Project: Annual Report, 1970–71.

[34] TNA MH 154/433, Letter from Mr Chadwell, Home Office to Mr Ogbourne, CDP, 21 June 1971; TNA MH 154/433, Note of an office meeting between Dr Sippert and Mr Eversfield (DHSS) and Mr Searchfield and Dr Mitcheson (CDP), 23 April 1971.

[35] TNA MH 154/430, Points arising from LBA working party on drug addiction, M.H. Bruce, Social Work Service Officer, June 1972; and TNA MH 154/430, London Boroughs Association, Report of General Purposes Committee, 22 November 1972.

[36] TNA MH 154/433, Letter from Geoffrey Finsburg, Joint Parliamentary Under Secretary of State, DHSS, to John Fraser MP, regarding the funding of CDP, 22 October 1982.

[37] Alex Mold, '"The Welfare Branch of the Alternative Society"? The Work of Drug Voluntary Organisation Release, 1967–1978', *Twentieth Century British History*, 17, 1, 2006, pp. 50–73.

working in the drugs field.[38] Government funding for such organisations was part of a wider move towards greater statutory funding for voluntary groups, but in the case of illicit drugs there was an added impetus as the 'outsider' status of voluntary organisations was useful for dealing with a hard-to-reach group for whom statutory services were not always appropriate. This was a different pattern from that seen in the case of ASH, whose outsider image was used by those on the inside (within government) to achieve specific policy objectives. Yet, for drug groups, working closely with government did raise a number of issues. The consequences of changing outside/inside relationships will be explored in relation to a different type of group working in the drugs field: those operating at a national level.

National voluntary organisations

The growth of the street agencies was paralleled by the development of national voluntary organisations in the drug field. One was the Institute for the Study of Drug Dependence (ISDD). The ISDD was the brainchild of Frank Logan, a former Home Office and United Nations Division of Narcotics official. In 1967, Logan had been trying to write an article about drug use and had found that not only was there a lack of factual information on the topic, but there was also no obvious library or collection to turn to for help in locating relevant material.[39] Logan decided to create an institution where individuals could gain access to published work on drugs, and also 'to provide a centre where the subject [drug use] is under continuous study'.[40] Jasper Woodcock, who began work at the ISDD in 1969 as an information officer and later became the Institute's director, stated that there was a perceived need for neutral, objective information about drug use. The ISDD was therefore set up on the basis that the information it provided would be without bias; that it would be believable by everybody.[41] The Institute was intended to be 'non-political and entirely objective

[38] Modern Records Centre, University of Warwick, hereafter MRC, MSS.171/4/14, *Release 67–77: Tenth Anniversary Publication*, pp. 13–14.
[39] J. Woodcock, 'The Growth of Information: The Development of Britain's National Drug Misuse Information Resource', in J. Strang and M. Gossop (eds), *Heroin Addiction and Drug Policy: The British System* (Oxford, 1994), pp. 304–310.
[40] TNA FD 23/1949, Proposal for setting up an Institute for the Study of Drug Addiction and related questions, 1967.
[41] Interview conducted by Alex Mold and Virginia Berridge with Jasper Woodcock, 10 November 2004.

in its approach. While aiming to cooperate with Government Departments
. . . it would be free to express its own views.'[42] Logan thought that the
ISDD's independence could be guaranteed by its 'non-governmental' or
'non-official' status: that there was a particular need for a voluntary, as
opposed to statutory, body in this area. To some degree, it would appear
that the state concurred. Sir Harold Himsworth, deputy chairman of the
Medical Research Council, remarked in 1968: 'I personally think that there
is a great deal to be said for a voluntary body in a field concerned with [an]
illness in which suspicion on the part of the patients is the characteristic
feature. These views are not only my own. I have checked with Godber [the
Chief Medical Officer] . . . and they are his also.'[43]

The ISDD opened on 1 April 1968, and was initially based in the attic of
the Royal Society's Chandos House, near Oxford Circus, moving to a house
in West Hampstead in 1973.[44] A reference library of material on drug use
was assembled and catalogued, a task begun by volunteer amateurs and
later continued by professional library and information staff. The Institute
also developed its research into drugs, setting up a research unit in 1972
which employed the organisation's first full-time staff.[45] It was through this
research that the ISDD had the potential to influence government policy
on drugs, despite their stated aim to be neutral and objective.

In its early days, the ISDD was reluctant to accept statutory funding
as it was felt it might compromise its reputation for independence. As a
result, the Institute was initially funded from charitable sources.[46] But, in
1972, the DHSS offered the ISDD a grant of £10,000 over three years to
enable the organisation to develop the library and employ professional
staff. Woodcock argued that the ISDD 'by then felt sufficiently secure in its
independence to accept'.[47] When the ISDD faced closure a few years later
as a result of a financial crisis, the DHSS stepped in, and by 1977 the government department was providing core deficit funding, supporting the
ISDD in its key activities.[48] However, Woodcock was quick to point out
that the ISDD was only receiving between 40 and 50 per cent of its income

---

[42] TNA FD 23/1949, Proposal for setting up an Institute for the Study of Drug Addiction and
related questions, 1967.
[43] TNA FD 23/1949, Letter from Himsworth to Amory, 4 June 1968.
[44] Woodcock, 'The Growth of Information', pp. 305–307.
[45] Interview with Woodcock.
[46] *Ibid.*; Woodcock, 'The Growth of Information', pp. 304–307.
[47] Woodcock, 'The Growth of Information', p. 307.
[48] Interview with Woodcock.

from the DHSS, a situation, he maintained, that allowed the Institute to retain a considerable degree of independence.[49] The former ISDD director recalled a couple of occasions when the DHSS had attempted to influence how the organisation allocated its resources, but in each case he stated that he was able to tell the department that 'none of our activities are solely funded by you . . . and so you have absolutely no business telling us how to allocate the money'. Woodcock said that the ISDD were able to tell the DHSS to 'Go away basically, and both times they went away.'[50]

This remarkable degree of tolerance on the part of the state can perhaps be explained by the importance the government placed on the ISDD's work. A letter from a DHSS official to a counterpart in the Department of Education and Science observed that the 'ISDD is considered by those working in the field of drug abuse to be fulfilling a useful role'.[51] Another official recorded after a visit to the ISDD that he was 'very impressed with the quality of the Institute's achievements'.[52] Woodcock himself felt that the DHSS had allowed the ISDD to retain its independence because 'they must have thought there was some value' in their work.[53] Even when the ISDD controversially published a guide to glue sniffing, promoting harm-reduction techniques before these were official policy, and there was a media furore, the Department only wanted reassurance that it was not government money which had funded the guide. Once reassured, they were happy to leave the issue alone.[54] It would seem that the DHSS was prepared to allow the ISDD to retain its freedom as the organisation was already fulfilling a role which the state valued.

Yet, the government did not deal with all voluntary organisations in the drugs field in the same way. A somewhat different relationship with the state can be observed in the experiences of another national drug voluntary organisation: the Standing Conference on Drug Abuse (SCODA), which grew out of a series of meetings held by voluntary organisations working in the drugs field in the early 1970s. SCODA was created in 1972 to coordinate the activities of drug voluntary organisations. Its aims were: first, to provide a forum where information on the pattern of drug use could be

---

[49] *Ibid.*

[50] *Ibid.*

[51] TNA FD 23/1949, Letter from Mrs P.A. Lee, DHSS, to Mrs D.M. White, Department of Education and Science, 12 December 1975.

[52] TNA FD 23/1949, Note for the file by M. Ashley-Miller, 18 May 1973.

[53] Interview with Woodcock.

[54] *Ibid.*

shared and where policy recommendations could be formulated; second, to identify needs and assist in developing services; and finally, to encourage research into drug use, evaluate services and stimulate the training of agency staff.[55] To fulfil these aims SCODA carried out a range of activities. They took on a considerable degree of policy and campaigning work, but also provided services to drug voluntary organisations, such as holding meetings between different groups, providing training and producing a newsletter.[56]

Alongside the services SCODA offered voluntary groups were the services it offered to the government. SCODA saw one of its main functions as being to 'bridge the communications and information gap between street level agencies and government ministries'.[57] The potential value of this 'in between' role was clearly recognised by the state: in 1972, SCODA received a three-year grant from the DHSS to fund its work.[58] A SCODA worker from this period noted that 'Government always likes to have a mechanism for communicating to a wider audience rather than [to] have to deal individually with every single body.'[59] Indeed, there was a more general policy shift towards the creation of coordinating bodies for the voluntary sector. In 1978 the Wolfenden Committee examined the role played by intermediary bodies at the local and national level in coordinating voluntary action and recommended that more of these groups be established. Wolfenden suggested that these bodies should have functions very similar to those of SCODA, such as identifying areas of need, offering services to other organisations, and representing the views of these groups to the statutory sector. Moreover, Wolfenden also recommended that these organisations be funded by the government, as they would have little charitable appeal.[60]

SCODA clearly fitted into this model in terms of its functions and in terms of its level of statutory support. Throughout the 1970s the DHSS provided SCODA with its sole source of income, so that by the end of the

[55] DL 14039, The First SCODA Report, 1974.

[56] MRC MSS.171/3/18/8, Letter from Bob Searchfield, Coordinator of SCODA, to Don Aitken at Release, 5 February 1974; SCODA, *Drug Problems: Where to Get Help* (London, 1986); DL 26430, Report of the conference 'Ten Years After', held 1 July 1976.

[57] DL 14039, The First SCODA Report, 1974.

[58] *Ibid.*

[59] Interview conducted by Alex Mold with a SCODA worker, 25 February 2005.

[60] Joseph Rowntree Trust, *The Future of Voluntary Organisations*, pp. 100–145.

decade SCODA was in receipt of over £38,000 a year.[61] The DHSS justified this financial assistance (for which they had to have special authority from the Treasury) as SCODA operated 'in a field unattractive to the public and if unsupported [SCODA] would have to compete for funds with its member agencies whose direct service has more immediate appeal'.[62] Attached to this funding, however, were an increasing number of conditions. In 1976, the DHSS decided to review its support for voluntary organisations working in the drugs field and asked SCODA to submit a report on their current work and its future directions.[63] Yet, when SCODA's policy and campaigning work during the 1970s is examined, there seems to have been no obvious attempt by the DHSS to influence SCODA's work. A SCODA worker stated that 'No assistant secretary at the DoH [Department of Health] ever found me quiet and calm to follow what I was told to do if I thought they were wrong.'[64] From the outset, observers from the DHSS and the Home Office, as well as the LBA, sat on SCODA's management committee, but these individuals do not appear to have exerted any influence over SCODA's work. Indeed, SCODA was at times openly critical of the government's policy on illegal drugs and of statutory service provision. A SCODA worker asserted that 'it was perfectly reasonable to receive funding [from the state] but also to criticise [the government]'. The voluntary sector, he argued, was the 'loyal opposition'.[65] SCODA was, for example, able to point to the weaknesses in statutory services as it saw them, and also to campaign successfully against additional controls being placed on barbiturates.[66] SCODA's close relationship with the state may actually have helped the organisation to become more effective in its campaign work. For example, as a result of its trusted position, SCODA gained access to the Advisory Council on the Misuse of Drugs (ACMD), the government's main consultative body on illegal drug use, and it was able to influence policy in a number of areas, particularly around service provision for barbiturate users.

Voluntary organisations in receipt of statutory funds were clearly afforded a considerable degree of independence throughout the late 1960s

---

[61] DL 32718, SCODA Annual Report 1978–79.
[62] TNA MH 154/1192, Background notes on SCODA by DHSS, no date [1976].
[63] DL 29050, SCODA Annual Report, 1976–77; TNA MH 154/1192, Future Directions for SCODA: a report to the DHSS.
[64] Interview with a SCODA worker.
[65] *Ibid.*
[66] *Ibid.*

and early 1970s. Taking money from the state actually seems to have enhanced the reputation of some agencies and allowed them access into policy-making circles. ASH and the ISDD, for example, were both recipients of statutory funding, although their input into policy operated in different ways. The rationale of the two organisations was not totally dissimilar – there was even some discussion of occupying joint premises in the early 1970s – but the ISDD focused on information for policy, while ASH used science in policy in a more overtly activist way. Yet neutrality for drugs meant in practice a stance which helped to question the status quo. Simply providing unbiased information about the relative harms of different substances and their effects helped to undermine some of the more extreme opposition to drug use.

By the end of the 1970s there were signs that statutory and voluntary agencies were increasingly working together in addressing the drug problem. New kinds of 'hybrid' services, like the City Roads Crisis Intervention Centre, which aimed to stabilise the most chaotic drug users before referring them on for further treatment, combined statutory and voluntary approaches.[67] All of this would suggest that the support provided by the state to voluntary organisations during the 1960s and 1970s did not necessarily usher in the supposed 'rolling back of the state' in the 1980s, but was instead indicative of a situation where voluntary organisations were viewed as an increasingly essential part of the response to a difficult and growing problem. A partnership between voluntary organisations and the state was being formed during the 1960s and 1970s, one which allowed for considerable flexibility on both sides.

Conclusion

At first glance, an examination of public health activism and the provision of local and national services for drug users in the 1960s and 1970s seems to point to a series of dichotomies. The tension between 'outsider' and 'insider' groups and between 'old' and 'new' types of voluntary action can be seen in the very different origins and modes of operation of ASH, the CDP, the ISDD and SCODA. Yet, upon closer analysis, such clear

[67] A. Jamieson, A. Glanz and S. MacGregor, *Dealing with Drug Misuse: Crisis Intervention in the City* (London, 1984).

132

distinctions appear to melt away. ASH drew on the image of a new social movement organisation and 1970s radicalism; in reality it was supported by government to play a key role in government policy making. Its outsider image was crucial to its insider status. The CDP began life outside the mainstream of treatment services but came to rely on inside support in the form of statutory funding. The ISDD and SCODA initially found themselves outside the core of drug policy making, but through government funding actually moved some way inside the policy community. Similarly, both new and old styles of voluntary action can also be observed in the activities of these groups. Drug groups, like the CDP, appeared to be rooted in the counter-culture, but also relied on more traditional models of voluntary action for financial assistance and practical support.

The overlapping of inside and outside groups, and the breakdown between the old and the new, raises broader questions about how to characterise and explain voluntary action in Britain during the 1960s and 1970s. The newness of the new social movement model has been shown to be in need of revision. We are not denying that some aspects were novel. For example, the rationale of the ISDD lay in the provision of unbiased 'information' for policy; that of ASH lay in the use of 'science' as an activist tool within policy. While the role of information itself was not new, we can see in its enhanced position, and also that of science, the beginnings of the 'evidence-based revolution' which became so prominent in policy making in the 1980s and after.[68] In both of the areas examined in this chapter, organisations were operating in an 'in between space' between NSM radicalism (for smoking) and the counter-culture (for drugs), and government policy. There were new styles of pressure group activity for public health, which were not separate from government, but rather part of a policy balancing act. Science and the media began to perform an essential double act in this developing relationship. Drugs service organisations were less science- and media-focused but no less part of this 'in between space'. Drawing on long-standing traditions of voluntary activity and concern, they also operated within a new counter-cultural milieu. Both sets of organisations were led by new types of non-medical radical professionals, and the influence of doctors and psychiatrists, although significant, was less dominant than in areas such as mental health. Government was prepared to fund the new and alternative voices but not to dictate or determine their activities; the

[68] Berridge, *Making Health Policy*.

relationship was more equal. Service provision and pressure group activity, and their interaction with government, present a more complex picture than has been characterised to date.

What this series of case studies suggests, therefore, is that our understanding of the supposed tension between the 'outside' and the 'inside', and the 'old' and the 'new', in the 1960s and 1970s needs to encompass the ways in which both old and new drew on each other. This is not simply to argue that there was nothing 'new' about the new social movements of these decades, but rather to suggest that NSMs operated within a social and political landscape that retained many of its existing features.[69] Such a situation required individuals and organisations to draw on the new social movement model in a variety of different ways. The air of radicalism attached to NSMs could allow access to government and policy-making circles, as well as enabling organisations to engage with a hard-to-reach clientele. But, at the same time, groups found that they also needed professional and political connections to survive and to operate effectively. In between the old and the new, dynamic voluntary organisations flourished. This kind of activity might evade easy categorisation, but it should not escape our attention.

Acknowledgements

This chapter is based on funding from different sources: primarily the Wellcome Trust's funding of Virginia Berridge's study of smoking policy; and Economic and Social Research Council research grant RES-000-23-0265, 'Drug user patient groups, user groups and drug policy, 1970s–2002', on which Virginia Berridge was principal investigator and Alex Mold research fellow. Our thanks are due to these funders, and to the organisers and audience of the British Academy conference on voluntarism at which Virginia Berridge's comment on voluntarism in the 1970s was originally given.

---

[69] Craig Calhoun, for example, points out that the new social movement model can also be used to explain earlier social movements. See C. Calhoun, '"New Social Movements" of the Early Nineteenth Century', *Social Science History*, 17, 3, 1993, pp. 385–427.

7
Faith, charity and citizenship

Christianity, voluntarism and the state in the 1980s

ELIZA FILBY

The development of Christian charity and the association between faith and voluntarism more generally in post-war Britain has received scant attention from scholars.[1] There has been a tendency either to assume its decline in modern secular Britain, or not to make a demarcation between religious and secular care at all. This however obscures the particular role that faith organisations have played in welfare provision and the distinct challenges that they have faced amidst increasing secularisation. This chapter will attempt to explore these themes by detailing the experiences of Christian, chiefly Anglican, community-based action during the 1980s. The first section charts how the faith sector adapted to the new post-war secular world of statutory welfare. It will then provide a specific examination of the churches' collaboration with the Manpower Services Commission (MSC) on unemployment schemes during the early part of the 1980s. The final part explores how the Church and Christian agencies developed a more critical and independent position by challenging the Conservative government's approach to welfare, voluntarism and charity. It will also analyse how the Church encountered problems when it communicated this more politicised message to its conservative laity. The broad

---

[1] There has been renewed interest in religiously-inspired community action triggered by New Labour's support for faith communities: see M. Harris, *Organising God's Work: Challenges for Churches and Synagogues* (Basingstoke, 1998); G. Smith, *More than a Little Quiet Care: The Extent of the Churches' Contribution to Community Work in East London in the 1990s* (Aston, 1998). In terms of historical work, see G. Finlayson, *Citizen, State and Social Welfare* (Oxford, 1994).

aim here is to show how Christian social thought and the changing political landscape profoundly shaped religious organisations and the definition and ethos of charity itself.

The Christian voluntary sector in the secular welfarist age

The second half of the twentieth century witnessed two significant developments that appeared to spell the end of Christian-inspired voluntary action in Britain. The first of these was the establishment of a universal statutory welfare system promising care 'from cradle to grave', which, initially at least, seemed to render charitable provision no longer necessary. The second process, of equal importance, was the dramatic collapse in Christian worship in Britain from the 1960s onwards, which saw attendance drop by one-third and denominational affiliation decrease by 45 per cent.[2] The rapid decline in congregational numbers was coupled with a retraction in other forms of Christian associational culture and the secularisation of the public sphere. So the argument goes, if the 'secular turn' had destroyed the sense of Christian social obligation, then statutory welfare had rendered such activity unnecessary. The most recent exponent of this declinist analysis is historian Frank Prochaska, who judges that the development of the welfare state rid the churches and church charities of their social purpose, which in turn triggered the complete collapse of Christian belief, philanthropy and voluntary effort in British society. For Prochaska, the story is one of replacement, whereby 'the ministries of state gradually displaced the ministries of religion as founts of hope and charity'.[3]

Yet, there is a need to interrogate this convenient and tidy narrative a little further, not least the two developments on which it is based. Britain undoubtedly experienced a significant secular turning point in the 1960s; however, this process was by no means absolute. There remained a strong residual Christian identity within society, while the churches continued to have an important presence in the local community and so too their leaders on the national stage.[4] In respect to the welfare state, it soon became clear

[2] C.G. Brown, *Religion and Society in Twentieth-Century Britain* (Harlow, 2006), p. 278.
[3] F. Prochaska, *Christianity and Social Service in Modern Britain: The Disinherited Spirit* (Oxford, 2006), p. 25.
[4] G. Davie, *Religion in Britain since 1945: Believing without Belonging* (Oxford, 1994); K.N.

that it had not solved the problem of poverty and that the non-profit sector could continue to thrive alongside statutory services. Far from being a period of decline, the history of the post-war voluntary movement is in fact marked by the way in which it successfully adapted and reshaped its activities around statutory provision.[5] Christian charities, like their churches, undoubtedly faced a distinct challenge in these years; however the story is one of reformulation rather than retreat. One important development was the shift in emphasis to the developing world, yet domestic agencies also flourished too.[6] Christian-founded organisations such as Dr Barnardo's, the Church of England Children's Society and the Shaftesbury Project continued to be at the forefront of delivering care to children and the disabled, while the Church Housing Association, established in 1924, had by the 1980s developed into one of the main providers of homes for the elderly, families and the homeless. Parishes remained the central location for Britain's fund-raising efforts and community action, despite the development of a more non-religious form of local activism in the 1970s. Christians also continued to make up the majority of the nation's army of charity workers. A survey conducted in the 1980s by the National Council for Voluntary Organisations (NCVO), for example, calculated that over 70 per cent of volunteers described themselves as 'religious persons', and over half of these were active adherents, attesting to the continual correlation between faith and service.[7]

This is not to say that Christian agencies did not adapt, for one of the notable aspects of the faith sector in the post-war period was the way in which it acclimatised to the new secular culture. This transition is most obviously illustrated in the re-branding of organisations. The Church of England Children's Society, for example, dropped the first part of its title, while the Temperance Council of Christian Churches was renamed the Churches Council on Alcohol and Drugs because 'temperance' was thought to have 'archaic' overtones.[8] These specific examples are illustrative of a broader shift away from the nineteenth-century evangelical charitable tradition and an embracement of the style, approach and

Medhurst and G.H. Moyser, *Church and Politics in a Secular Age* (Oxford, 1988); E. Filby, 'God and Mrs Thatcher' (unpublished PhD thesis, University of Warwick, 2010).

[5] Finlayson, *Citizen, State and Social Welfare*, ch. 4.

[6] For a full list of Anglican charities operating in the 1980s, see *The Church of England Year Book* (London, various years).

[7] D. Gerard, *Charities in Britain: Conservatism or Change?* (London, 1983), p. 79.

[8] Lambeth Palace Library, MS 3758, TCCC 15/1/78, fol.26.

methods of the modern secular voluntary movement. One major change was the loosening of the hold of Victorian morality in the realm of Christian charitable provision.[9] In this, charities had followed the lead of the Protestant churches which, as Hugh McLeod has shown, supported the liberalisation of the nation's moral code in the 1960s.[10] An evangelical and missionary purpose, which had characterised Victorian charities, was also notably less explicit in those of the late twentieth century.[11] Christian volunteers were acutely aware of the evangelical potential of their community work, yet this was now seen as a beneficial by-product, rather than a definite aim, or indeed a measure of success. This period also saw organisations move away from a distinct denominational identity, which again paralleled developments within the Christian churches.[12]

While it would be an exaggeration to talk of this process as the 'secularisation of Christian charity', there is little doubt that by the 1980s there was a certain blurring of the distinction between 'sacred' and 'secular' care. Importantly, however, Christian conviction and a sense of 'doing God's work' remained the central motivation for the employees, volunteers and supporters of these faith agencies, both large and small.[13] The development of a more secular outlook was particularly obvious within Anglican organisations, which, because of their ties to the Church of England, felt a special obligation to serve citizens of all faiths and none. Naturally, this process was less evident in Catholic agencies and not true at all for the Jewish and Muslim voluntary sector, which catered exclusively for their own faith groups, often serving to strengthen religious identity.

As the ethos of Christian organisations changed, so did their language and tactics. Conscious of the predominantly secular climate in which they now operated, these charities shifted from an evangelical to a more ethical discourse and a marketing of causes to both Christians and 'men of goodwill'. Inspired by the pressure-group activism of the 1960s (in which a number of Christians had been involved), faith agencies developed into much more politically conscious bodies, an identity which, as we shall see,

---

[9] Finlayson, *Citizen, State and Social Welfare*, p. 332. It is important not to over-generalise, for such a change was not as evident in Catholic and evangelical charities. Moreover, just because these organisations officially adopted a more liberal position, it did not always follow that this was the attitude of those administering the care.

[10] H. McLeod, *The Religious Crisis of the 1960s* (Oxford, 2007), ch. 10.

[11] Prochaska, *Christianity and Social Service*, p. 19.

[12] P.A. Welsby, *A History of the Church of England, 1945–1980* (Oxford, 1984).

[13] Finlayson, *Citizen, State and Social Welfare*, pp. 330–331.

only strengthened in the polarised climate of the 1980s. In this respect, their links with the Church were crucial. The Anglican bishops emerged as important spokesmen for the sector and, through their presence in the House of Lords and in the media, were able to wield an authority and influence even beyond that of the voluntary sector's umbrella organisation, the NCVO. The Bishop of Southwark, in his capacity as both a religious leader and President of the National Federation of Housing Associations, proved particularly effective in vocalising the concerns of the non-profit housing sector during this period. Also crucial was the Anglican Board for Social Responsibility (BSR), the Church's think-tank, which acted as an important communication point, hosting regular meetings with the NCVO and reporting the concerns of the sector through its publications and submissions to Whitehall. The presence of Geoffrey Holland of the MSC on one of the BSR's boards proved pivotal during the early collaboration with the MSC. This was in addition to the Church's parish system, network of industrial chaplains, and diocesan and national synods, all of which provided crucial channels of contact, support and action.

In the late 1970s, the widespread disillusionment with statutory welfare was coupled with a renewed appreciation for the innovative, flexible and localised nature of voluntary provision. The vision for a mixed economy of care, as set out in the Wolfenden Report of 1978, was duly welcomed by faith agencies encouraged by this recognition and greater potential for cooperation with the state.[14] The fact that the Conservative Party's 1979 manifesto (unlike Labour's) had pledged to extend the work of non-profit agencies in health, welfare and employment pointed towards a potentially rewarding era when Mrs Thatcher eventually entered Number 10.[15]

Practical Christianity: the churches, the MSC and unemployment in the 1980s

Mrs Thatcher's first term in office was characterised by rising dole queues, industrial strikes and widespread urban riots, as the nation's workforce was forced to adjust under a severe economic recession.[16] With unemployment

---

[14] *Ibid.*, ch. 4.

[15] http://www.conservative-party.net/manifestos/1979/1979-conservative-manifesto.shtml (accessed 10 March 2010).

[16] Numbers of registered unemployed reached a peak of 3.2 million in 1986: C. Cook and J. Stevenson, *The Longman Companion to Britain since 1945* (Harlow, 2000), p. 182.

soon reaching over 3 million, the government set about expanding the work of the MSC, a quango responsible for employment and training services. Under the newly appointed chairman David Young, and with a substantially increased budget of over £200 million, the MSC was handed the task of getting people back into work, either through paid employment or community volunteering. Government initiatives – such as the Youth Training Scheme (YTS) for school-leavers, the Opportunities for Volunteering Programme, providing unpaid work experience for the unemployed, and the Community Programme, placing the long-term unemployed on local projects – were introduced to supplement the already-existing Urban Programme. As the names of these programmes suggest, it was envisaged that the voluntary sector would be a crucial player in the implementation of these schemes. Thus, the early 1980s saw unparalleled state investment in non-governmental agencies; for the Urban Programme alone funding increased from £18 million to £76 million between 1980 and 1986.[17]

The aim of MSC investment was to tackle the problem of unemployment at a local level. The Church, with its ready-made infrastructure of buildings, leaders and volunteers, was suitably poised to make a significant contribution. Faith groups readily embraced this new opportunity, with the early 1980s seeing numerous Church-MSC-sponsored schemes spring up across the country.[18] How did these local initiatives operate? Help for the unemployed came in various forms, from counselling and self-help groups to resource centres, training and business co-operatives. Ecumenical collaboration between local churches was commonplace, even in sectarian Belfast, where MSC schemes acted as a practical outlet for Catholic–Protestant dialogue.[19] Many churches also worked with secular voluntary organisations as well as trade unions, local government and trades councils. In Wolverhampton, for example, partnership between the MSC and the diocese of Lichfield resulted in the setting up of a YTS centre for sixty trainees.[20] In Avon, Methodist and Anglican representatives, with the help of local industry leaders and MSC funds, converted an old factory site into workshops for new businesses and subsequently managed to secure

---

[17] B.D. Jacobs, 'Charities and Community Development in Britain', in A. Ware (ed.), *Charities and Government* (Manchester, 1989), p. 95.

[18] *Action on Unemployment: 100 Projects with Unemployed People* (London, 1984).

[19] *Ibid.*, p. 124. There is no evidence of inter-faith cooperation, which is not surprising given that this dialogue was in its early stages in this period.

[20] *Ibid.*, p. 113.

a grant from the EEC Social Fund to expand the project.[21] Monies from the MSC were also given to the Lancaster Council of Churches to transform a disused Methodist hall into an advice and volunteering centre for the unemployed.[22] Most of the impetus came from ecumenical church councils, although other Christian organisations also took a leading role. British Youth for Christ, an evangelical group founded by Billy Graham in 1946, for example, part-funded and led over sixty-three resource centres for the young unemployed across Britain.[23] Some churches also acted as managing agents for the government's Community Programme, such as the Bristol Churches Group, which was in charge of a budget of £1.5 million and oversaw twenty-one different schemes.[24] A survey of 100 church-led MSC projects in 1984 found that eleven were directing MSC Community Programme grants, while thirty-three were running YTS programmes and thirty-two were supporting schemes for small businesses.[25] All this activity was a significant undertaking for local churches, requiring a level of skill and commitment which many clergy and volunteers had had little training or preparation for.

In an effort to coordinate and encourage such activity, an umbrella organisation funded by the churches was launched in 1982 called Church Action with the Unemployed (CAWTU). The aim of this organisation was twofold: first, to mount an information campaign on unemployment to inspire Christians into action; and second, to act as a communication point for churches and faith groups interested in applying for government grants. In the words of CAWTU's founders, it was not only to organise the 'ambulance work' but also to counter 'the generally hostile British attitudes to the unemployed'.[26] Educating Christians on the extent, breadth and social ramifications of unemployment, CAWTU leaders considered, would have the twin advantages of instilling a more sympathetic attitude towards those out of work and galvanising the parishes into action. Thus CAWTU literature, addressed to both clergy and the laity, overflowed with tips on how

---

[21] *Ibid.*, pp. 14–15.

[22] *Ibid.*, p. 67.

[23] *Unemployment: What Can Be Done?* (London, 1981), p. 17.

[24] *Action on Unemployment*, p. 13.

[25] *Ibid.*, pp. 135–138.

[26] Lambeth Palace Library, Board for Social Responsibility Papers, Industrial and Economic Affairs Committee (hereafter LPL, BSRP, IEAC), Minutes and Papers 1980–1, Minutes of the Industrial Committee, 8 October 1980, p. 2.

to become better informed on the unemployment problem, from visiting the local job centre to talking to those out of work.[27] More imaginative suggestions included the plotting of a graph comparing local unemployment figures and weekly parish attendance with the wide disparity presumably serving to highlight where Christians' energies should be directed.[28] There was an implicit assumption, therefore, that Christian volunteers were broadly middle-class (or at least employed), and were very much the providers rather than receivers of aid. A suggestion from one CAWTU leaflet reveals the assumed socio-economic profile of volunteers in its proposal that parishes set up 'a board of directors' made up of business leaders, lawyers and company executives, 'often just the kind of people you have in your congregations'.[29]

CAWTU aimed at convincing parishioners that community action for the unemployed was an appropriate manifestation of faith, as one leaflet evoking the parable of the Good Samaritan encouraged: 'Do not pass by on the other side . . . . Use your Church as an Action Centre for new hope.'[30] Another CAWTU pamphlet entitled *4 Million Reasons to Care* urged that, in this time of national crisis, citizens in the pew needed to extend their confessional obligations beyond 'mowing the churchyard or arranging the flowers' and into society: 'It is now that the Church as a body of Christians must take the lead, both corporately and individually', it claimed.[31] By presenting this as a 'call to arms' and a duty of citizenship, the implication was that such involvement was a spiritual rather than a political act.

According to its founders, CAWTU was founded to 'promote practical work by the churches' and would not delve 'into the causes or possible economic solutions'.[32] In this way, CAWTU's message was distinctly non-political, framing the unemployment crisis as an inevitable consequence of post-industrialisation, rather than a critique on government policy. Despite this, there is evidence that some schemes utilised these funds for more 'political' means. In Hampshire, Industrial Mission priests in alliance with

---

[27] *Unemployment: What Can Be Done?*, p. 17.

[28] *Ibid.*, p. 15.

[29] LPL, BSRP, IEAC, Minutes and Papers 1980–1, 'Action on Unemployment', p. 12.

[30] *Opportunities for Adults: A Guide to Help Get You Started* (London, 1984).

[31] P. Elsom and D. Porter, *4 Million Reasons to Care: How Your Church Can Help the Unemployed* (Bromley, 1985), pp. 7, 49.

[32] LPL, BSRP, IEAC, Minutes and Papers 1980–1, 'Unemployment and the Churches', 23 June 1981.

local trade union representatives obtained MSC funds to set up an advice centre run by the unemployed. Its political ambitions soon became clear when it launched a 'take up your rights' campaign for those on benefits.[33] The centre was opposed by the city council and lost its MSC funding after a year. What was deemed 'political', however, was highly contestable and its acceptability largely dependent on where the activity took place. The tensions in Hampshire contrasted with the fortunes of the Furness Churches' Unemployment Resource Group in Cumbria which, with the help of MSC funds, established itself as a campaigning group and success-fully tabled a motion at its diocesan synod advocating the extension of benefit rights for the long-term unemployed.[34] The fact that this group pursued their political aims through an ecclesiastical rather than a political forum points to a blurring of the boundaries between religious and political action and is illustrative of how experiences at the grassroots level were able to filter into official Anglican structures.

Despite good intentions, it was easy to label CAWTU-inspired efforts as paternalistic. This was a familiar charge in respect to Christian charity, and one which both CAWTU and the MSC seemed desperate to avoid. In 1980, when the idea of CAWTU was initially being muted, Geoffrey Holland agreed that the MSC would part-fund its educational material only on the condition that it avoided 'the concept of the haves coming down to help the have-nots'.[35] Conscious of this, CAWTU literature thus urged parish-ioners to avoid thinking in terms of 'charity', but to approach these efforts as a 'cooperative alliance'.[36] Clergy and volunteers were also advised to consult the unemployed at every stage and to facilitate (but not lead) the setting up of self-help groups for those out of work.[37] Yet, questions pertaining to the paternalistic nature of all this activity persisted. Writing in 1984, the vicar of St Matthew's Church in Brixton, the Rev. Matthew Hind, whose parish had been central in restoring community relations in the aftermath of the Brixton riots, reflected on the negative implications of this paternalistic mindset: 'Too many of us assume that we *know* on behalf of others and are surprised when the others vote with their feet when

---

[33] *Action on Unemployment*, pp. 57–58.
[34] *Ibid.*, pp. 31–32.
[35] LPL, BSRP, IEAC, Minutes and Papers 1980–1, Minutes of the Industrial Committee, 8 October 1980, p. 2.
[36] Elsom and Porter, *4 Million Reasons*, p. 131.
[37] *Mutual Help Groups and Resource Centres: A Guide to Help Get You Started* (London, 1984).

offered the fruit of our arrogant decisions.'[38] The fact that CAWTU had confined its message to the Church's chief constituency, the middle classes, meant that however much CAWTU wished to avoid encouraging a paternalistic form of charitable aid, it did not really offer a serious challenge or alternative to it.

MSC regulations stipulated that investment needed to be of benefit to the local area and not simply the congregation or parish. This meant that although it was not possible to obtain funds to construct places of worship, the renovation of a church by unemployed 'volunteers' was entirely permitted. This was an opportunity that was duly welcomed by parishes at a time when many churches were being forced to close or had fallen into disrepair. In Leeds, for example, the Community Programme financed the restoration of All Souls Church which had been threatened with closure, providing work for thirty employees and the local area with a youth club.[39] Similarly, a parish in Sheffield used MSC-sponsored volunteers to restore its organ 'back to its nineteenth century glory' and to transform part of the church building into a crèche and IT centre.[40] Some Anglicans felt that such activity displayed a worrying confusion of priorities, for, as one rector in Liverpool observed, parishes should not view MSC funds as simply 'a cheap way of getting repairs done to church halls'.[41] In 1984, the director of the William Temple Foundation, the Rev. Tony Addy, raised these concerns with the BSR, arguing that by engaging in such activity the Church was sacrificing its credibility and values in order to serve its 'own interests'.[42] Only the most cynical would accuse local churches of being entirely motivated by their own gain, yet it does indicate that their input was not entirely selfless and that the relationship between the MSC and faith agencies was to some extent reciprocal. It also raised the somewhat thorny issue of public monies being used to support religious organisations, a subject which would become increasingly problematic in subsequent decades, particularly over public investment in Islamic organisations, schools and charities.

For this period at least, clergy were generally optimistic about the positive impact of this engagement with the community, especially the

---

[38] *Action on Unemployment*, p. 7.

[39] *Ibid.*, pp. 118–119.

[40] *Ibid.*, pp. 91–92.

[41] *Ibid.*, p. 78.

[42] LPL, BSRP, IEAC, Minutes and Papers 1984, Tony Addy, 'MSC and the Management of Unemployment', p. 13.

144

opportunity it afforded for evangelising to the un-churched masses. Rev. Matthew Hind articulated the views of many of his fellow clergymen when he enthused: 'for the first time for many decades, there exists a situation in which that major group of the nation, working men and women, may be able to form a relationship with representatives of the churches'.[43] A desire to reverse working-class alienation from Anglicanism had been one of the central motivations behind Christian social action since the industrial revolution, and, in this sense, the 1980s were no different, although these evangelical ambitions were perhaps less explicit. CAWTU did not demand that clergy preach the Word, only that they build a long-lasting relationship with those in receipt of church aid. While there was little evidence that this contact resulted in a significant growth in churchgoing, it did demonstrate the continual relevance of the Christian faith and the churches as social agents in a secular society. Anglican leaders in particular were conscious of the fact that its voluntary agencies and community work, like its schools, provided the Church with legitimacy and purpose in an age when its position as the established Church was continually in question.

After 1987, with unemployment numbers steadily decreasing, the Conservative government decided to dramatically cut and reorganise the MSC, forcing many centres and schemes to abruptly cease their activities. A large majority of these had been partly, or, in some cases, entirely, dependent on MSC funds, which is a testimony to the success of this partnership, but also an indication of a dangerous over-reliance on this investment.[44] It is clear, however, that many parishioners and priests had felt overwhelmed by the responsibility of running these projects.[45] Like their secular partners, faith groups were also uneasy about the government's re-classification of the unemployed as 'volunteers', believing it to be a corruption of the voluntary ethic which relegated legitimate unpaid workers to a secondary role. These concerns at ground level were also felt by the BSR. As early as 1984, the BSR had come to the conclusion that the Church's 'collusion with the government' needed to be reassessed and that a more 'critical distancing' was needed in future.[46]

Collaboration with the MSC posed a major dilemma for faith groups. A natural Christian inclination to help the disadvantaged and an

---

[43] *Action on Unemployment*, p. 5.
[44] *Ibid.*, pp. 139–140, 135.
[45] T. Addy and D. Scott, *Fatal Impacts? The MSC and Voluntary Action* (Manchester, 1987), p. 7.
[46] LPL, BSRP, IEAC, Minutes and Papers 1984, Letter from the Bishop of Coventry, 9 December 1983; and Minutes of the Industrial and Economic Affairs Committee, 22 February 1984, p. 1.

enthusiasm for collaboration with the state was quickly replaced with a concern that the churches had become 'managing agents' for government schemes and that these initiatives were merely a bandage measure that did not address the source of the problem. Collaboration with the MSC had been justified on the grounds that cooperation was more constructive than criticism (in the words of CAWTU, 'it is better to light a candle than curse the darkness'), yet the experiences with the MSC coupled with a growing discontent about the direction of social and economic policy eventually forced the Church and its agencies to adopt a more critical position.[47]

Politicised theology: challenging the discourse of the New Right

According to the secretary of the BSR, Giles Ecclestone, writing in 1985, the contemporary role of the Church was 'not so much to take over the Samaritan role from statutory agents, as to question a system which puts so many people into the ditch'.[48] The most successful example of this new political prophecy was the report into urban poverty, *Faith in the City*, published in 1985.[49] The impetus for the report had come from the Anglican grassroots, rather than the ecclesiastical hierarchy, out of a concern that both the Church and government were neglecting the problem of social deprivation which lay behind the urban disturbances of 1981. In a direct address to the government, the Commissioners reaffirmed the primacy of the state in the provision of social services and its responsibility to deal with the deep-rooted structural inequalities within British society. The report also proposed a reformulation of the relationship between statutory and non-statutory agencies based on long-term investment and continuity.[50] In respect to the Church of England, the report recommended a reorganisation of its urban ministry and a Church Urban Fund for investment in inner-city projects. In terms of content, the report was far from radical yet it presented a vision of urban life which was hard to either dispute or defend. Voluntary agencies had contributed to the report in

---

[47] LPL, BSRP, IEAC, Minutes and Papers 1980–1, 'Action on Unemployment', p. 11.

[48] G. Ecclestone, 'Coping with Caring', *Crucible*, January–March 1985, p. 2.

[49] *Faith in the City: The Report of the Archbishop of Canterbury's Commission on Urban Priority Areas* (London, 1985).

[50] *Faith in the City*, p. 191.

significant ways, with notable representatives on the Commission as well as evidence from leading charities.[51] The message within *Faith in the City* was representative of what most Christians were saying in the 1980s, reinforcing the primacy of statutory over charitable aid, and countering the Thatcherite vision of the voluntary sector.

It has already been demonstrated that the Conservative government's encouragement of the non-profit sector was matched by greater financial investment. This enthusiasm was not simply a pragmatic desire for 'welfare on the cheap', but linked to an ideological distrust of state bureaucracy which Conservatives believed restricted economic growth, destroyed community spirit and curtailed the liberty and potential of the individual.[52] Charity, philanthropy and voluntarism, on the other hand, were heralded as the holy trinity of civic culture, which strengthened individual responsibility and provided the foundations on which social harmony, liberty and national prosperity were based. Whenever Mrs Thatcher spoke of charity, she would always evoke a typical Victorian scene; one which was socially conservative, middle-class and religiously-inspired. It was this Victorian voluntary spirit, she claimed, which had been a fundamental part of her upbringing under the guidance of her father – Rotarian, lay-preacher and Alderman – Alfred Roberts. 'I owe whatever I have been able to do to the upbringing which I had from a very very good Rotarian', she had declared on receiving the International Rotary Award in 1988.[53] Mrs Thatcher often alluded to how her 'Victorian' upbringing had shaped her political vision, yet in respect to the voluntary sector, the allusions to the nineteenth century were even more deliberate. For just as Mrs Thatcher sought to resurrect Victorian *laissez-faire* capitalism and industrial spirit, so she also consciously evoked the independent, altruistic and communitarian culture which she believed complemented this economic order.[54] According to Mrs Thatcher, the civic and moral impulse which lay behind

---

[51] Sir Richard O'Brien (Chair) was former Chairman of the Manpower Services Commission. Robina Rafferty of the Catholic Housing Aid Society and Linbert Spencer, Chief Executive of Project Fullemploy were also members of the Commission.

[52] Finlayson, *Citizen, State and Social Welfare*, pp. 353–357.

[53] Margaret Thatcher, Speech on receiving International Rotary Award (Grantham Rotarians), 12 December 1988, http://www.margaretthatcher.org/speeches/displaydocument.asp?docid=107416 (accessed 10 March 2010).

[54] The Jewish charitable tradition and philanthropic model in the United States was also frequently cited, but Mrs Thatcher tended to draw upon the Victorian tradition as it reinforced the idea that such 'spirit' was a fundamental part of British national character.

the religious and economic prosperity of the nineteenth century had been crushed under the imposition of an oppressive welfare state in the twentieth. This 'spirit', she would often claim, would be resurrected once more under the Conservatives.[55] This was not only a convenient (and inaccurate) reading of history, but also one that ignored the fact that the contemporary voluntary movement was now fully professionalised, politicised and inextricably tied to the state.

Mrs Thatcher presented charity as a non-political endeavour beyond partisanship, one that belonged to the moral rather than the political sphere. Any notion that charity could have an explicitly political output was dismissed outright as corrupting and compromising the moral integrity of charitable endeavours. It goes without saying of course that Mrs Thatcher was herself offering a highly partisan interpretation of charity, as she demonstrated in a speech entitled 'Dimensions of Conservatism' in 1977:

> In a market economy, people are free to give their money and their time for good causes. They exercise their altruism on their own initiative and at their own expense, whether they give directly and personally through institutions, charities, universities, churches, hospitals. When the state steps in, generosity is increasingly restricted from all sides.[56]

Rejecting the notion of taxation as a form of altruism, the understanding was that compulsory taxation deprived citizens of their free will, whereas charitable giving, in contrast, allowed them to exercise their moral virtue. A false dichotomy was created between voluntarism, the market economy and individual altruism on the one hand, and compulsory taxation, state welfarism and dependency culture on the other. The Conservative Party's promotion of voluntarism and charity was, therefore, not just a peripheral interest but a fundamental aspect of the moral and libertarian vision of Thatcherism. This philosophical outlook may have been at the root of government thinking and was undoubtedly central to Mrs Thatcher's public doctrine, yet its implementation proved not to be as coherent and instead was rather patchy and slightly haphazard.[57]

[55] Margaret Thatcher, Speech to the Per Cent Club, 8 December 1988, http://www.margaret thatcher.org/speeches/displaydocument.asp?docid=107413 (accessed 11 March 2010).
[56] Margaret Thatcher, Iain Macleod Memorial Lecture, 'Dimensions of Conservatism', 4 July 1977, http://www.margaretthatcher.org/speeches/displaydocument.asp?docid=103411 (accessed 10 March 2010).
[57] Finlayson, *Citizen, State and Social Welfare*, pp. 353–401; 'Witness Seminar: Voluntary Action in 1980s Britain', NCVO, 11 December 2009.

Mrs Thatcher's protestations on the moral superiority of voluntarism inevitably provoked a response from the Church, but not one she expected nor particularly welcomed. As early as 1981, in the year that the Prime Minister had publicly declared that the voluntary sector rather than the state was at the 'heart' of the nation's social care,[58] the Bishop of Liverpool in a Lords debate on public service cuts put forward a different view: 'Voluntary organisations important as they are, cannot carry the main load of caring for the neediest. The belief that the community as a whole has that responsibility expresses an important moral principle in our country.'[59] The bishop warned against seeing the voluntary sector as an alternative to state services, reminding the House that the two sectors were linked, not least financially in that restrictions on the public purse would inevitably affect the non-profit sector. The prelate's statement aimed at directly countering the Conservatives' ideological vision of voluntarism and charity. The experience with the MSC over the next couple of years only served to highlight the need for the Church to challenge the government's expectations and to set out in stark terms the true style, substance and limitations of the voluntary sector in Britain.

This assertion by Church leaders on the appropriate position of voluntary agencies was linked to their unyielding belief in the Christian basis of the welfare state. On countless occasions, Anglican prelates reaffirmed their belief in the Christian ethos of statutory welfare as a manifestation of the Biblical doctrine of fellowship. Thus, paradoxically, in the face of the New Right's claims of the moral superiority of the non-profit sector over the state, it was the Church and its associate voluntary bodies which became the leading defenders of centralised bureaucratic care. In their objections to the Social Security Act of 1985, Christian charities, for example, opposed the creation of the Social Fund, not only because it would put pressure on their resources, but also because in their view it would destroy the connection between citizenship and welfare rights, which had underlined Beveridge's original vision.[60] Similarly, housing charities questioned the principle of a property-owning democracy and

---

[58] Margaret Thatcher, Speech to the Women's Royal Voluntary Service National Conference, http://www.margaretthatcher.org/speeches/displaydocument.asp?docid=104551 (accessed 12 March 2010).
[59] Hansard, *Parliamentary Debates*, vol. 419, 8 April 1981, cols 547–548.
[60] LPL, BSRP, Social Policy Committee, Reform of Social Security: Response of the BSR to DHSS Green Paper; and Church Action on Poverty Archives, Manchester, 'A Review of the

reinforced the moral responsibility of the state to build council houses. Meanwhile, the BSR produced a report entitled *Christian Reflections on the Welfare State*, offering a theological endorsement of state welfarism.[61]

In the second half of the 1980s, the government introduced the payroll-giving scheme and lowered personal taxation out of a belief that a 'wealthy nation should be a giving nation'. These initiatives again were met with a cautious reaction from Anglican leaders, who judged that the twin policies of incentivising charity and reducing the individual tax burden were a corruption of citizenship and an abdication of governmental responsibility. In a letter to the *Church Times*, the Bishop of Manchester stressed that although charity was important, it was not in his view 'morally superior to action in the political field which is absolutely vital – and often far more effective – if greater justice both within and outside our nation is to be achieved'.[62] Similar sentiments were voiced by his fellow prelate, David Sheppard, of Liverpool, a year later: 'Charity', he affirmed 'merely reflects the lack of contact and understanding between parts of divided Britain, charity is discriminate and dictated by preferences or prejudices, whereas indiscriminate contribution through taxation is a greater example of collective giving and "belonging to one body".'[63] Here Sheppard sought not only to respond to the government's prioritisation of charity, but also to remind the nation that even in the era of Live Aid and Comic Relief, charity could not supersede taxation in its capacity to do good or as an exercise of citizenship.[64]

In his history of the decline of the voluntary sector and charity in modern Britain, Frank Prochaska contends that the 'evocation of a voluntary and philanthropic ethic drummed up by Margaret Thatcher fell on deaf ears' because 'such sentiments were being voiced in a world that had lost its Christian underpinnings'.[65] Yet this decade saw the established Church articulate a contrasting concept of Christian altruism manifested through the state while it denounced Mrs Thatcher's vision of self-help and the charitable ethic as immoral and un-Christian. A Christian appreciation of

Government Green Paper on Social Security', September 1985; see also Finlayson, *Citizen, State and Social Welfare*, pp. 369–371.

[61] *Not Just for the Poor: Christian Perspectives on the Welfare State* (London, 1986).

[62] *Church Times*, 19 September 1988.

[63] Liverpool Record Office, Sheppard papers, Additional Deposit Box I, Part II, Addresses, lectures and other papers 1989, Church Action on Poverty Lecture 1989, p. 14.

[64] Finlayson, *Citizen, State and Social Welfare*, p. 404.

[65] Prochaska, *Christianity and Social Service in Modern Britain*, p. 162.

institutionalised welfare did not, of course, replace a theological under-standing of charitable obligation, but its long association had to a certain extent been undermined, not because of secularisation, but because statism had been anointed with a Christian outlook.

The position of the Church in the 1980s reflected the evolution of Christian social thought over the preceding 100 years. The seeds of Christian socialism had been sown in the nineteenth century, yet it was not until the first half of the twentieth that these ideas had crystallised. Crucial in their development were former Archbishop of Canterbury William Temple, who had set out the theological case for the post-war settlement, and R.H. Tawney, whose writings on the Christian basis of equality were hugely influential in undermining the historic association between Protestantism and capitalist values.[66] These ideas were developed further still amidst the political and cultural upheavals of the 1960s, the growth of liberation theology in South America, and greater involvement in the developing world, which together generated new insights and gave exposure to radical notions of social justice. This development of a more resistive and politicised theology obviously took various forms, some more radical than others, yet in general terms it had the effect of reformulating the meaning and scope of Christian charity around a politicised framework and imbuing activists with a theo-political outlook which changed the nature and ethos of the churches and their associate organisations accord-ingly. The Charities Act, as it then stood, bestowed charitable status on those organisations which operated for the relief of poverty or for the advancement of religion, but not those which campaigned on a political platform. What the Christian social activism of the Thatcher decade had confirmed, however, was that religious faith, the cause of poverty and political action were now inextricably linked.

Yet how did this more radical message filter down to the parishes? If CAWTU aimed at inspiring a practical response, then the Commissioners of *Faith in the City*, in contrast, hoped to provoke a political reaction. The report did not simply seek to challenge the government but also to prick the social conscience of the middle classes. As the Bishop of Liverpool confirmed in a letter to the Chief Rabbi, the report had been 'chiefly aimed at suburban Britons, who all too easily seem to blame those who have been

---

[66] William Temple, *Christianity and the Social Order* (London, 1942); R.H. Tawney, *Religion and the Rise of Capitalism: A Historical Study* (London, 1926). For a historical overview, see Edward Norman, *Church and Society in England, 1770–1970* (Oxford, 1976).

left behind'.[67] Here Sheppard's comments were reflective of the then widespread perception (not without some truth) that the middle classes, embittered by the experience of the 1970s and seduced by the Thatcherite culture of self-interest in the 1980s, were unsympathetic to the plight of the poor and had lost faith in the principles of social democracy. This was also at a time when images of 'absolute' poverty in the developing world and 'relative' poverty at home were juxtaposed in the public consciousness. The merit of *Faith in the City*, therefore, as *Church Times* journalist Patrick Duggan confirmed, was the way in which it prompted Christians, who were heavily involved in the cause of overseas aid, to reflect upon 'the impoverishment of whole communities barely a few miles away from their own homes'.[68]

One of the principal recommendations in *Faith in the City* had been the establishment of a Church Urban Fund (CUF) to inject money into the Church's urban ministry. It was envisaged that over half of the Fund's income would come from the Church's own congregations, with each diocese allocated a specific target in accordance with its wealth and capability. As a way of rousing enthusiasm and faith in the cause, the Church focused on mobilising and informing the laity on the pressing issue of urban poverty. Through its newly established network of *Faith in the City* officers, and with help from its voluntary organisations, the Church organised an impressive array of programmes, activities and literature, including a popular version of the report (which sold over 65,000 copies), a video documentary entitled *Does Anyone Care?*, and a link-up programme connecting wealthy parishes with those in deprived areas. In the diocese of York, for example, the Mothers' Union organised *Faith in the City* awareness days, which regularly attracted over 100 participants. A professional theatre company was also commissioned to tour the dioceses with *Up the Wall*, a contemporary parable endorsed by the Bishop of Oxford, who thought it a 'superb drama, wonderfully acted and containing the right mixture of humour and challenge'.[69] Services were held in Westminster Abbey and Coventry Cathedral marking the launch of the appeal, while a specially-composed CUF prayer was read out in every parish in the land, blessing the work of the Fund and calling for hope for the 'powerless'

---

[67] Liverpool City Archives, Sheppard Papers, Urban Priority Areas Box, *Faith in the City* file, Letter to the Chief Rabbi, 4 March 1986.
[68] *Church Times*, 6 December 1985, p. 8.
[69] *Winchester Churchman*, No. 317, August 1989, pp. 4–5.

and 'healing and renewal' for the nation's cities.[70] Anglicans responded positively to this challenge, with congregations across all dioceses donating time, energy and money to the Fund. It was clear that targets would not be met simply through the weekly collection plates and Anglicans proved themselves to be particularly resourceful at coming up with entertaining and creative ways of raising money. The Winchester diocesan newsletter, for instance, was overflowing with examples of committed parishioners doing their bit for the cause, such as Lady Prideaux, who auctioned off fifty of her homemade red church kneelers, and vicar's wife Mrs Virginia Sutherland, who organised an open day for visitors to view her 'English Vicarage Garden'.[71]

It is unlikely that Lady Prideaux considered the auctioning of her church kneelers as a political act, but there was little doubting the political slant of the CUF campaign. The point of all these educational efforts was not simply to inspire benevolence and giving, but to challenge the laity's preconceptions of social equality and the nature of poverty by urging them to think in terms of structural, rather than material, deprivation. As *Faith in the City* explained, 'Poverty is not only about shortage of money. It is about rights and relationships; about how people are treated and how they regard themselves.'[72] The emphasis was on social justice for the underprivileged coupled with an interrelated understanding of wealth and poverty, one which entreated the laity to consider why, in the words of theologian John Atherton, 'Etons and Harley Streets will always mean Liverpool 8s and Grunwicks.'[73] In this, the *Faith in the City* Commissioners had aimed at directly challenging the self-interest of the affluent, as the report declared: 'The combination of our private preferences and the rami-fications of our political choices are returned to us here as the geographical dimension of an unequal society.'[74] Underlying this message was the imposition of a stratified (albeit a rather limited) 'two nations' framework on both society and the Church, whereby the freedom, wealth and joy experienced by 'comfortable Britain' was positioned alongside the powerlessness, poverty and misery faced by the urban poor. This was the

---

[70] *Winchester Churchman*, No. 305, August 1988, p. 7.
[71] *Winchester Churchman*, No. 304, July 1988, p. 8; and No. 305, August 1988, p. 7.
[72] *Faith in the City*, p. 195.
[73] J. Atherton, *The Scandal of Poverty: Priorities for an Emerging Church* (London, 1983), p. 15. Atherton had served on the *Faith in the City* commission and was an advisor to the BSR.
[74] *Faith in the City*, p. 25.

manner through which the Church's social witness was articulated: to 'comfortable Britain' on behalf of the poor, with very little intervention or initiative from the poor themselves. This discourse combined sociological understandings of powerlessness and social exclusion with theological notions of fellowship and Christian obligation articulated through the language of social citizenship and the common good. Yet, this was a discursive veil, which disguised a distinctly political position. The York Diocesan newsletter from 1989, for example, asked parishioners to consider the following questions:

> Am I by conviction an individualist (stand on your own two feet) or a corporate person (let's share the burden)?
>
> Who is the poorest person I know?
>
> How did I measure that poverty?

It then advised churchgoers to talk to 'one who is deprived' to understand who was not 'benefiting from our prosperous economy'.[75] Although the piece avoided using explicit partisan labels or phrases, the political (and indeed the party-political) implications of the answers were clear.

The Church's politicised prophecy did not go unchallenged, however, and voices of discontent could be heard from both 'comfortable Britain' and those working in deprived areas. For urban clerics, the Church's protestations were judged to be distanced from and irrelevant to the reality on the ground. For one clergyman based in the industrial heartlands of South Yorkshire then suffering from acute unemployment and strikes, these 'sermons' amounted to little more than 'armchair middle class piety'.[76] Others questioned the purpose of a message entirely directed towards the affluent, which, as one Children's Society worker pointed out, was preoccupied with the 'need to remember the poor, something the poor themselves are unable to forget'.[77] At the same time, there was also a rising chorus of protest from both clergy and laity resentful of the Church leadership's relentless criticism of its core middle-class membership and its somewhat apologist and virtuous portrayal of the urban poor. Lay synod member James Pringle spoke for many Anglicans when, during the

[75] York University Library, Borthwick Institute, PC 62.12.YOR, York Diocesan leaflet, February 1989.
[76] I. Gaskell, 'Rotherham and Barnsley: A Parable of Coal and Steel', *Crucible*, July–Sept 1985, p. 1114.
[77] J. Hasler, 'With You Always – but Absent?', *Crucible*, January–March 1987, pp. 12–14.

debate on *Faith in the City*, he interjected: 'may I remind the Synod that comfortable Britain and urban priority Britain . . . both need a Saviour? That the Gospel is for rich and poor?'[78] These objections reflected a deeper concern amongst some Anglicans that the Church leadership were unduly prioritising its social over its evangelical mission.

By 1993, the CUF diocesan appeal had generated £18 million; however, this impressive figure disguises some of the problems the CUF encountered, particularly the lack of enthusiasm for its 'educational' campaign.[79] In 1995, only 18 per cent of inner-city parishes and 21 per cent of non-urban churches were still involved in the linking-up programme. Revealingly, many cited unbridgeable class and cultural differences, even though a number of churches were engaged in a similar scheme with African parishes.[80] Winchester was one such diocese where the appeal achieved limited success, with the initial campaign only raising £20,000, far short of its half a million goal. Parishioners were believed to be uncomfortable with the CUF's political, rather than evangelical, emphasis and were unresponsive to appeals they felt sought to capitalise on a middle-class sense of guilt.[81] Similar misgivings had surrounded the British Council of Churches' (BCC) Race Relations Fund, which also encountered opposition from parishioners concerned by its political orientation. The fact that the BCC had donated money to the controversial Liverpool 8 Defence Committee, an organisation campaigning against police brutality, seemed to confirm the subversive leanings of the Fund.[82]

In specific relation to the CUF and the issue of poverty, criticism of the Church's position was largely due to the fact that the majority of Anglicans were Conservative voters and were suspicious of what they considered to be left-leaning tendencies within the church leadership. If *Faith in the City* had revealed the Church to be ideologically opposed to the government, then the broader reaction within the parishes also revealed the extent of a political divide within Anglicanism.[83] The parallel with

---

[78] *Proceedings of the General Synod*, 17, 1, 5 February 1986 (London, 1987), p. 139.

[79] R. Farnell *et al.*, *Hope in the City? The Local Impact of the Church Urban Fund* (Sheffield, 1994), p. 7.

[80] G. Bowpitt, *The Clergy in the Local Community: A Summary* (York, 1999), p. 29.

[81] *Winchester Churchman*, No. 306, September 1988, p. 1. Between 1987 and 1993, only 4.5 per cent of grants went directly on evangelical projects: Farnell *et al.*, *Hope in the City?*, p. 12.

[82] The Liverpool 8 Defence Committee was set up to monitor police brutality against the Afro-Caribbean community.

[83] In the 1987 election it was calculated that 63 per cent of the Anglican laity voted

155

overseas aid charities helps to further illuminate this point. Even though the tactics of education and mobilisation were the same, overseas aid was a less contentious issue in that it tended not to conflict with individual political beliefs and, thus, was more easily defined as a legitimate cause for Christian concern. By contrast, the issue of domestic poverty, when framed in the language of social Anglicanism, or even the moralised public doctrine of Mrs Thatcher, directly crossed the boundaries between faith and politics. Thus, the CUF campaign encountered opposition because it was seen by some to be demonstrative of a dangerous and inappropriate convergence between religious and political beliefs, one which politicised charity and corrupted the notion of giving in the name of Christ.

A report assessing the impact of the CUF in its first decade concluded that, although the Fund had provided huge investment in the Church's urban ministry, it had retreated from pursuing its more political and theological objectives. The initial campaign, it judged, had not penetrated 'comfortable Britain' and had been replaced with a 'less contentious frame of reference' so as to ensure unequivocal support from the Church.[84] Despite this switch from a political to a more practical message, the CUF was still an impressive undertaking, one that showed the Church to be 'putting its money where its mouth was' in respect to urban poverty. Between 1988 and 1993, for example, the CUF invested over £17 million in 700 projects.[85] Like the MSC-funded schemes, the initiative more often than not came from the clergy, out of a desire to position the local parish in service to the community. Lack of time, resources and lay apathy continued to be an issue, although the introduction of specific urban ministry training into ordination courses meant that the new generation of priests were better equipped to deal with these challenges. One major development in this period, the ordination of women, also signalled an important change. With the majority of this new workforce employed in urban parishes, women emerged as crucial leaders in community faith-based action.[86]

In his 1983 study of charities in Britain, David Gerard saw a clear distinction between secular organisations, which tended to be politically radical and socially liberal, and religious charities, which he classified as

Conservative: *The Times*, 1 July 1988. For a social-economic profile of Anglican congregations, see Medhurst and Moyser, *Church and Politics in a Secular Age*, ch. 10.
[84] Farnell *et al.*, *Hope in the City?*, p. 143.
[85] *Ibid.*, p. 1.
[86] Bowpitt, *The Clergy in the Local Community.*

socially conservative.[87] The story of faith voluntary action in the 1980s does not strictly fit Gerard's neat categorisation. As has been suggested here, the faith sector increasingly became a space for critical and political action, which, although not 'radical' in Gerard's terms, still amounted to a substantial moral challenge to the Thatcher government. Yet as it did so, it encountered serious opposition from its more conservative support base. This points to the crucial issue that although faith is an important factor in motivating volunteers and charitable efforts, the *interpretation* of that faith is equally crucial in directing the way in which this charitable obligation is undertaken.

The 1980s thus proved an important juncture in the history of faith-based voluntary action and charity. An initial enthusiasm for working with the state in alleviating unemployment soon dissipated as agencies and churches struggled under the pressures of operating MSC schemes. These experiences on the ground fuelled an already rising political consciousness within the sector, resulting in a change of tack towards a more confrontational approach with the government. The publication of *Faith in the City* was crucial in crystallising this message, as Church leaders, the Synod, and Christian voluntary organisations mounted an effective challenge to the Thatcherite discourse on welfare, voluntarism and citizenship. In this, the faith sector was not saying anything significantly different from their secular partners; however a Christian critique proved highly effective in undermining the moral credibility of Thatcherism. Faith organisations were distinct from their secular counterparts in other ways too. They were more likely to encounter suspicion and hostility from the left, as was the case in Liverpool, when, during the rates crisis, the churches found themselves caught in the crossfire between central and local government when they offered to fulfil the role of social services if the council went bankrupt. Meanwhile, as the Church adopted a more political position, this generated a feeling of unease amongst more conservative Anglicans, who felt that a political bias was dominating the Church's agenda. Yet, these problems should not detract from the fundamental contribution of the Church and its associated bodies to local communities suffering from acute hardship, and, perhaps equally as important, their role in shaping the moral contours of debate about welfare during this crucial decade.

---

[87] Gerard, *Charities in Britain*, p. 83.

8

Voluntary action, New Labour and the 'third sector'[1]

PETE ALCOCK

Introduction

The focus of this chapter is on the changing policy environment for voluntary action under the New Labour governments at the turn of the twenty-first century. This was a period of rapid policy change, with a rise in the profile of voluntary action to rival, if not outstrip, that in any of the earlier periods discussed in this book. This rising profile was also accompanied by terminological change and debate. Throughout much of the previous century in the UK, the focus of academic and policy concern was on what was generally referred to as the 'voluntary sector', extended later to include also the 'community sector', as we will return to discuss briefly below. This is to some extent a particularly British concept. Elsewhere different concepts are employed, including the 'non-profit sector' (common in the United States) and the 'non-statutory sector' (in continental Europe). These different terms reflect the politics and ideologies of varied national contexts and cultures, although they also aim to encompass rather different constituencies within these umbrella terms. The voluntary sector is not the same thing everywhere, something explored in a collection by Evers and Laville, and the more recent UK debate is explained in an article by Alcock.[2]

[1] The support of the Economic and Social Research Council (ESRC), the Office of the Third Sector (OTS) and the Barrow Cadbury UK Trust is gratefully acknowledged. The work was part of the programme of the joint ESRC, OTS, Barrow Cadbury Third Sector Research Centre.
[2] A. Evers and J.-L. Laville (eds), *The Third Sector in Europe* (Cheltenham, 2004); P. Alcock, 'A Strategic Unity: Defining the Third Sector in the UK', *Voluntary Sector Review*, 1, 1, 2010, pp. 5–24.

However, what was distinctive about the recent New Labour period in the UK was that it saw the development of a new concept, the third sector, aiming to capture a new, and broader, notion of what could, and should, be the focus of political and policy attention. Adoption of the term third sector dated in particular from the creation of the Office of the Third Sector (OTS) in 2006, which brought together policy coordination for the voluntary and community sector with previously separate support for social enterprise and co-operatives and mutuals, and was part of a deliberate attempt by government to expand the reach of policy intervention into areas not traditionally associated with voluntary action in the country. To quote the definition employed on the OTS website, 'The term encompasses voluntary and community organisations, charities, social enterprises, cooperatives and mutuals both large and small.'[3]

At the beginning of the new century, therefore, a broader third sector replaced the more established focus on voluntary action, which had been the concern of much of the analysis presented elsewhere in this book. This has meant that both policy and analysis have had to embrace a larger slice of organisational activity. The third sector includes not only the traditional charities but also industrial and provident societies, community interest companies, and companies limited by guarantee. In 2007, the *Civil Society Almanac*, compiled by the National Council for Voluntary Organisations (NCVO), put the total number of potential organisations covered by this wider definition at 870,000.[4]

However, other political changes have, in effect, operated to narrow the field of policy and analytical concern. This is because of the devolution of political control to the independent administrations in Scotland, Wales and Northern Ireland since 2000. Third sector policy is one of the policy arenas which have been devolved, and now separate policy initiatives are being pursued in each of these three countries, delivered by separate offices within the different administrations, although in practice rather similar policy directions have been followed in all three of the devolved administrations.[5] Devolution has fragmented UK policy, and, therefore, the focus

---

[3] See OTS web archive at www.cabinetoffice.gov.uk.
[4] D. Kane, J. Clark, S. Lesniewski, J. Wilton, B. Pratten and K. Wilding, *The UK Civil Society Almanac 2009* (London, 2009), p. 9.
[5] P. Alcock, 'Devolution or Divergence? Third Sector Policy across the UK since 2000', in G. Lodge and K. Schmuecker (eds), *Devolution in Practice: Public Policy Difference within the UK* (London, 2010).

of this chapter is primarily upon the policy environment that developed in England under the Labour administrations at Westminster from 1997.

Context

The policy environment of the New Labour era was informed by the legacies of the longer history of policy change as well as by the priorities and innovations of the government. This is a relationship that can be traced back to the Statute of Charitable Uses of 1601, but it is the last century or so of development that has been most influential, and in particular the changing policy environment which flowed from the implementation of the public welfare provisions of the welfare state.

Much of what we now regard as public welfare provision was initially provided, in some form at least, by voluntary organisations, and the introduction of state welfare in the last century could perhaps be seen in simple terms as a gradual replacement of voluntary action by public support. In fact, however, the history of the changing relations between the state and the third sector over this period is a more complex one than this simple model of displacement suggests. In an overview of this history, Lewis identifies three major shifts in terms of the relationship between the sector and the state.[6]

The three shifts can be characterised as producing three, or now four, eras of engagement for voluntary action in its relations with the state. First, in the nineteenth century, was the era of voluntary organisations as the providers of services, with little competition or interference from the state. Then, as public services developed in the first half of the twentieth century, voluntary action remained as a complementary form, providing services where public provision was absent or under-developed, such as hospital services and social care. In the middle of the century, the welfare state reforms of the late 1940s introduced more comprehensive public provision, for instance through the National Health Service, and following this, voluntary action moved to a supplementary role, providing additional or

---

[6] J. Lewis, 'Reviewing the Relationship between the Voluntary Sector and the State in Britain in the 1990s', *Voluntas: International Journal of Voluntary and Nonprofit Organizations*, 10, 3, 1999, pp. 255–270. See also G. Finlayson, *Citizen, State and Social Welfare in Britain 1830–1990* (Oxford, 1994); B. Harris, 'Voluntary Action and the State in Historical Perspective', *Voluntary Sector Review*, 1, 1, 2010, pp. 25–41.

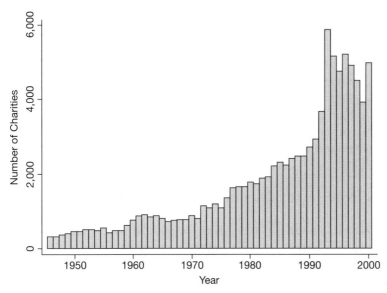

Figure 8.1 Growth in charity registrations from 1945 to 2000[7]

specialist services, such as hospice care, or challenging state services, for instance in Citizens Advice Bureaux. At the turn of the new century, we entered a new era in state and voluntary sector relations which has been characterised as one of partnership, as we will explore in more detail below.[8]

Thus, the simple model of a decline in the scale of voluntary action as state welfare developed is far from an accurate portrayal of a complex set of changing relations, as some of the other chapters in this book also explore. There is also no evidence of a decline in the numbers of voluntary organisations over this period; indeed analysis from the Third Sector Research Centre (TSRC) suggests a more or less continual process of growth over the latter half of the twentieth century, albeit that changes in registration criteria complicate the picture after 1990 – see Figure 8.1.

The changing policy environment of the post-war period has been explored in more depth by Kendall, who argued that, over this time, there was first a move from incremental 'charity-centric' institution

---

[7] Graph produced by Peter Backus, TSRC.
[8] J. Lewis, 'New Labour's Approach to the Voluntary Sector: Independence and the Meaning of Partnership', *Social Policy and Society*, 4, 2, 2005, pp. 121–133.

building, with no policy focus on any broader sector, to 'voluntary sector'-oriented incremental consolidation, influenced critically by the Wolfenden Report of 1978.[9] 6 and Leat analysed the policy discourses of this post-Wolfenden period to argue that these discourses operated in effect to create the voluntary sector as a site for policy interest.[10] This led up to the third phase in Kendall's analysis, which followed the Deakin Commission and Michael's Labour Party paper on partnership, with a shift to a discourse of partnership and a more directive policy regime that Kendall called 'hyperactive mainstreaming', and the creation of the third sector.[11]

The new third sector discourse

The most recent Labour government phase of third sector policy making can be traced back to the consolidation of discourse about the sector in the 1990s. As Lewis explained, in the 1980s the predominant policy discourse was that of New Public Management efficiency and effectiveness, and the role of voluntary organisations as potential alternative providers to state welfare.[12] This market-style, contractual, environment was criticised by some third sector commentators as potentially undermining sector values and independence; and it did not initially include any positive policy engagement with the sector.[13] However, in the early 1990s a more supportive policy dialogue began to develop – for instance, in the 1994 'Make a Difference' initiative to provide support for volunteering, delivered through the Home Office.[14]

---

[9] J. Kendall, *The Voluntary Sector: Comparative Perspectives in the UK* (London, 2003); J. Kendall, 'The Third Sector and the Policy Process in the UK: Ingredients in a Hyperactive Horizontal Policy Environment', in J. Kendall (ed.), *Handbook of Third Sector Policy in Europe: Multi-level Processes and Organised Civil Society* (Cheltenham, 2009); Wolfenden Committee, *The Future of Voluntary Organisations* (London, 1978).

[10] P. 6 and D. Leat, 'Inventing the British Voluntary Sector by Committee: From Wolfenden to Deakin', *Non-Profit Studies*, 1, 2, 1997, pp. 33–47.

[11] Commission on the Future of the Voluntary Sector, *Meeting the Challenge of Change: Voluntary Action into the 21st Century* (London, 1996); Labour Party, *Building the Future Together: Labour's Policies for Partnership between the Government and the Voluntary Sector* (London, 1997); Kendall, 'The Third Sector and the Policy Process in the UK'.

[12] Lewis, 'Reviewing the Relationship between the Voluntary Sector and the State'.

[13] D. Billis and M. Harris (eds), *Voluntary Agencies: Challenges of Organisation and Management* (Basingstoke, 1996).

[14] J. Davis Smith, 'Volunteers: Making a Difference?', in M. Harris and C. Rochester (eds),

162

The Voluntary Services Unit in the Home Office became more active in promoting and supporting voluntary action in the 1990s, commissioning the Centris Report.[15] More significant was the Deakin Commission, which reported three years later.[16] This was an independent inquiry established by the NCVO and chaired by an academic, Nicholas Deakin. Its remit was to review the challenges facing the voluntary sector in the coming new century and to outline how these might be met. The recommendations focused significantly on relations between government and the sector and argued that these could be improved through a more structured and proactive approach by both sides. It was suggested that this could be framed within an over-arching concordat, governing, directing and improving policy and practice in relations between the two.

The Deakin Commission was independent of government, but Deakin himself had had a close affiliation with the Labour Party as well as with the voluntary sector. His report was in some ways an anticipation of the policy environment that a New Labour government might wish to embrace. And in 1997 Labour published its own review of relations with the sector, led by Alun Michael, who had been appointed by Tony Blair to lead new policy thinking on this issue.[17] As Kendall explained, Deakin, Michael and other leading policy agents played a critical role in the development of a new discourse on the need for a formal and structural review of state and voluntary sector relations in the mid-1990s, which the new government in 1997 proved able and willing to take up.[18]

Much has been written about the broad thrust of New Labour politics and policy and the extent to which it was distinctive and innovative.[19] Central to the new policy environment, however, at least in the early years, was the notion of a third way for public policy planning.[20] The third way was intended to capture a rejection of public service policy planning that relied primarily on the state (as supposedly was the case with previous

Voluntary Organisations and Social Policy in Britain: Perspectives on Change and Choice (Basingstoke, 2001).
[15] B. Knight, *Voluntary Action* (London, 1993).
[16] Commission on the Future of the Voluntary Sector, *Meeting the Challenge of Change.*
[17] Labour Party, *Building the Future Together.*
[18] Kendall, 'The Third Sector and the Policy Process in the UK'.
[19] S. Driver and L. Martell, *New Labour,* 2nd edn (Cambridge, 2006); A. Chadwick and R. Hefferman (eds), *The New Labour Reader* (Cambridge, 2003).
[20] T. Blair, *The Third Way* (London, 1998); A. Giddens, *The Third Way: The Renewal of Social Democracy* (Cambridge, 1998).

Labour governments) or the market (as had been the case under the Thatcher governments of the 1980s). It also drew on the New Public Management notion that what mattered in service delivery was 'what worked' rather than who provided it. Much rhetoric permeated the third way discourses, and critics pointed out there was nothing new in promoting reliance on a mix of state and market forces, or in being concerned to ensure that service delivery was effective. But, in the context of voluntary sector policy development, it created a potentially new space for a proactive role for the sector as a tailor-made alternative to both the state and the market.

By being explicitly not-the-state and not-the-market, the third sector could offer a genuine alternative provider base. A government seeking to celebrate and promote such welfare mixing was, therefore, likely to embrace voluntary and community activity, and to seek to bring it into the mainstream of political debate and policy planning.[21] This is just what Labour did, not just mainstreaming third sector policy, but doing so 'hyperactively'.[22]

An enhanced role for voluntary action within the third way was supported early on by the Prime Minister, Tony Blair, in a speech to the NCVO Annual Conference: 'History shows that the most successful societies are those that harness the energies of voluntary action, giving due recognition to the third sector of voluntary and community organisations.'[23] And at a similar event six years later, the man who would succeed him as Prime Minister, the then Chancellor Gordon Brown, expressed similar sentiments, talking of a 'Transformation of the third sector to rival the market and the state, with a quiet revolution in how voluntary action and charitable work serves the community'.[24]

Blair's quote was an early example of the use of the term 'third sector' by the government, a point to which we will return below. The new engagement with the sector was also welcomed by key practitioners within it, who embraced the partnership theme which, as we shall see, became the leitmotif of New Labour policy. For instance, Sir Stuart Etherington, Chief Executive of the NCVO, opened a speech in 2002 with the words:

[21] R. Macmillan and A. Townsend, 'A "New Institutional Fix"? The "Community Turn" and the Changing Role of the Voluntary Sector', in C. Milligan and D. Conradson (eds), *Landscapes of Voluntarism: New Spaces of Health, Welfare and Governance* (Bristol, 2006).
[22] Kendall, 'The Third Sector and the Policy Process in the UK'.
[23] T. Blair, Speech to National Council for Voluntary Organisations, Annual Conference, February 1999.
[24] G. Brown, Speech to National Council for Voluntary Organisations, Annual Conference, February 2004.

164

> This is an exciting and challenging time for people working in the voluntary
> sector. Over the past five years we have seen a growing understanding of,
> and emphasis on working with, the voluntary sector across government.
> Partnership working has become the norm . . .[25]

In addition to speeches, there were a range of government documents
outlining the dimensions of the new relations between the state and the
third sector (discussed in more detail below), together with a cross-cutting
review on the role of the sector in the delivery of public services as part
of the Comprehensive Spending Review, and a joint report on future
planning for an ever wider role for the sector in social and economic
regeneration.[26]

In an analysis of the broader ideological context of New Labour policy
development, Kendall went on to argue that what had been created by the
discourses on third sector policy since the mid-1990s was a 'decontested
space' for voluntary action at the centre of modern democratic society.[27]
This notion that both government politicians and policy makers, and third
sector practitioners and protagonists, had developed a shared discourse
around the desirability of a new partnership between government and the
sector in policy planning was explored further by Alcock.[28] He argued that
what had emerged from this discourse was a 'strategic unity' amongst all
the key agents and agencies, who had a collective interest in maintaining
and developing the third sector as a space for policy intervention and
forward planning. In the space of around a decade, therefore, the Labour
governments had translated the emerging discourses of the mid-1990s into
a new era of state and third sector relations with ever greater expectations
about the role that the sector could play across society and the support that
was needed from government to underpin this.

---

[25] S. Etherington, 'Delivery: The Role of the Voluntary Sector', Public Management and Policy
Association Lecture, 22 October 2002.
[26] HM Treasury, *The Role of the Voluntary and Community Sector in Service Delivery: A Cross
Cutting Review* (London, 2002); Cabinet Office and HM Treasury, *The Future Role of the Third
Sector in Social and Economic Regeneration: Final Report*, Cm 7189 (London, 2007).
[27] J. Kendall, 'Losing Political Innocence? Finding a Place for Ideology in Understanding the
Development of Recent English Third Sector Policy', Third Sector Research Centre, Working
Paper 13, 2010.
[28] Alcock, 'A Strategic Unity'.

Institutional change

Central to the new era of partnership between the state and the third sector was the building of new institutions to act as sites for policy development and delivery. In the 1980s and 1990s, the location for policy interface with the voluntary and community sector had been the Voluntary Services Unit within the Home Office. The Labour government's first strategy was to rebrand and expand this. In 2001, it became the Active Community Unit (ACU) and received an additional £300 million three-year budget to underpin a programme of engagement and support for the sector aimed at promoting voluntary activity. This was followed by the creation of the Civil Renewal Unit with a wider remit to promote citizenship and community action, but with a focus too on the role of voluntary action in this. These were then merged with a separate Charities Unit to create a larger entity within the Home Office, the Active Communities Directorate, expanding further the policy reach and the budgetary commitment.

New institutions were not only being built up within the Home Office. In the Treasury a new Charity and Third Sector Finance Unit was created in 2006 to coordinate fiscal policy for the sector. And it was the Treasury in 2002 that initiated the cross-cutting review of the role of the sector in service delivery, which led to some of the major investment programmes outlined below. The review was revisited in 2004 and 2005, with further investment and a continuing concern to ensure that support for the sector was included in mainstream financial planning within the Comprehensive Spending Reviews.[29]

In 2001 the government also created a Social Enterprise Unit (SEU) within the then Department of Trade and Industry (DTI) to provide coordination and support for social enterprises. This was a new term developed to apply to third sector organisations which traded as businesses but had explicit social and/or environmental purposes and used their surpluses to reinvest in the business rather than paying out dividends to shareholders. In practice this form of activity has been around for a long time, and could include for instance the co-operatives created in the nineteenth century. The broader area of the social economy, within which businesses with a social purpose operate, is also one well recognised and

[29] HM Treasury, *Cross Cutting Review: Follow-up of the Role of the Third Sector in Service Delivery* (London, 2004); HM Treasury, *Exploring the Role of the Third Sector in Public Service Delivery and Reform* (London, 2005).

established in continental Europe.[30] However, they became a new focus for political and policy concern within the UK at the turn of the new century, in part because of the expectation (or hope) that they could play a critical role in economic regeneration and neighbourhood renewal by promoting business and social development in rundown areas. A powerful lobby developed to promote social enterprises as a new form of third sector activity, at the heart of Labour's third way.[31] By 2001, this had led to the creation of the SEU and the development of Community Interest Companies (CIC) as a new legal form for social enterprise.

One of the recommendations of the Deakin Commission had been that the law on the definition and regulation of charities should be reviewed and updated, in particular because it dated back to the seventeenth century. The Labour government also took forward this proposal and in the Charities Act of 2006, for the first time in over four centuries, charity law was simplified and the definition of charities more closely refined.[32] All charities now needed to demonstrate 'public benefit' in order to register, and to secure or retain the benefits of tax relief, although much of the practical implementation of this new definition was left to the Charity Commission to develop.

By the mid-2000s, a range of new institutions and legal forms had been created to provide a new structure for relations with the voluntary and community sector. Indeed, if anything, it was the wide range of institutions that was itself creating potential problems for policy coordination and practical engagement. So, in 2006, the process of institution building was rationalised, and given even higher political profile, by the creation of a new Office of the Third Sector, based at the heart of government within the Cabinet Office. The OTS was constituted by a merger of the Active Communities Directorate from the Home Office and the SEU from the DTI, although some of the civil renewal activities of the former Directorate were, at the same time, transferred to the new Department for Communities and Local Government – and the Charity and Third Sector Finance Unit remained in the Treasury.

The OTS took over coordination of all government policies and investments for the sector, giving it a portfolio and a budget much larger

---

[30] Evers and Laville, *The Third Sector in Europe*, ch. 1.

[31] K. Peattie and A. Morley, *Social Enterprises: Diversity and Dynamics, Contexts and Contributions* (London, 2008).

[32] Cabinet Office, *Private Action, Public Benefit: A Review of Charities and the Wider Not-for-Profit Sector* (London, 2002).

than its separate constituents. In 2009, it also took over control of the Social Exclusion Taskforce, which had started out in 1998 as a separate unit within the Cabinet Office. The move of social enterprise support from the DTI was not popular with all in the social enterprise community, but the OTS moved quickly to establish its credentials here with the publication of a new Social Enterprise Action Plan.[33]

The creation of the OTS also meant that there was now a Minister for the Third Sector, within the Cabinet Office team; the first incumbent was Ed Miliband, later himself a senior Cabinet member. It also meant that a Director for the Office had to be appointed. The first person to hold this position was a significant appointment, for the post went to Campbell Robb. Robb had previously worked at the NCVO as its policy lead and had a strong base within the voluntary and community sector. His appointment was a clear indication that partnership between the government and the sector could lead to transfer of people as well as ideas and resources, and that a sector perspective and experience would be valued at the centre of government.

Perhaps because of Robb's experience and commitment, the OTS moved quickly to establish formal mechanisms for engagement with the sector, establishing an Advisory Body of senior sector representatives and a group of strategic partners with whom they would work in delivering funding and other support to third sector organisations. They also worked to establish links across government to ensure that third sector engagement reached into major service departments, recruiting senior civil servants as 'third sector champions' in each department.

Perhaps the most significant feature of the OTS, however, was what its title revealed about the organisational and conceptual base for policy under the Labour governments. The Office's remit was the third sector, and not just the voluntary and community sector. The merger with the SEU was critical in this, and was evidence of a clear intention by government to bring social enterprise and voluntary action into the same political and policy space. As the definition employed on the OTS website explained: 'The term encompasses voluntary and community organisations, charities, social enterprises, cooperatives and mutuals both large and small.'[34]

In an analysis of the policy discourses of the 1970s and 1980s, 6 and Leat argued that these had operated to create the voluntary and community

---

[33] Office of the Third Sector, *Social Enterprise Action Plan: Scaling New Heights* (London, 2006).
[34] See OTS web archive at www.cabinetoffice.gov.uk.

sector as an entity.[35] The creation of the OTS in the early twenty-first century, in effect, did the same thing for the third sector. Carmel and Harlock explored this in a rather more critical vein, arguing that, in this way, the third sector was a product of a new discourse of governance through which agencies previously outside of formal policy planning could be constituted as a 'governable terrain' and, therefore, a site for policy intervention and, potentially, control.[36] The policy makers did, of course, have an active interest in securing the sector as a distinct entity. But it was not just policy makers who contributed to this new consensus. In 6 and Leat's study of the invention of the voluntary sector, practitioners also played a leading role; and, as Kendall later discussed, many of the leading protagonists in more recent debate and practice acquired a shared interest in promoting and supporting the notion of a third sector as a distinct and homogeneous entity.[37]

Capacity building and investment

One of the reasons for the support from sector practitioners for the new discourses of third sector partnership was the considerable benefits that flowed to third sector agencies and organisations from the programmes of investment set up to provide practical support to back up the rhetoric of greater third sector involvement in service delivery and civil renewal. One of the issues addressed by the Deakin Commission was the capacity of third sector organisations to deliver on their own commitments and mission, and to engage more actively with government. Although some, especially the larger and well established organisations, were well placed to do this, and to take advantage of the new forms of engagement, many others were not; and both government and sector policy makers were concerned that the new environment of partnership should not be extended only to a small handful of larger and already more influential organisations within the sector. As a result, therefore, institutional change was accompanied by formal regulation and guidance, and by financial investment, to support partnership.

[35] 6 and Leat, *Inventing the British Voluntary Sector by Committee.*
[36] E. Carmel and J. Harlock, 'Instituting the "Third Sector" as a Governable Terrain: Partnership, Procurement and Performance in the UK', *Policy and Politics*, 36, 2, 2008, pp. 155–171.
[37] Kendall, *Losing Political Innocence?*

A recommendation of the Deakin Report had been the need for some proactive formalisation of relations between public and voluntary sector agencies in the form of a governing 'concordat'. This was taken up quickly by the government after 1997, and, in 1998, they established a national Compact in England to provide a framework for relations between central government and third sector organisations, implementing the principles, if not the terminology, of Deakin.[38] Similar Compacts, with much the same aims and structure, were implemented shortly after in Scotland, Wales and Northern Ireland. The national Compact was also promoted as a model for local compacts to be developed between local authorities, National Health Service agencies and other public bodies, and the representatives of the local third sector. Over the next few years, local compacts were implemented in virtually all local areas.[39]

However, the Compact was a framework for relations, not a legally binding document, and it required both parties to undertake proactive engagement with its guidance and procedures to make it work. This led to difficulties both nationally and locally, with some government departments and agencies much more willing and able to engage with the Compact protocols than others, and to criticism from practitioners that, in some cases, not enough was being done to translate documentary rhetoric into practical reality. The result was that national guidance was then issued on a number of key matters of concern, such as whether, and how to ensure that, the full costs of voluntary organisations were included in contracts.[40] Later, an independent agency, the Compact Commission, was established by government to oversee its implementation and promote good practice under it. The Compact was also a framework for partnership: third sector organisations had to play their part as active parties; this led to the creation of another new agency, Compact Voice, to coordinate and promote engagement with the sector.

Despite the criticisms and the limitations, the Compact became a leading feature of new government commitments to engaging with the third sector. It has also led policy makers to recognise that coordination and partnership may require more than just formal agreement. In particular, for third sector

---

[38] Home Office, *Compact on Relations between Government and the Voluntary and Community Sector in England*, Cm. 4100 (London, 1998).

[39] G. Craig, M. Taylor, M. Wilkinson and S. Monro, *Contract or Trust? The Role of Compacts in Local Governance* (Bristol, 2002).

[40] Home Office, *Funding and Procurement: Compact Code of Good Practice* (London, 2005).

organisations to engage in the partnership arrangements that flow from the Compact, including securing funding under contracts to deliver services for government, investment may be needed to build up their organisational capabilities and practical skills.

There had been previous examples of government support for organisational development in voluntary action and social enterprise in the twentieth century, but this had largely been confined to the work of national agencies operating within particular fields of social action, such as the Housing Corporation in supporting housing associations. Kendall has referred to these as vertical structures for support, and he contrasted them with the horizontal dimensions that were introduced after 1997.[41] Following the principles underlying the Compact, horizontal support was aimed at building up the capacity of all third sector organisations, whatever the focus of their mission or activity – although, as we shall see, inevitably not all could in practice benefit from this.

It was the Treasury-led cross-cutting review of 2002 which led to the development of significant new initiatives to support third sector organisational development in England, and, because this was linked to the Comprehensive Spending Review, it led to new streams of investment for this. The first example of this was the Futurebuilders fund – initially £125 million over three years from 2005 to 2008 – to provide grants or loans to third sector organisations to help equip them to bid for public funding.

The investment in Futurebuilders was expanded to £215 million and continued for 2008 to 2011, although delivery of the programme was transferred to a new independent agency, the Adventure Capital Fund, which later established the Social Investment Business (SIB). The SIB went on to become a major source of investment support for third sector organisations. It also administered the £70 million Communitybuilders fund, established by the Department for Communities and Local Government and the OTS in 2008 to provide support for small local and community-based organisations, and the £100 million Social Enterprise Investment Fund, established by the Department of Health, to provide support for social enterprises bidding to deliver health and social care services. It became a major source of financial support for voluntary action and social enterprise, therefore, much of it provided in the form of loans, which, in principle at least, could secure the basis for an ongoing investment fund for the sector as these were repaid and could be re-invested.

[41] Kendall, *The Voluntary Sector*.

In addition to the horizontal funding provided through the SIB, the government introduced another programme in 2004 called ChangeUp, to provide support for infrastructure agencies delivering capacity building services to third sector organisations. Infrastructure agencies operate at a national level, for instance the NCVO, but also at local and regional levels – most local authority areas have a local Council for Voluntary Service coordinating and supporting local organisations. There are also service-based, or vertical, infrastructure agencies, such as the National Association of Citizens Advice Bureaux (now called Citizens Advice), and these too have national and local manifestations. All have been supporting voluntary action for decades. However, the ChangeUp programme provided significant additional resources of £150 million for such infrastructure support, directed at particular organisational needs, such as workforce development and information technology. After 2006, ChangeUp was delivered by a separate government agency established by the OTS called Capacitybuilders. This led some commentators to refer to these horizontal investment initiatives as the builders programmes; and certainly the theme of investing in building up the capacity of organisations runs through them all.

Public funding through the builders programmes has been a major boost to horizontal support for voluntary action over the last decade or so, but it has not been the only source of such support. Independent funding from charitable trusts and foundations has always been an important source of support for organisational development within the sector, with some well known providers, such as the Nuffield Foundation or the Baring Foundation, playing key roles in promoting and developing third sector capacity. However, a major new source of independent support was created in the 1990s in the National Lottery Charities Board (now Big Lottery Fund or BIG), to distribute a proportion of the income from National Lottery ticket sales to third sector organisations. BIG grew significantly over the first decade of the century as lottery sales increased, and it provided over £2.8 billion for investment in voluntary and community action, much of which was linked to organisational capacity building and development. As a source of horizontal investment in the sector, BIG support was in some ways even more influential than government funding; and, as relatively independent of government policy priorities, it was also able, in practice, to reach a wider range of third sector organisations. By the end of the 2000s, therefore, it had become a central feature of the new environment of capacity building and investment.

Partnership

The public investment in capacity building for the third sector in the UK, supplemented by other new resources, such as BIG, led to a step change in horizontal support for voluntary action in the new century. Never before had so much public investment been available to the sector, and, as a result, the sector itself grew significantly over the decade or so after 1997. This growth was captured by the annual *Almanac* produced by the NCVO. In 2009, this revealed that income for general charities (only a part of the broader third sector) over the period from 2000 to 2007 had increased from £24.2 billion to £33.3 billion, with around 31 per cent of this coming from statutory sources.[42]

These additional resources expanded both the scope and the scale of voluntary action and social enterprise. They also meant that third sector organisations were better equipped to secure funding and develop their business; indeed much of the funding was tied specifically to such organisational development. They also raised the profile of the sector within politics and policy making more generally. Delivery of horizontal support required policy makers to engage with the sector to identify priorities, distribute resources and monitor outcomes. At the same time, sector representatives were encouraged, and required, to review their own structures and priorities and to engage with politicians and policy makers in the development and delivery of programmes of support. Kendall had described this as 'hyperactive mainstreaming', and it had significant consequences for voluntary action and third sector organisation within the UK.[43]

As we mentioned earlier, if this new engagement could be captured in one word, then that word was partnership.[44] Partnership was the term frequently used by government to describe the new form of engagement that underpinned investment and support. The Compact was described as 'an expression of the commitment of Government and the voluntary and community sector to work in partnership'; and this spirit of collaboration was also embraced by key sector representatives, such as in the quote from Etherington from the NCVO above.[45] Partnership working required both

---

[42] Kane *et al.*, *The UK Civil Society Almanac 2009*, pp. 29–36.
[43] Kendall, 'The Third Sector and the Policy Process in the UK'.
[44] Lewis, 'New Labour's Approach to the Voluntary Sector'.
[45] Home Office, *Compact on Relations between Government and the Voluntary and Community Sector in England*, para. 4; Etherington, *Delivery: the Role of the Voluntary Sector*.

sides to work towards common frameworks and common goals. After 1997, there was a willingness on the part of the leading agents in government and the third sector to do just this.

There was a broader policy context to this new spirit of partnership, however. One of the key drivers here was the expanding role of third sector organisations in the delivery of public services. Third sector organisations have always played a central role in delivering public services – the National Society for the Prevention of Cruelty to Children (NSPCC), created in 1884, was providing child protection services long before the creation of local authority children's departments. However, this role began to grow in the 1980s, as the Conservative governments sought to explore alternatives to state monopoly of welfare services, and expanded further in the health and social care field after the implementation of 'community care' in the 1990s.[46] After 1997, Labour's commitment to a third way for policy development and the promotion of a mixed economy of welfare providers placed third sector delivery of public services at the centre of policy planning. The concern to ensure that users of services were given a choice in service access, and to focus on the outcomes of policy provision (what works), rather than the input (who provides), provided an opportunity for third sector organisations to bid for and secure contracts to deliver public services, particularly in areas such as health and social care and community empowerment, where they already had a strong record.

The shift to contract funding for service delivery also had a significant impact on third sector organisations, however. It required them to acquire skills and experience in procurement processes, contract negotiation, cost allocation, and reporting and evaluation. It was the need to equip organisations with these skills and competences which was behind much of the 'builders' investment discussed above, and the consequences for the structure of the sector have been clear to see. Whilst income from statutory sources grew from £8.4 billion to £12 billion from 2000 to 2007, all of this additional income came from contract funding, with grant funding even declining slightly from £4.6 to £4.2 billion.[47]

The expansion of contract funding for service delivery was warmly welcomed by some in the sector, for instance, the Association of Chief

---

[46] J. Kendall and M. Knapp, 'Providers of Care for Older People: The Experience of Community Care', in M. Harris and C. Rochester (eds), *Voluntary Organisations and Social Policy in Britain: Perspectives on Change and Choice* (Basingstoke, 2001).

[47] Kane et al., *The UK Civil Society Almanac 2009*, p. 40.

Executives of Voluntary Organisations (ACEVO) and their chief executive, Sir Stephen Bubb, who championed an ever greater role for third sector service delivery as an alternative to a bureaucratic state and a profit-oriented market.[48] However, contract funding was not without its problems, not least the need for organisations to acquire new skills, and the 'transactional costs' of securing and delivering on contracts themselves. It also meant that the services provided were driven by the needs, and priorities, of government funders, rather than the missions of organisations themselves. And some have expressed concerns that this could threaten the more general independence of the sector.[49]

Service delivery was not the only driver behind the new partnership between government and the third sector, however. In his introduction to the Compact in 1998, the then Prime Minister, Tony Blair, talked about the government's mission to support voluntary and community organisations and said this was because, 'They enable individuals to contribute to the development of their communities. By so doing they promote citizenship, help to re-establish a sense of community and make a crucial contribution to our aim of a just and inclusive society.'[50]

The role that third sector organisations can play in promoting citizenship and civic engagement has long been recognised as a key dimension of voluntary action, and has been articulated theoretically by Putnam in his world-famous work on voluntary organisations and social capital.[51] Putnam was an early advisor to the New Labour administrations on social capital and civic engagement, and his ideas amongst others were instrumental in convincing the government that another reason for supporting the third sector was the contribution that it could make to democratic politics through promoting engagement in social action. In 2003, the Home Office published a strategy document on *Building Civil Renewal* and

[48] Association of Chief Executives of Voluntary Organisations, *Communities in Control* (London, 2004).

[49] M. Smerdon (ed.), *The First Principle of Voluntary Action: Essays on the Independence of the Voluntary Sector in Canada, England, Germany, Northern Ireland, Scotland, United States of America and Wales* (London, 2009).

[50] Home Office, *Compact on Relations between Government and the Voluntary and Community Sector in England*, p. 1.

[51] R. Putnam, *Making Democracy Work: Civic Traditions in Modern Italy* (Princeton, NJ, 1993); R. Putnam, *Bowling Alone: The Collapse and Revival of American Community* (New York, 2000).

established a separate Civil Renewal Unit to provide support for third sector partnership in community-based regeneration activity.[52]

The Civil Renewal Unit was merged into the OTS in 2006, although some of its budget and activities were transferred to the Department for Communities and Local Government. This suggested something of a division between this dimension of policy engagement and partnership, and the Treasury-led support for public service delivery. Both were aimed at horizontal support for partnership action through building the capacity of third sector organisations, and both were instrumental in expanding voluntary action and raising the profile of the third sector; but they had rather different aims (service provision, and community engagement) and, in practice, were often targeted on different parts of the third sector (larger service-focused charities and social enterprises, and smaller community groups). Service delivery also tended to be supported through contracts for provision, whilst support for civic renewal was more likely to take the form of grants.

One effect of this was to threaten a bifurcation within the sector, between the larger, well-funded delivery organisations, and the smaller, less well-established community groups. That the former were more likely to share the aims of their public funders and the latter were more likely to be challenging, or even campaigning against, public agencies made this division potentially more politically problematic too – for both government and third sector partners. The divide was sometimes presented as creating a distinction between the insiders (compliant and welcome partners) and the outsiders (challenging and potentially threatening opponents); although, as Craig *et al.* explained, in practice the distinctions between engagement and challenge in relations between third sector organisations and public agencies were more complex and nuanced than this simple bi-modal model might suggest.[53]

The divisions between different third sector organisations flowing from these different strands of government support for the sector were also reflected in the ideologies and discourses which underpinned such strands. As discussed above, the notion of a single third sector was, at best,

---

[52] Home Office, *Building Civil Renewal: Government Support for Community Capacity Building and Proposals for Change* (London, 2003); Home Office, *Firm Foundations: The Government's Framework for Community Capacity Building* (London, 2004).

[53] G. Craig, M. Taylor and T. Parkes, 'Protest or Partnership? The Voluntary and Community Sectors in the Policy Process', *Social Policy and Administration*, 38, 3, 2004, pp. 221–239.

one constructed from a 'strategic unity' within policy discourse, based on the mutual benefits which both government and sector agencies could extract from a unified space for policy intervention and practice development.[54] And, in an analysis of the ideological debates which lay behind these discourses, Kendall argued that fractures existed here, based on different emphases or dimensions within the partnership model: from higher regulation to lower regulation, and from higher engagement to lower engagement.[55] From these dimensions of partnership relations, he identified an unfolding ideological differentiation, with three different 'constellations' or 'camps' emerging, supporting different models of partnership, and potentially different levels and means of engagement and support:

- Consumerist ideologies – largely based on quasi-market public service delivery concerns, promoting the sector as an alternative to state and market failure.
- Civil revivalist ideologies – with a state-led focus on third sector contributions to civil order, promoting the sector as a response to a perceived democratic deficit.
- Democratic renewal ideologies – with a community focus on group action and engagement of local citizens, promoting the sector as a vehicle for community empowerment.

In one sense, of course, this was hardly surprising or concerning. The third sector has always been known to be an aggregation of a wide range of different shapes and sizes of organisations engaging in an almost infinite range of activities, from major international service providers like Oxfam to the local church playgroup – once tantalisingly described by Kendall and Knapp as 'a loose and baggy monster'.[56] And, though fractured, these ideological camps have all co-existed within a broader consensus on the values of partnership between the state and a collective third sector. However, what this more nuanced analysis revealed was that the policy environment created by the New Labour governments after 1997 had a more complex dynamic than the simple notion of partnership might at first suggest, and also that the third sector, which came together to engage with this partnership, was itself a fractured unity.

[54] Alcock, 'A Strategic Unity'.
[55] Kendall, *Losing Political Innocence?*
[56] J. Kendall and M. Knapp, *The Voluntary Sector in the UK* (Manchester, 1996).

Conclusion

Throughout the thirteen years of New Labour government after 1997, voluntary action enjoyed a higher profile in political debate and policy planning than at almost any point in its long history. The government openly committed itself to promoting and supporting an active partnership with the sector, and sector agencies came together to embrace and engage with this in a climate of sectoral unity that was unprecedented. What is more, this new united third sector expanded to include social enterprises, co-operatives and mutuals, which would not in earlier times naturally be seen as belonging to a collective third sector. A shared discourse of policy and practice, thus, created a new third sector and placed it at the centre of a new third way for policy development.

However, the policies and practices of the new Labour era had their roots in a longer history of engagement between voluntary action and government support and intervention. Furthermore, the unity of discourse in policy and practice was, at most, only a strategic unity, based in large part on the mutual benefits which both government and the third sector could gain from the practice (and in some cases the appearance) of partnership working. Government policy has been less holistic and coordinated than this in the past, and could become less so in the future; and the strategic unity, which was constructed within the third sector to engage with the New Labour partnership agenda, could fragment and divide in a changed political and policy landscape.

This begs the question, of course, to what extent third sector partnership was an exclusively New Labour idea – especially since a new Conservative-Liberal coalition government has explored some similar themes in its concept of 'the Big Society'. This is not the place to speculate about recent and future policy development; but, in practice, there is evidence that many of the positive features of closer government and third sector relations are shared by the other major UK political parties. In particular, in 2008, the Conservatives published a 'Green Paper' on third sector policy development, which echoed and endorsed many of the key elements of recent Labour policy developments.[57]

However, much of the positive engagement in partnership by both government and the third sector has been driven by the high levels of

---

[57] Conservative Party, *A Stronger Society: Voluntary Action in the 21st Century* (London, 2008).

financial support that was available through the OTS and the builders programmes in England, and through analogous provisions within the devolved administrations in Scotland, Wales and Northern Ireland. The ability of government to sustain such support in the aftermath of the severe economic recession of 2008 to 2009 will be open to question, especially after the series of cuts launched in late 2010. Whilst political support for partnership may be broad and deep, therefore, economic support for an expanding process of engagement and support may be hard to deliver – and, without this, the unified discourses of partnership may fragment into competition within the sector, and challenge to government agencies no longer able to meet the demands of all. Whatever happens to the politics and ideology of voluntary action, therefore, economic pressures may mean that, in time, history may judge the New Labour era to have been a high water mark in partnership between the state and the sector.

Index

Community Drug Project (CDP) 116,
    123–6, 133
Community Interest Companies (CICs)
    19, 167
'community sector' 158, 159, 166–8, 173
community-based street agencies 123–7,
    130
Compact agreements 19, 170–1, 173
Comprehensive Spending Review 165,
    166, 171
Conservative Party
    Anglicanism 155–6
    'Big Society' agenda 4, 24, 178
    Christian voluntary sector 135
    expansion of voluntary agencies 139,
        174
    ideology 16
    interwar years 55, 58
    rent strikes 101
    tenant group politics 107, 108
    Thatcherism 17, 147–9, 152, 157
    see also New Right
consultation 111–12
consumer empowerment 92
consumerism 6–7, 48, 99, 113, 177
contract funding 174–5
Cooksley, Peter 29n7
Co-operative Guilds 52
co-operative movement 28, 55, 73, 159,
    166, 178
co-option 14
Coronary Prevention Group (CPG) 121
Council Tenants Action Committee 102
Craig, G. 176
Crosland, Tony 85, 92
Crossley, Nick 123
Crossman, Richard 15, 70, 81, 85–6
Cutler, Horace 102–3

Dahrendorf, R. 95
Daube, Mike 114, 118–19, 120
De Vries, Jacqueline 45
Deakin, Nicholas 15, 16, 18, 69–93, 163
Deakin report (1996) 3, 162, 163, 167,
    169–70
Dean, Malcolm 107
declinist narratives 1–2, 6–7, 10, 49
    see also 'golden age' of voluntarism
democracy 9, 94, 113
    active 80, 86

interwar associational voluntarism 48,
    55–6
participatory 92, 110
socialist principles 76
tenant groups 21–2, 105, 110, 111
democratic renewal ideologies 7–8,
    177
democratisation 21, 48, 53–7, 67–8
Department for Communities and
    Local Government 167, 171, 176
Department of Health and Social
    Security (DHSS) 119, 126, 128–9,
    130–1
Department of Trade and Industry
    (DTI) 166, 167, 168
devolution 159–60
Director General of Voluntary
    Organisations (DGVO) 30–1, 36–40,
    41, 44
disability 98
Dr Barnardo's 17, 137
drugs services 116, 121, 122–32
Duggan, Patrick 152

Ecclestone, Giles 146
economic conditions 9–10
Edinburgh, voluntary groups in 96
Edwardian era 5, 28
Edwards, Dr Griffith 123–4, 125
environmentalism 6, 9, 98
Etherington, Sir Stuart 164–5
evangelicalism 138, 144–5
Evers, A. 158
'evidence-based revolution' 133

Fabian Society 73, 74
Faith in the City (1985) report 17, 146–7,
    151–2, 153, 155, 157
faith organisations *see* Christian
    voluntary sector
Fascism 56, 57
feminism 6
Filby, Eliza 17, 135–57
Finlayson, Geoffrey 29
First World War 5, 14–15, 27–46
    Director General of Voluntary
        Organisations 30–1, 36–40, 41, 44
    fund-raising techniques 35–6
    medical services 35
    National Relief Fund 31–4